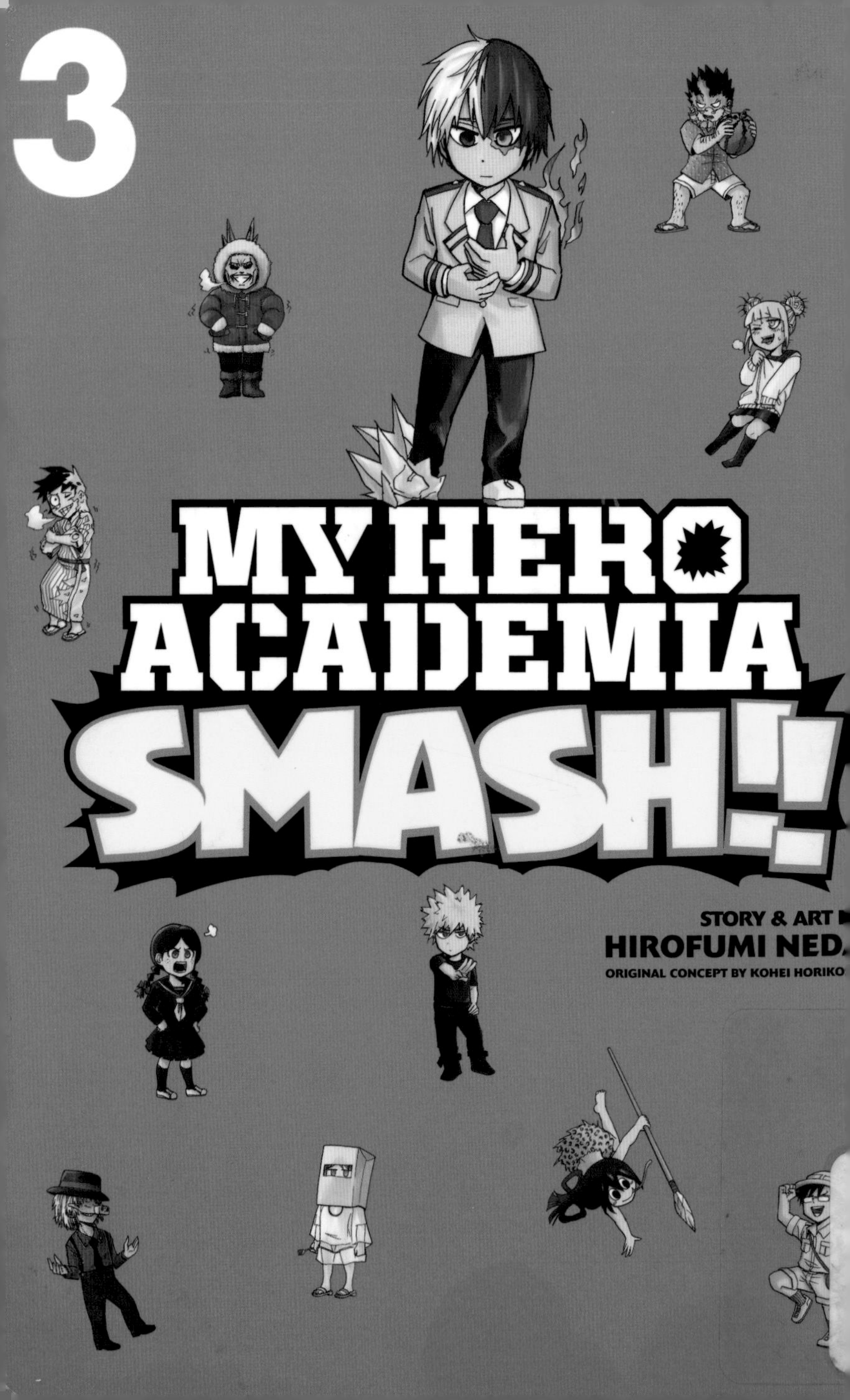
3
MY HERO ACADEMIA
SMASH!!
STORY & ART
HIROFUMI NED
ORIGINAL CONCEPT BY KOHEI HORIKO

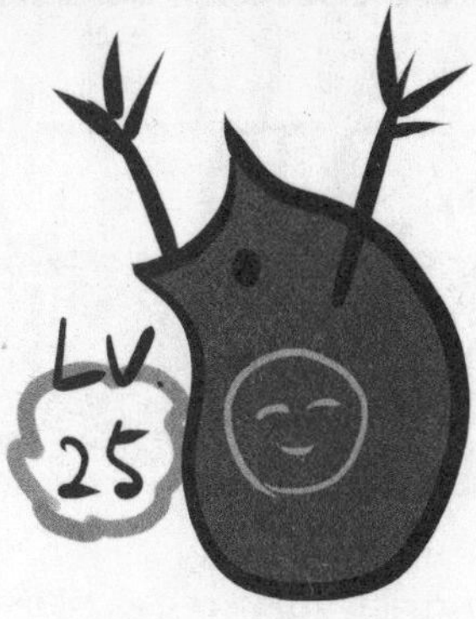
LV.
25

Hirofumi Neda

I'm constantly wondering if any of what I'm doing is really okay, so when people tell me, "I like *Smash!!* too," I feel like an abandoned kitten being thrown some table scraps. Though I'm more like a raggedy old dude standing there, trembling...

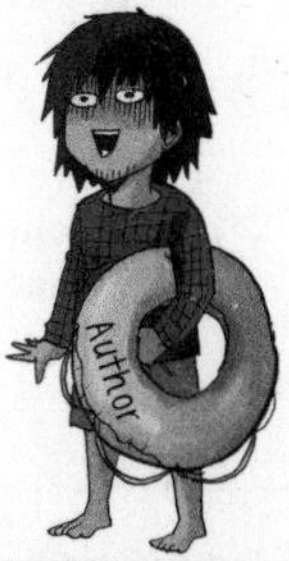
Author

HIROFUMI NEDA began his professional career as a manga artist in 2007, winning the Akatsuka Prize Honorable Mention for his short story "Mom Is a Spy." After publishing several other short stories, he began working as an art assistant to Kohei Horikoshi on *Oumagadoki Zoo* and later on *My Hero Academia*.

KOHEI HORIKOSHI was born in Aichi, Japan, in 1986. He received a Tezuka Award Honorable Mention in 2006, and after publishing several short stories in *Akamaru Jump*, his first serialized work in *Weekly Shonen Jump* was *Oumagadoki Zoo* in 2010. *My Hero Academia* is his third series in *Weekly Shonen Jump*.

MY HERO ACADEMIA SMASH!!

VOLUME 3
SHONEN JUMP Manga Edition

STORY & ART BY HIROFUMI NEDA
ORIGINAL CONCEPT BY KOHEI HORIKOSHI

Translation/Caleb Cook
Touch-Up Art & Lettering/John Hunt
Designer/Julian [JR] Robinson
Editor/Hope Donovan

BOKU NO HERO ACADEMIA SMASH!!
© 2015 by Kohei Horikoshi, Hirofumi Neda
All rights reserved.
First published in Japan in 2015 by SHUEISHA Inc., Tokyo.
English translation rights arranged by SHUEISHA Inc.

Printed in the U.S.A.

Published by VIZ Media, LLC
P.O. Box 77010
San Francisco, CA 94107

10 9 8 7 6 5 4 3 2 1
First printing, February 2020

viz.com

shonenjump.com

PARENTAL ADVISORY
MY HERO ACADEMIA: SMASH!! is rated
T for Teen and is recommended for ages
13 and up. This volume contains fantasy
violence and crude/sexual humor.

MY HERO ACADEMIA SMASH!!

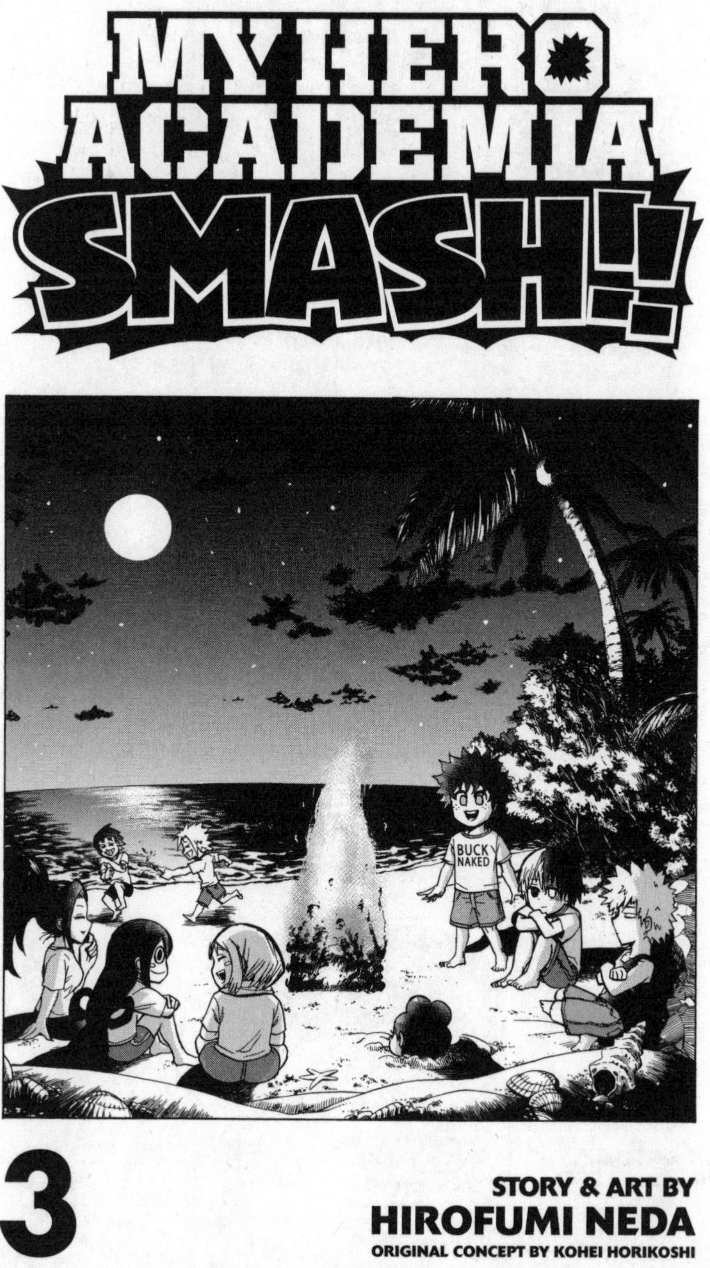
BUCK NAKED

3

STORY & ART BY
HIROFUMI NEDA
ORIGINAL CONCEPT BY KOHEI HORIKOSHI

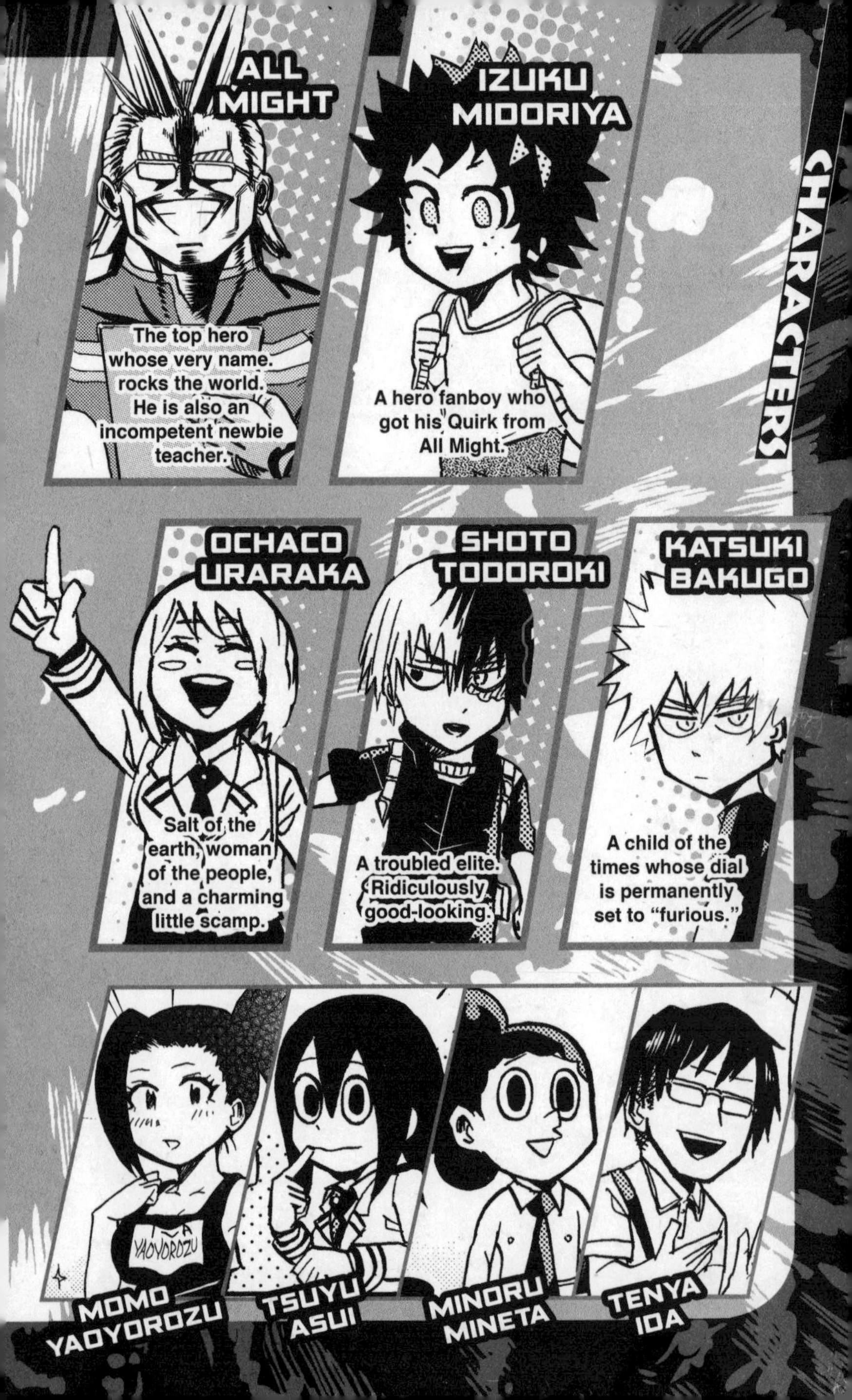
CHARACTERS
IZUKU MIDORIYA
A hero fanboy who got his Quirk from All Might.
ALL MIGHT
The top hero whose very name. rocks the world. He is also an incompetent newbie teacher.
KATSUKI BAKUGO
A child of the times whose dial is permanently set to "furious."
SHOTO TODOROKI
A troubled elite. Ridiculously good-looking.
OCHACO URARAKA
Salt of the earth, woman of the people, and a charming little scamp.
TENYA IDA
MINORU MINETA
TSUYU ASUI
MOMO YAOYOROZU
YAOYOROZU

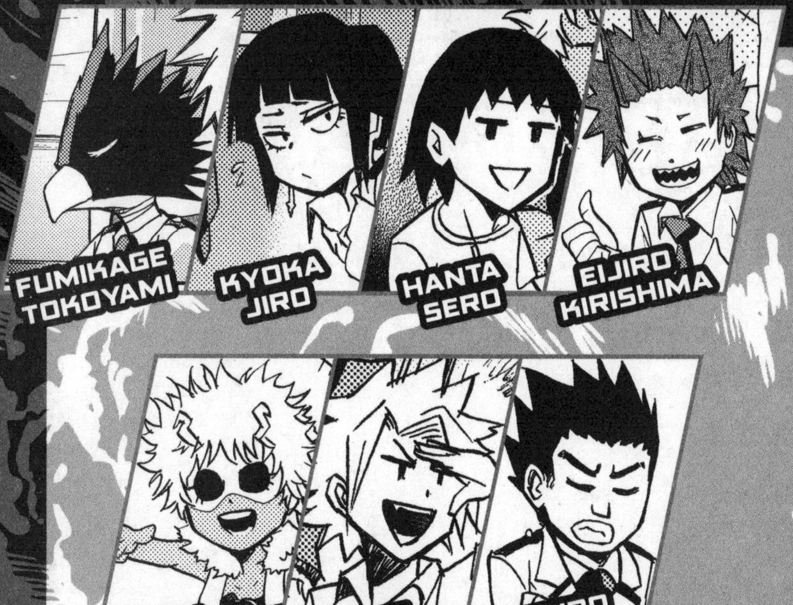
EIJIRO KIRISHIMA
HANTA SERO
KYOKA JIRO
FUMIKAGE TOKOYAMI
RIKIDO SATO
DENKI KAMINARI
MINA ASHIDO
KAMUI WOODS
MT. LADY
ENDEAVOR
SHOTA AIZAWA

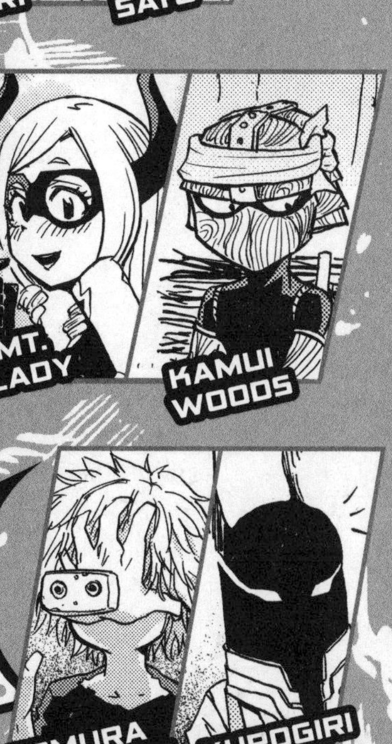
KUROGIRI
TOMURA SHIGARAKI

STORY

Izuku Midoriya has always idolized heroes—the people who use their Quirk powers to kick evil butt. A chance encounter with All Might gives him the Quirk he needs to attend U.A. High—an elite educational institution for heroes in training! Now there's never a dull moment at U.A.!!

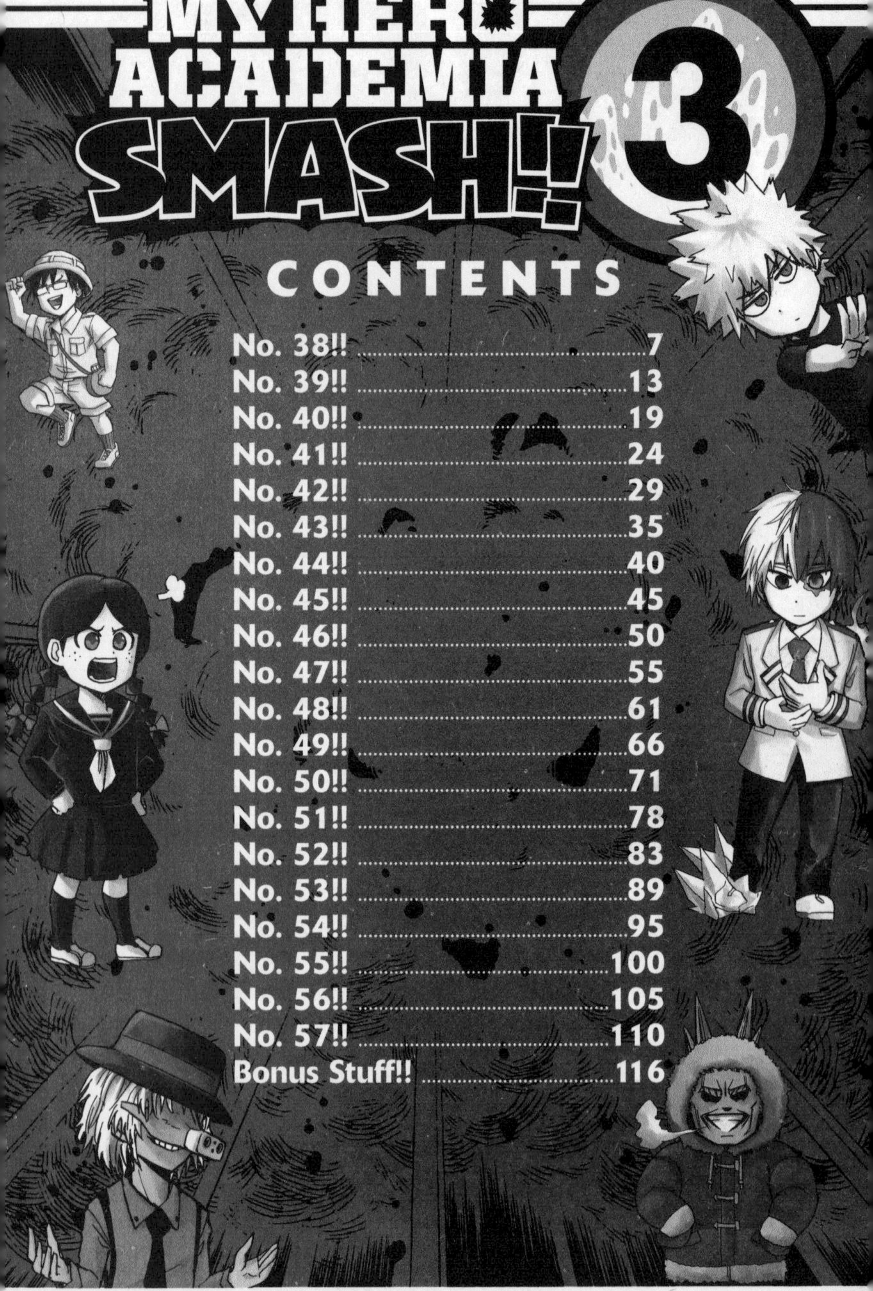

MY HERO ACADEMIA SMASH!! 3

CONTENTS

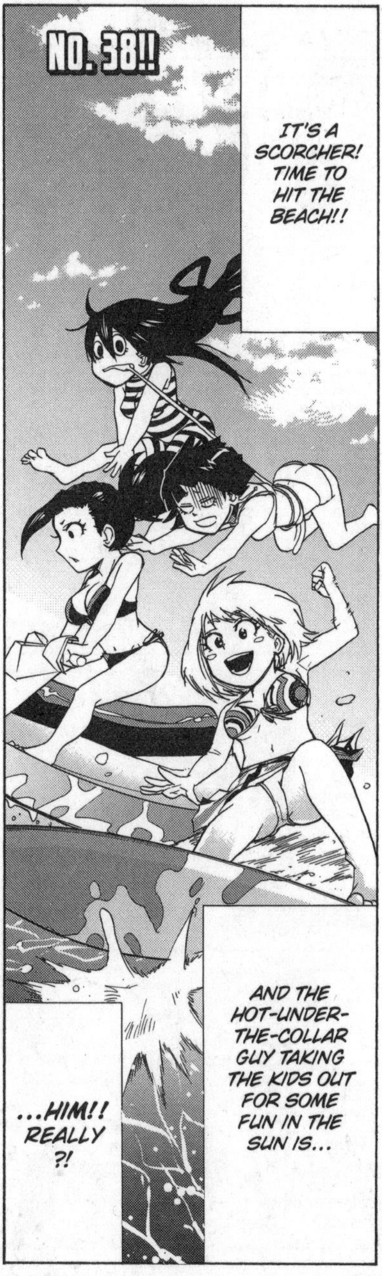
No. 38!!
IT'S A SCORCHER! TIME TO HIT THE BEACH!!
AND THE HOT-UNDER-THE-COLLAR GUY TAKING THE KIDS OUT FOR SOME FUN IN THE SUN IS...
...HIM!! REALLY?!

OPPORTUNISTS

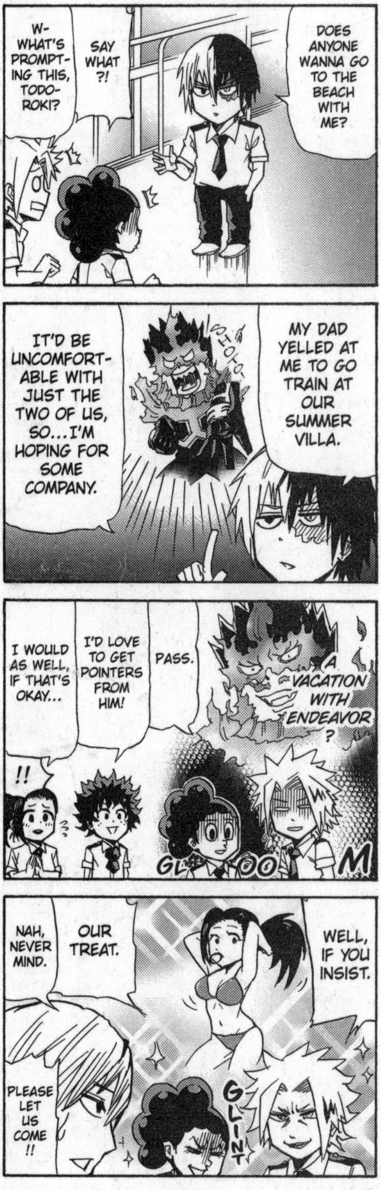
DOES ANYONE WANNA GO TO THE BEACH WITH ME?
SAY WHAT?!
W-WHAT'S PROMPTING THIS, TODOROKI?
MY DAD YELLED AT ME TO GO TRAIN AT OUR SUMMER VILLA.
IT'D BE UNCOMFORTABLE WITH JUST THE TWO OF US, SO...I'M HOPING FOR SOME COMPANY.
A VACATION WITH ENDEAVOR?
PASS.
I'D LOVE TO GET POINTERS FROM HIM!
I WOULD AS WELL, IF THAT'S OKAY...
!!
WELL, IF YOU INSIST.
OUR TREAT.
NAH, NEVER MIND.
GLINT
PLEASE LET US COME!!

DELUSIONAL DAD

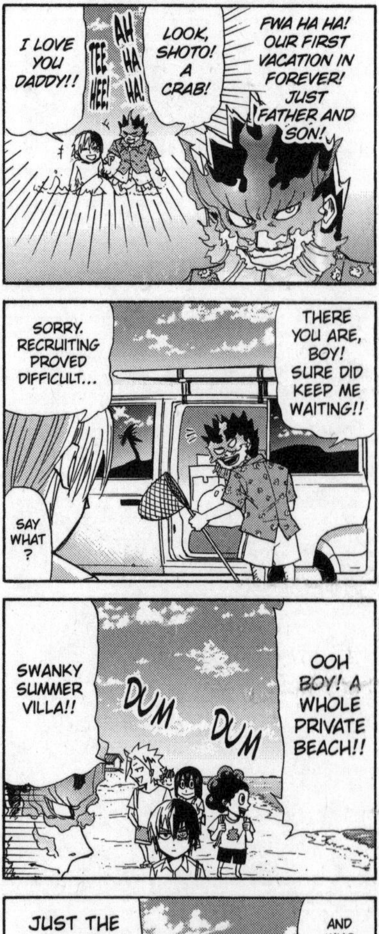
FWA HA HA! OUR FIRST VACATION IN FOREVER! JUST FATHER AND SON!
LOOK, SHOTO! A CRAB!
AH HA HA!
TEE HEE!
I LOVE YOU DADDY!!
THERE YOU ARE, BOY! SURE DID KEEP ME WAITING!!
SORRY. RECRUITING PROVED DIFFICULT...
SAY WHAT?
OOH BOY! A WHOLE PRIVATE BEACH!!
DUM
DUM
SWANKY SUMMER VILLA!!
AND WHO MIGHT THESE FREE-LOADERS BE...?
SPLASH
JUST THE TWO OF US WOULD'VE BEEN AWFUL. SO I INVITED THEM.
I SEE.

ONE PIECE

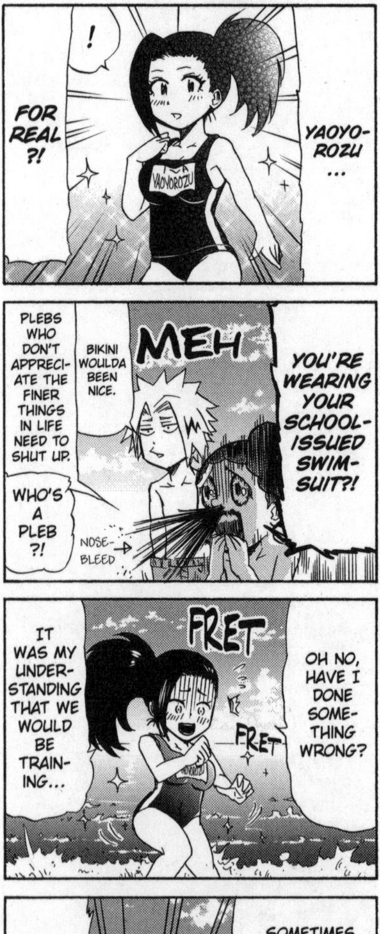
YAOYO-ROZU ...
!
YAOYOROZU
FOR REAL ?!
YOU'RE WEARING YOUR SCHOOL-ISSUED SWIM-SUIT?!
MEH
BIKINI WOULDA BEEN NICE.
PLEBS WHO DON'T APPRECI-ATE THE FINER THINGS IN LIFE NEED TO SHUT UP.
WHO'S A PLEB ?!
NOSE-BLEED
OH NO, HAVE I DONE SOME-THING WRONG?
FRET
FRET
IT WAS MY UNDER-STANDING THAT WE WOULD BE TRAIN-ING...
SOMETIMES YOU HAVE TO LET THE OCEAN WASH THINGS AWAY.
GAHHHH
I'LL BE GOOD, I SWEAR! C'MON, THE TIDE'S COMING IN!!

MISCALCULATION

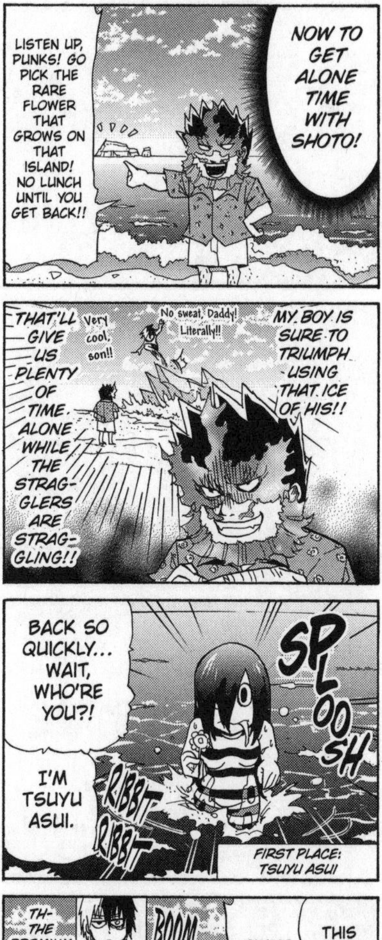
NOW TO GET ALONE TIME WITH SHOTO!
LISTEN UP, PUNKS! GO PICK THE RARE FLOWER THAT GROWS ON THAT ISLAND! NO LUNCH UNTIL YOU GET BACK!!
MY BOY IS SURE TO TRIUMPH USING THAT ICE OF HIS!!
No sweat, Daddy! Literally!!
Very cool, son!!
THAT'LL GIVE US PLENTY OF TIME ALONE WHILE THE STRAGGLERS ARE STRAGGLING!!
SPLOOSH
BACK SO QUICKLY... WAIT, WHO'RE YOU?!
I'M TSUYU ASUI.
RIBBIT RIBBIT
FIRST PLACE: TSUYU ASUI
THIS BBQ IS DELICIOUS.
GIMME MEAT!!
SECOND PLACE
BOOM
THIRD PLACE
TH-THE PREMIUM WAGYU BEEF I GRILLED UP JUST FOR SHOTO...
BOOM
BOOM

MALPRACTICE

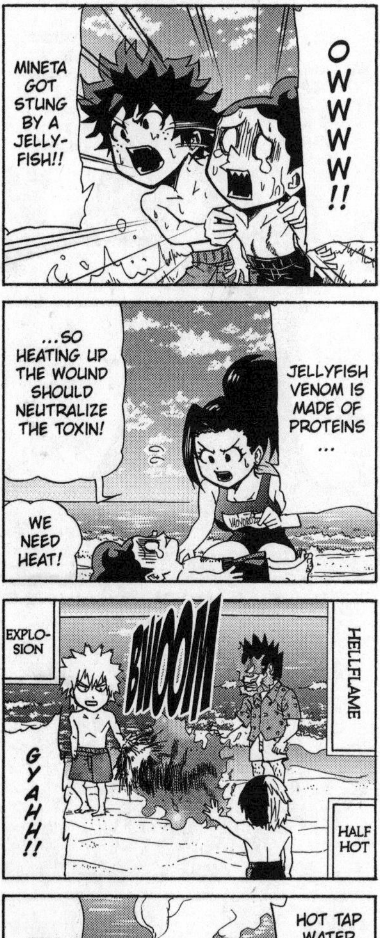
OWWWWW!!
MINETA GOT STUNG BY A JELLY-FISH!!
JELLYFISH VENOM IS MADE OF PROTEINS...
...SO HEATING UP THE WOUND SHOULD NEUTRALIZE THE TOXIN!
WE NEED HEAT!
HELLFLAME
HALF HOT
BWOOM
EXPLOSION
GYAHH!!
HOT TAP WATER WOULD HAVE DONE THE TRICK...
FSSH
FSSH
THAT BALMY 2,000 °C BLAST WORKED.

Number Three Hero Gets a Promotion

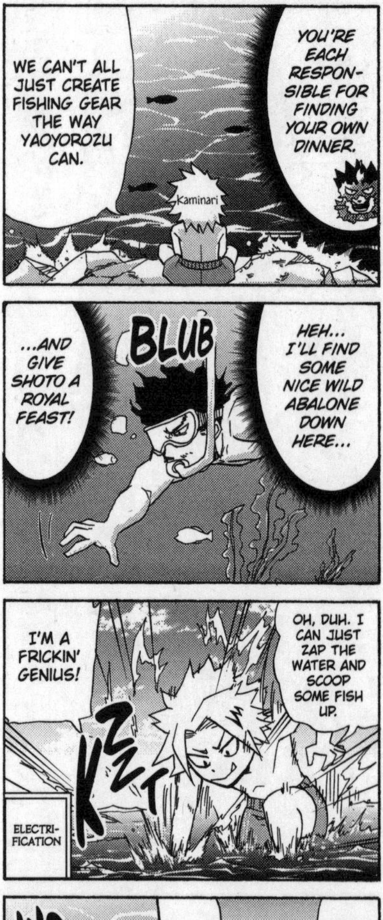
YOU'RE EACH RESPONSIBLE FOR FINDING YOUR OWN DINNER.
WE CAN'T ALL JUST CREATE FISHING GEAR THE WAY YAOYOROZU CAN.
Kaminari
HEH... I'LL FIND SOME NICE WILD ABALONE DOWN HERE...
BLUB
...AND GIVE SHOTO A ROYAL FEAST!
OH, DUH. I CAN JUST ZAP THE WATER AND SCOOP SOME FISH UP.
I'M A FRICKIN' GENIUS!
KZZZT
ELECTRIFICATION
ANYONE SEEN OLD FLAME-FACE?
YAYYY ...? NOT ME?
WORMP

Nose for Sugar

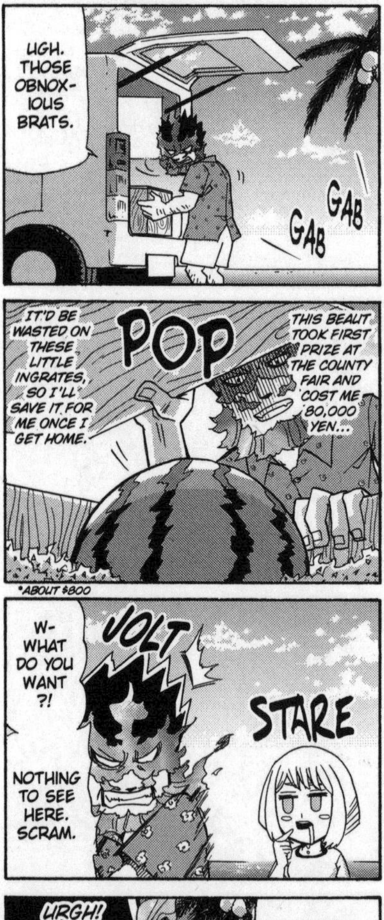
GAB GAB
UGH. THOSE OBNOXIOUS BRATS.
THIS BEAUT TOOK FIRST PRIZE AT THE COUNTY FAIR AND COST ME *80,000 YEN...
POP
IT'D BE WASTED ON THESE LITTLE INGRATES, SO I'LL SAVE IT FOR ME ONCE I GET HOME.
*ABOUT $800
STARE
JOLT
W-WHAT DO YOU WANT?!
NOTHING TO SEE HERE. SCRAM.
STARE
IF THERE'S A WATERMELON IN THERE, LET'S HAVE IT. MY FRIENDS ARE READY TO DIG IN.
URGH! THAT ROSY-CHEEKED PEST!!

PRICEY EMBRACE

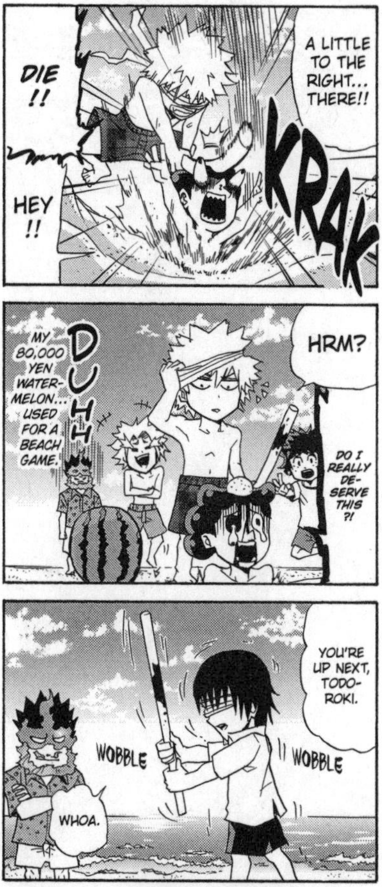
A LITTLE TO THE RIGHT... THERE!!
KRAK
DIE !!
HEY !!
HRM?
DO I REALLY DE-SERVE THIS ?!
DUHH
MY 80,000 YEN WATER-MELON... USED FOR A BEACH GAME.
YOU'RE UP NEXT, TODO-ROKI.
WOBBLE
WOBBLE
WHOA.
ACK... SORRY, WHOEVER YOU ARE.
THUD
Ahh... Worth every last yen...
BADUM

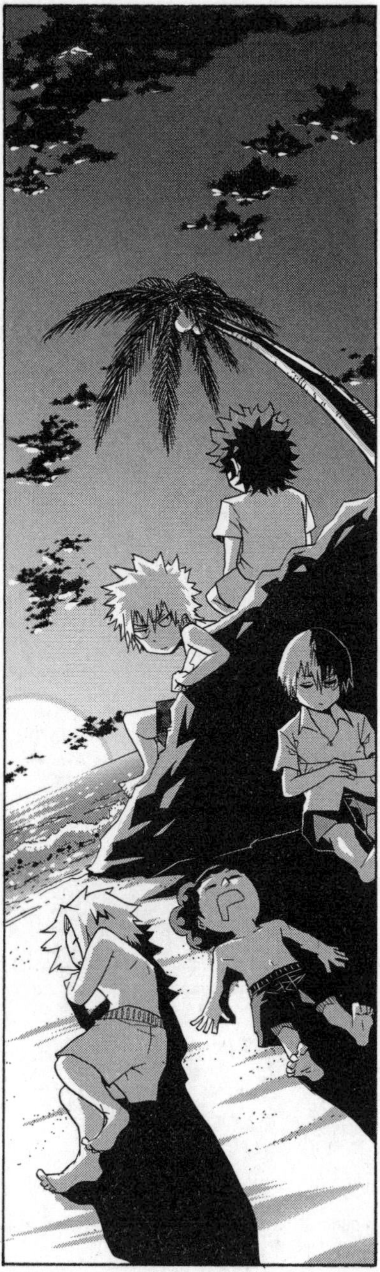

MY GOOD SIDE

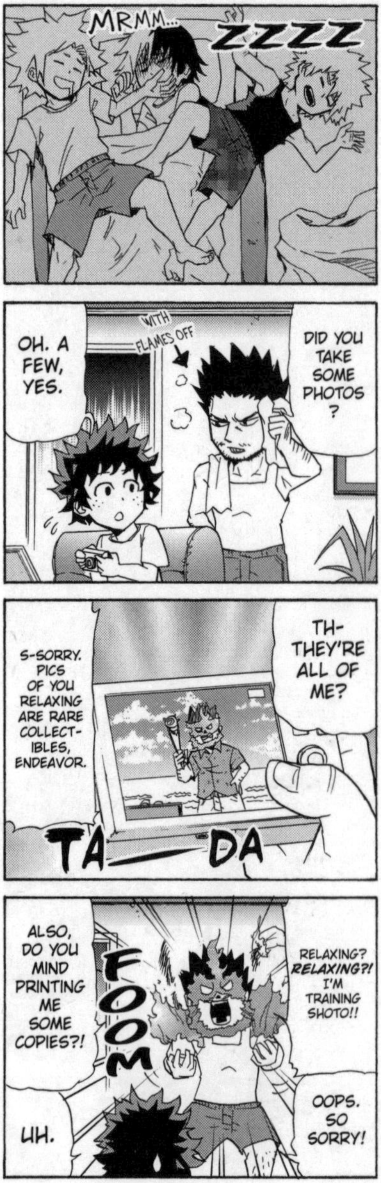
ZZZZ
MRMM...
DID YOU TAKE SOME PHOTOS?
WITH FLAMES OFF
OH. A FEW, YES.
TH-THEY'RE ALL OF ME?
S-SORRY. PICS OF YOU RELAXING ARE RARE COLLECT-IBLES, ENDEAVOR.
TA—DA
RELAXING? *RELAXING?!* I'M TRAINING SHOTO!!
FOOM
ALSO, DO YOU MIND PRINTING ME SOME COPIES?!
OOPS. SO SORRY!
UH.

WORTH A THOUSAND WORDS

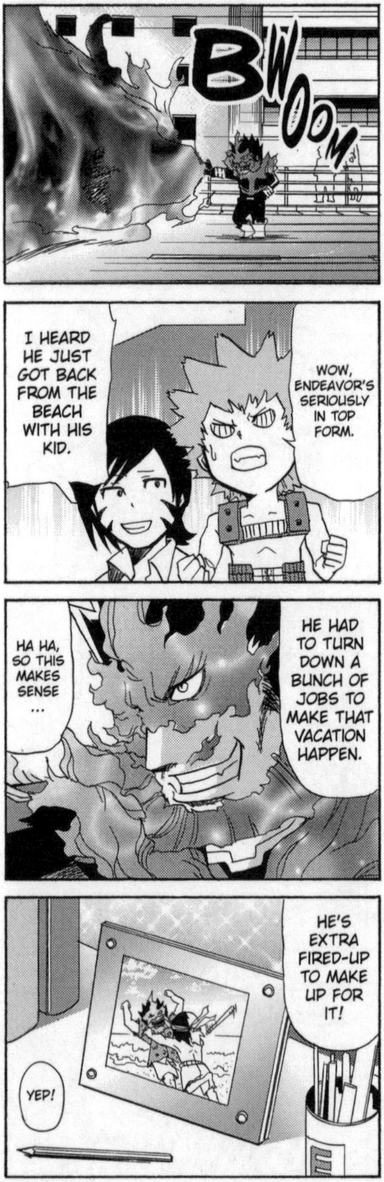
BWOOM
WOW, ENDEAVOR'S SERIOUSLY IN TOP FORM.
I HEARD HE JUST GOT BACK FROM THE BEACH WITH HIS KID.
HE HAD TO TURN DOWN A BUNCH OF JOBS TO MAKE THAT VACATION HAPPEN.
HA HA, SO THIS MAKES SENSE...
HE'S EXTRA FIRED-UP TO MAKE UP FOR IT!
YEP!

NO. 39!!
THE LEGENDARY RHINOCEROS BEETLE HAS LONG BEEN SOUGHT AFTER BY THOSE WHO YEARN FOR ADVENTURE.
WITH FLAMES OF DETERMINATION BURNING BRIGHT IN THEIR EYE SOCKETS, THESE FIVE BOYS HUNT FOR THAT ELUSIVE PREY!
THIS IS A CHAPTER ABOUT BUG HUNTING !!

FUSE, LIT

IT ALL BEGAN THREE DAYS AGO.
A RHINOCEROS BEETLE? WHAT'S THE BIG DEAL?
SHK
SHK
WELL, I WENT OUT AND CAPTURED THIS ONE LAST WEEK.
NEITO MONOMA, CLASS B
THE WILD ONES ARE A LITTLE MORE FEISTY.
I'VE GOT THREE MORE AT HOME, INCLUDING A FEMALE.
I DON'T SUPPOSE YOU SPOILED CLASS-A BABIES HAVE CAUGHT ANY YOURSELVES? HA HA!
JEALOUS? YOU COULD ALWAYS BUY A BORING OLD FARM-RAISED ONE AT THE PET SHOP.
WE'LL SHOW YOU, YOU BANGS-HAVING, DROOPY-EYED, COPYCATTING JERK!!
BLAZE

A Guy Thing

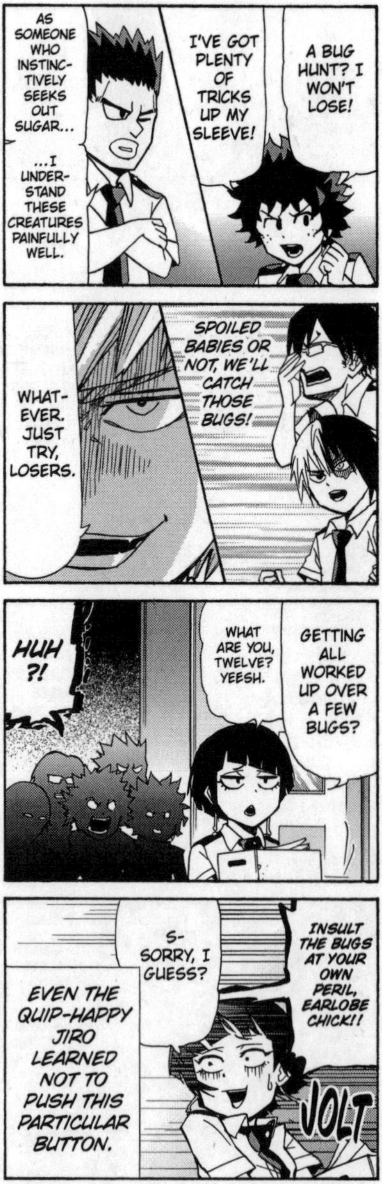
A BUG HUNT? I WON'T LOSE!
I'VE GOT PLENTY OF TRICKS UP MY SLEEVE!
AS SOMEONE WHO INSTINCTIVELY SEEKS OUT SUGAR...
...I UNDERSTAND THESE CREATURES PAINFULLY WELL.
SPOILED BABIES OR NOT, WE'LL CATCH THOSE BUGS!
WHATEVER. JUST TRY, LOSERS.
GETTING ALL WORKED UP OVER A FEW BUGS?
WHAT ARE YOU, TWELVE? YEESH.
HUH?!
INSULT THE BUGS AT YOUR OWN PERIL, EARLOBE CHICK!!
JOLT
S-SORRY, I GUESS?
EVEN THE QUIP-HAPPY JIRO LEARNED NOT TO PUSH THIS PARTICULAR BUTTON.

Machinations

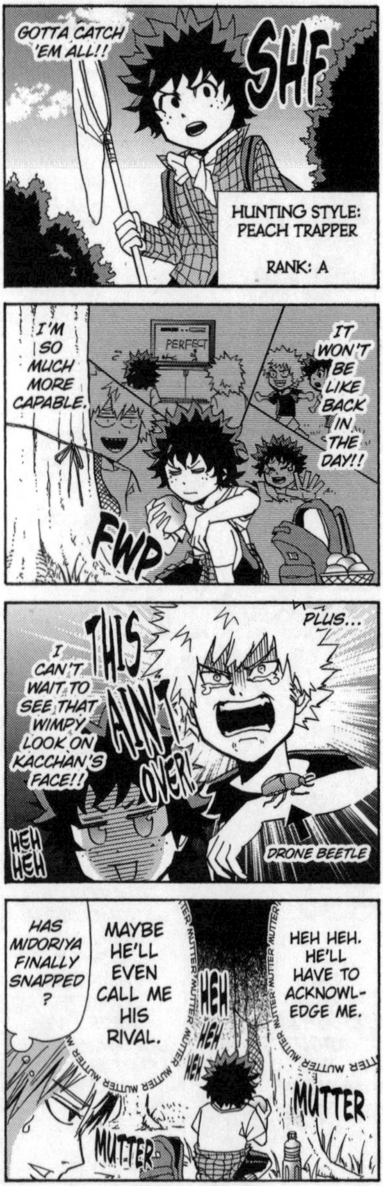
SHF
GOTTA CATCH 'EM ALL!!
HUNTING STYLE: PEACH TRAPPER
RANK: A
IT WON'T BE LIKE BACK IN THE DAY!!
PERFECT
I'M SO MUCH MORE CAPABLE.
FWP
PLUS...
THIS AIN'T OVER!
I CAN'T WAIT TO SEE THAT WIMPY LOOK ON KACCHAN'S FACE!!
DRONE BEETLE
HEH HEH
HEH HEH. HE'LL HAVE TO ACKNOWLEDGE ME.
HEH HEH HEH
MAYBE HE'LL EVEN CALL ME HIS RIVAL.
HAS MIDORIYA FINALLY SNAPPED?
MUTTER
MUTTER

ARMCHAIR HUNTER

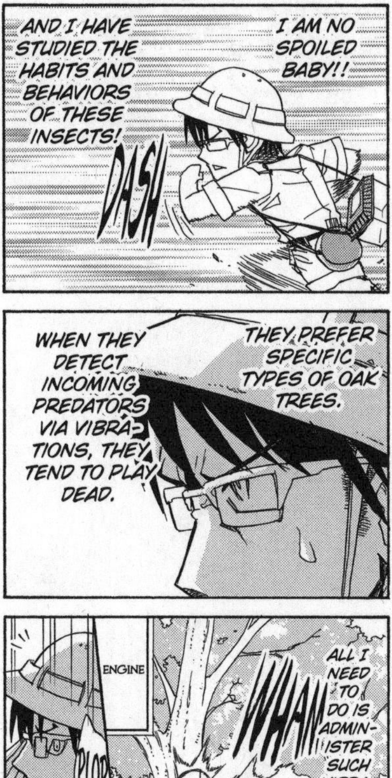
I AM NO SPOILED BABY!!
AND I HAVE STUDIED THE HABITS AND BEHAVIORS OF THESE INSECTS!
DASH
THEY PREFER SPECIFIC TYPES OF OAK TREES.
WHEN THEY DETECT INCOMING PREDATORS VIA VIBRATIONS, THEY TEND TO PLAY DEAD.
ALL I NEED TO DO IS ADMINISTER SUCH VIBRATIONS TO ONE OF SAID TREES, AND...
WHAM
ENGINE
PLOP
MWOHH?! WHAT FOUL CREATURES ARE THESE?!
FWASH
DON'T GO AROUND HURTING TREES, YOU IDIOTIC AMATEUR!!
HUNTING STYLE: KICKING TREES
RANK: B

A PRO'S NOSE KNOWS

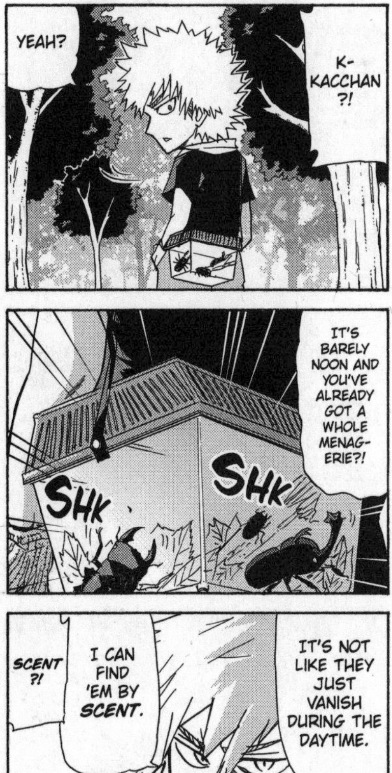
K-KACCHAN?!
YEAH?
IT'S BARELY NOON AND YOU'VE ALREADY GOT A WHOLE MENAGERIE?!
SHK
SHK
IT'S NOT LIKE THEY JUST VANISH DURING THE DAYTIME.
I CAN FIND 'EM BY SCENT.
SCENT?!
HUNTING STYLE: YEARS OF INSTINCT
RANK: S (FOR "SUPER")
AHA. FOUND LITTLE STAG AND DEEP MOUNTAIN STAG BEETLES.
CATCHING THEM WITH HIS BARE HANDS? HE'S TOO GOOD!
I MEAN, THEY'RE EASIER TO SNAG AT NIGHT, BUT WHATEVER.

BABY'S FIRST BUG HUNT

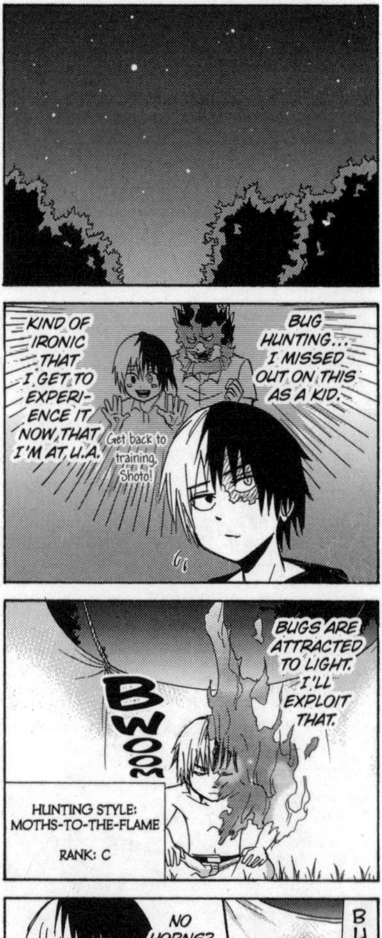
BUG HUNTING... I MISSED OUT ON THIS AS A KID.
KIND OF IRONIC THAT I GET TO EXPERIENCE IT NOW THAT I'M AT U.A.
Get back to training, Shoto!
BUGS ARE ATTRACTED TO LIGHT. I'LL EXPLOIT THAT.
BWOOM
HUNTING STYLE: MOTHS-TO-THE-FLAME
RANK: C
BUZZ
OH, THERE'S ONE.
NO HORNS? MUST BE A FEMALE RHINOCEROS BEETLE.
NOPE. JUST A DRONE BEETLE.

SWEETEST CATCH

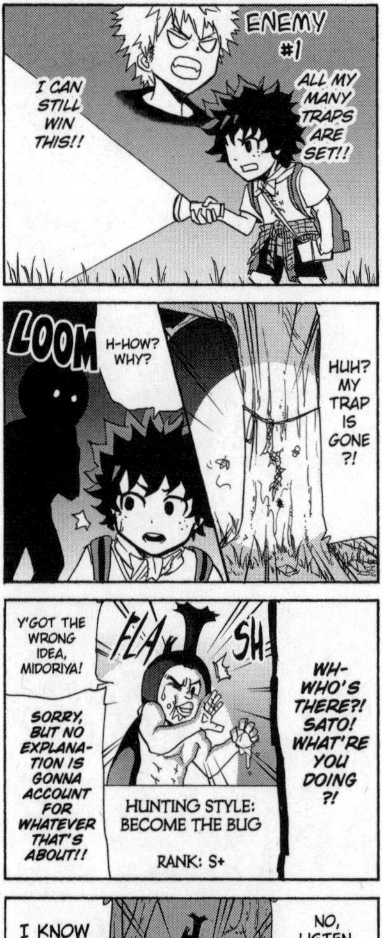
ENEMY #1
ALL MY MANY TRAPS ARE SET!!
I CAN STILL WIN THIS!!
HUH? MY TRAP IS GONE?!
H-HOW? WHY?
LOOM
WH-WHO'S THERE?! SATO! WHAT'RE YOU DOING?!
FLASH
Y'GOT THE WRONG IDEA, MIDORIYA!
SORRY, BUT NO EXPLANATION IS GONNA ACCOUNT FOR WHATEVER THAT'S ABOUT!!
HUNTING STYLE: BECOME THE BUG
RANK: S+
NO, LISTEN, IT'S CUZ MY QUIRK POWERS ME UP WHEN I EAT SUGAR!
I KNOW THAT!! AND IT DOESN'T EXPLAIN ANYTHING!
RIKIDOCUS SATOCUS CAPTURED!!

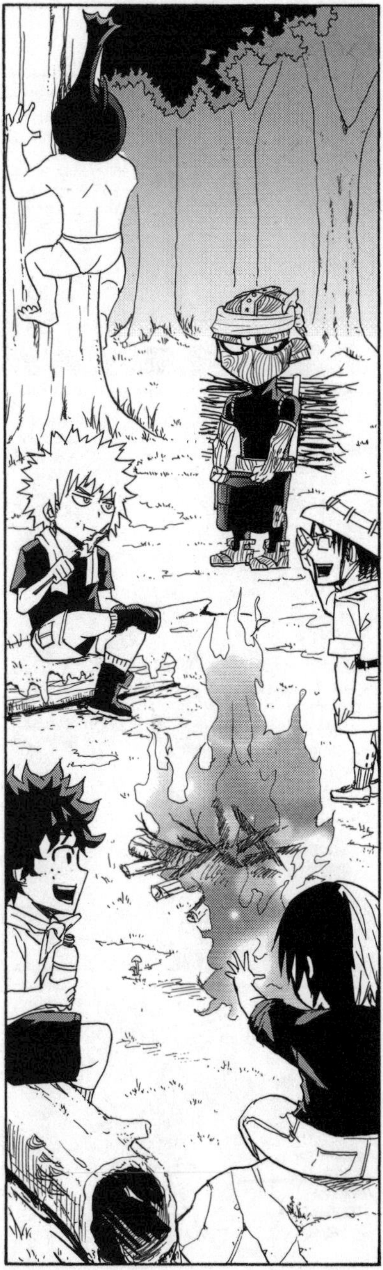

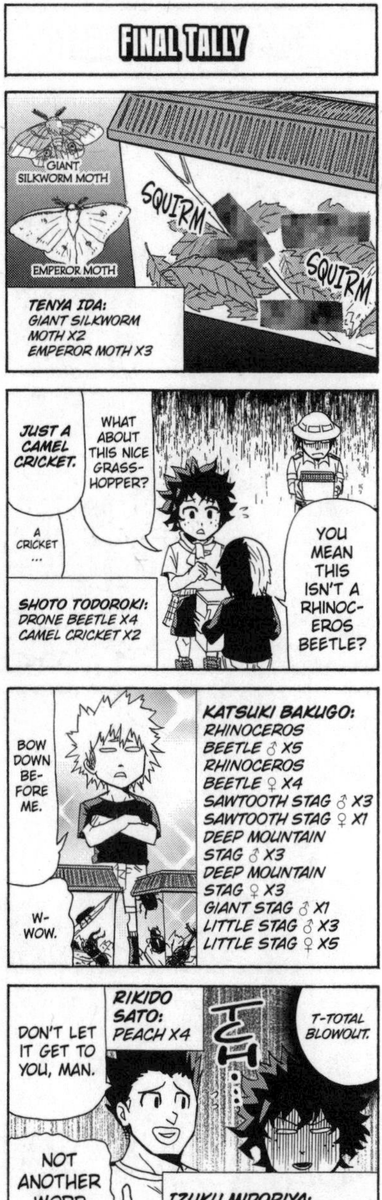
FINAL TALLY
SQUIRM
SQUIRM
GIANT SILKWORM MOTH
EMPEROR MOTH
TENYA IDA: GIANT SILKWORM MOTH X2 EMPEROR MOTH X3
YOU MEAN THIS ISN'T A RHINOCEROS BEETLE?
WHAT ABOUT THIS NICE GRASSHOPPER?
JUST A CAMEL CRICKET.
A CRICKET ...
SHOTO TODOROKI: DRONE BEETLE X4 CAMEL CRICKET X2
KATSUKI BAKUGO: RHINOCEROS BEETLE ♂ X5 RHINOCEROS BEETLE ♀ X4 SAWTOOTH STAG ♂ X3 SAWTOOTH STAG ♀ X1 DEEP MOUNTAIN STAG ♂ X3 DEEP MOUNTAIN STAG ♀ X3 GIANT STAG ♂ X1 LITTLE STAG ♂ X3 LITTLE STAG ♀ X5
BOW DOWN BEFORE ME.
W-WOW.
T-TOTAL BLOWOUT.
TCH...
RIKIDO SATO: PEACH X4
DON'T LET IT GET TO YOU, MAN.
IZUKU MIDORIYA: RHINOCEROS BEETLE ♀ X1 RIKIDOCUS SATOCUS ♂ X1
NOT ANOTHER WORD OUT OF YOU.

For the Love of Bugs

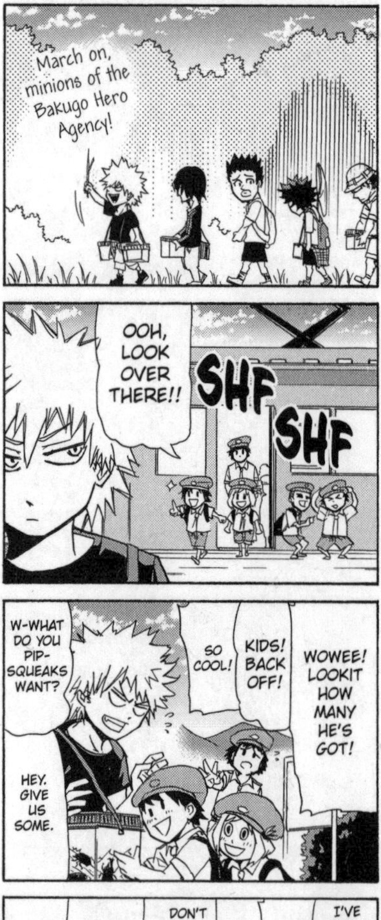
March on, minions of the Bakugo Hero Agency!
OOH, LOOK OVER THERE!!
SHF
SHF
WOWEE! LOOKIT HOW MANY HE'S GOT!
KIDS! BACK OFF!
SO COOL!
W-WHAT DO YOU PIP-SQUEAKS WANT?
HEY. GIVE US SOME.
I'VE GOT A FEMALE, BUT SHE'S ALL YOURS.
YAY!!
HERE'S MINE...
DON'T WANT YOUR DUMB DRONE BEETLE.
OR THOSE MOTHS. EW.
WHAT'S WRONG WITH YOU?

Supereffective

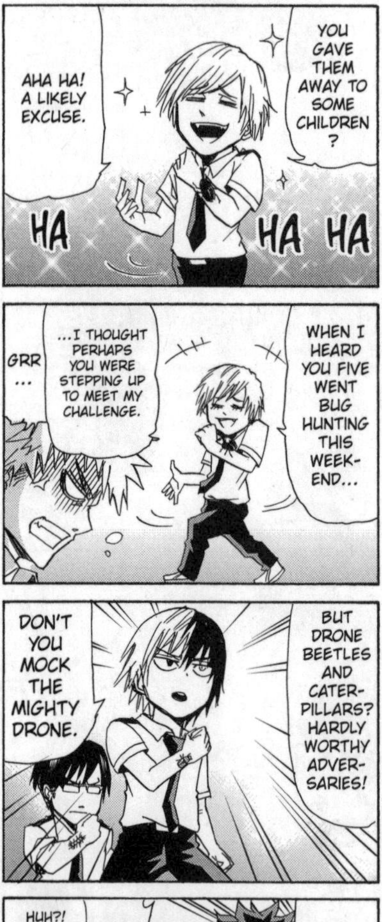
YOU GAVE THEM AWAY TO SOME CHILDREN?
AHA HA! A LIKELY EXCUSE.
HA HA HA
WHEN I HEARD YOU FIVE WENT BUG HUNTING THIS WEEK-END...
...I THOUGHT PERHAPS YOU WERE STEPPING UP TO MEET MY CHALLENGE.
GRR...
BUT DRONE BEETLES AND CATER-PILLARS? HARDLY WORTHY ADVER-SARIES!
DON'T YOU MOCK THE MIGHTY DRONE.
I CAUGHT A HUMAN (♂) TOO!! GO, RIKIDO!!
RIKI-RIKI!
HUH?! I'M NOT SURE WHAT THAT IS, BUT IT'S NO BUG...
TRAINER MIDORIYA'S HUMAN (♂) DEFEATED MONOMA.

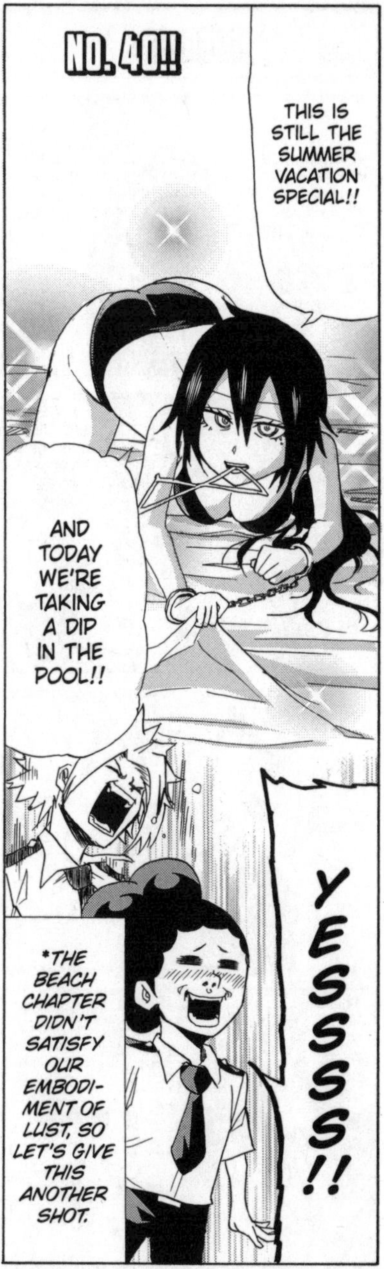
No. 40!!
THIS IS STILL THE SUMMER VACATION SPECIAL!!
AND TODAY WE'RE TAKING A DIP IN THE POOL!!
YESSSSS!!
*THE BEACH CHAPTER DIDN'T SATISFY OUR EMBODIMENT OF LUST, SO LET'S GIVE THIS ANOTHER SHOT.

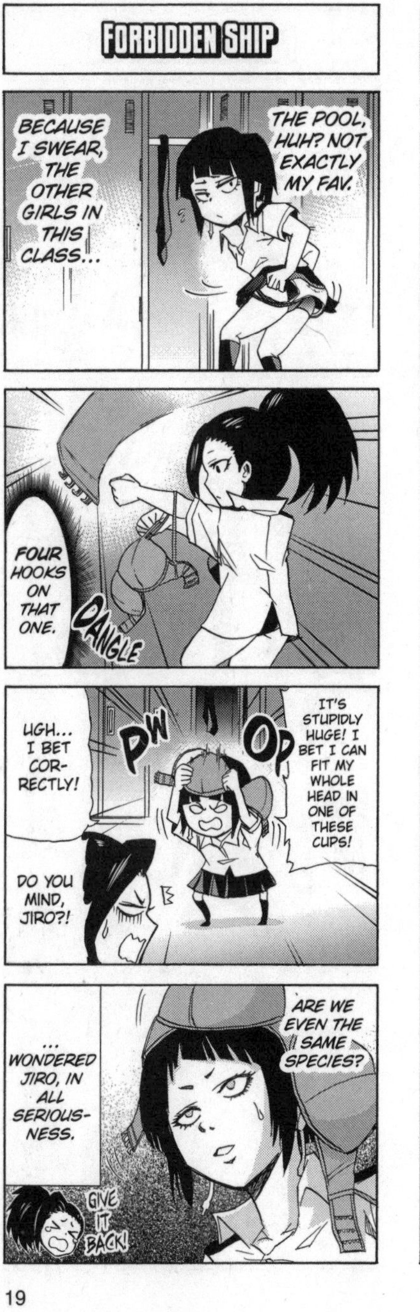
FORBIDDEN SHIP
THE POOL, HUH? NOT EXACTLY MY FAV.
BECAUSE I SWEAR, THE OTHER GIRLS IN THIS CLASS...
DANGLE
FOUR HOOKS ON THAT ONE.
IT'S STUPIDLY HUGE! I BET I CAN FIT MY WHOLE HEAD IN ONE OF THESE CUPS!
PWOP
UGH... I BET CORRECTLY!
DO YOU MIND, JIRO?!
ARE WE EVEN THE SAME SPECIES?
...WONDERED JIRO, IN ALL SERIOUSNESS.
GIVE IT BACK!

False Advertising

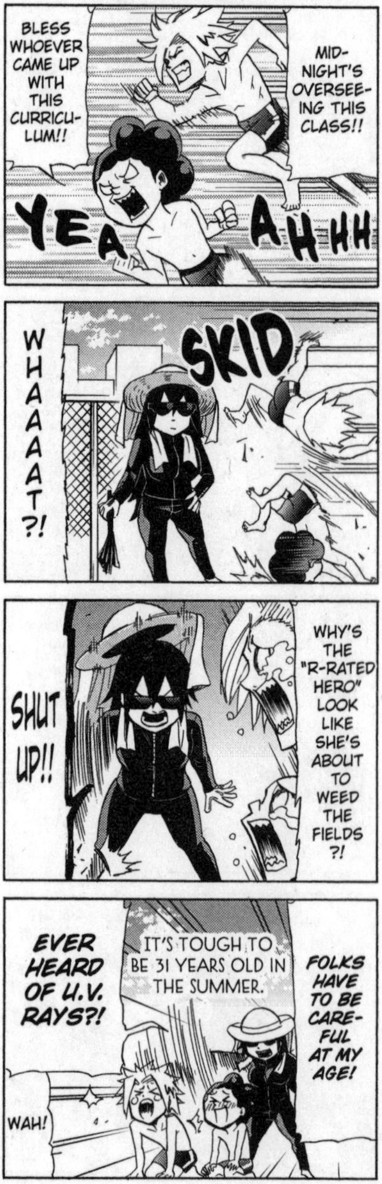

MID-NIGHT'S OVERSEE-ING THIS CLASS!!
BLESS WHOEVER CAME UP WITH THIS CURRICU-LUM!!
YEAAHHHH
SKID
WHAAAAT?!
WHY'S THE "R-RATED HERO" LOOK LIKE SHE'S ABOUT TO WEED THE FIELDS ?!
SHUT UP!!
FOLKS HAVE TO BE CARE-FUL AT MY AGE!
IT'S TOUGH TO BE 31 YEARS OLD IN THE SUMMER.
EVER HEARD OF U.V. RAYS?!
WAH!

It Burns

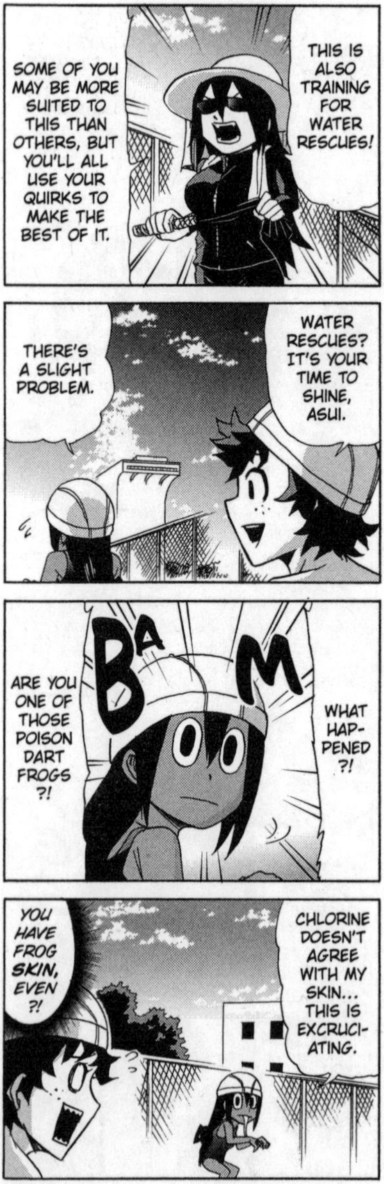

THIS IS ALSO TRAINING FOR WATER RESCUES!
SOME OF YOU MAY BE MORE SUITED TO THIS THAN OTHERS, BUT YOU'LL ALL USE YOUR QUIRKS TO MAKE THE BEST OF IT.
WATER RESCUES? IT'S YOUR TIME TO SHINE, ASUI.
THERE'S A SLIGHT PROBLEM.
BAM
WHAT HAP-PENED ?!
ARE YOU ONE OF THOSE POISON DART FROGS ?!
CHLORINE DOESN'T AGREE WITH MY SKIN... THIS IS EXCRUCI-ATING.
YOU HAVE FROG SKIN, EVEN ?!

HUMAN RESOURCES

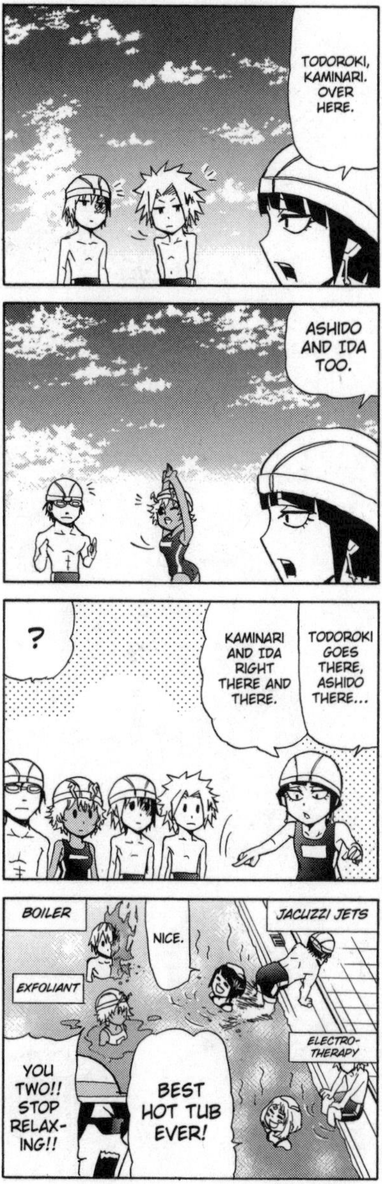
TODOROKI, KAMINARI. OVER HERE.
ASHIDO AND IDA TOO.
TODOROKI GOES THERE, ASHIDO THERE...
KAMINARI AND IDA RIGHT THERE AND THERE.
?
JACUZZI JETS
NICE.
BOILER
EXFOLIANT
ELECTRO-THERAPY
BEST HOT TUB EVER!
YOU TWO!! STOP RELAXING!!

CONTAMINANT

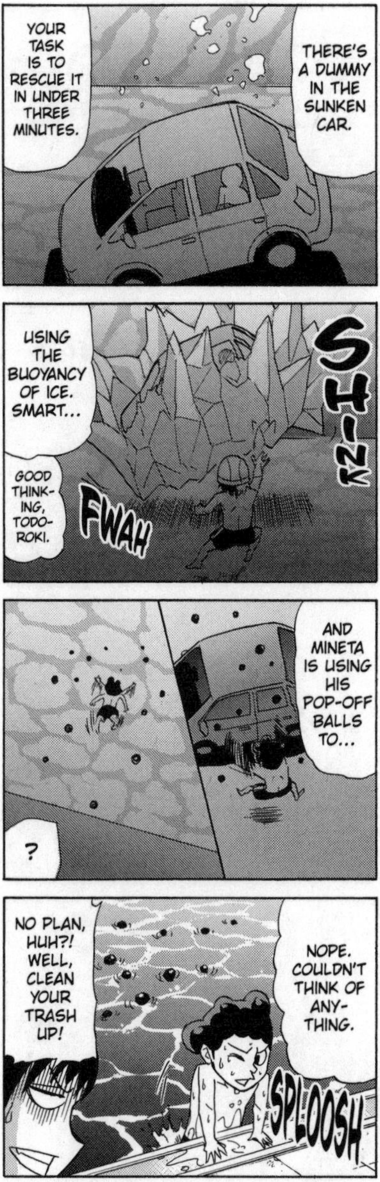
THERE'S A DUMMY IN THE SUNKEN CAR.
YOUR TASK IS TO RESCUE IT IN UNDER THREE MINUTES.
SHINK
USING THE BUOYANCY OF ICE. SMART...
GOOD THINKING, TODOROKI.
FWAH
AND MINETA IS USING HIS POP-OFF BALLS TO...
?
NOPE. COULDN'T THINK OF ANYTHING.
NO PLAN, HUH?! WELL, CLEAN YOUR TRASH UP!
SPLOOSH

NEPTUNIDA

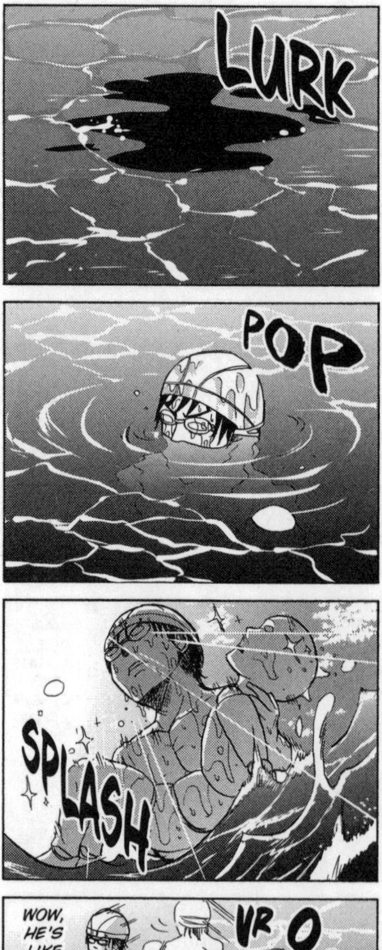
LURK
POP
SPLASH
VROOOM
WOW, HE'S LIKE SOME SORTA SEA GOD.
VROOM
ENGINE

CPR AVERSION

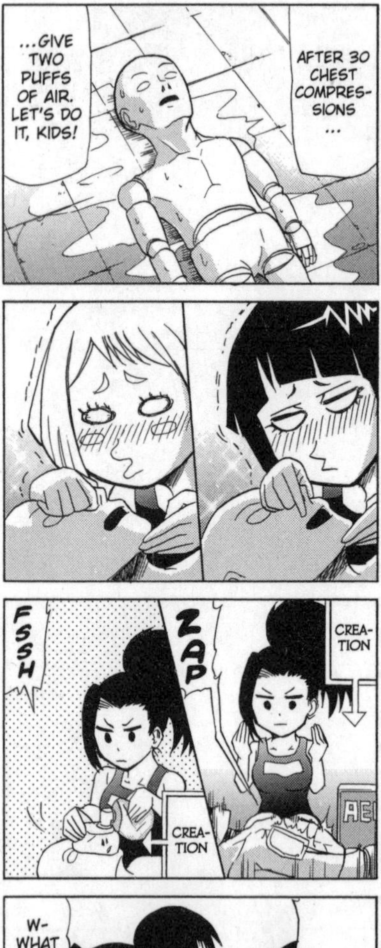
AFTER 30 CHEST COMPRES-SIONS ...
...GIVE TWO PUFFS OF AIR. LET'S DO IT, KIDS!
CREA-TION
ZAP
FSSH
CREA-TION
CHEATER !!
W-WHAT ?

Mouth Envy

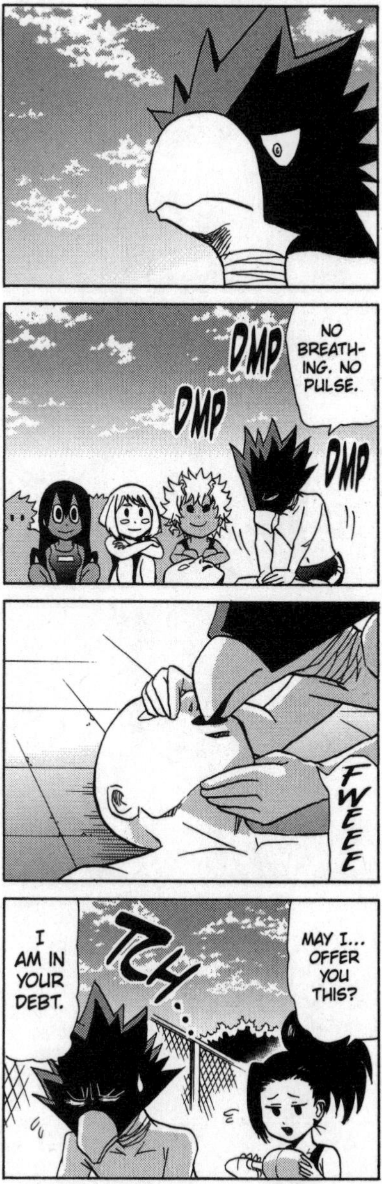
NO BREATH-ING. NO PULSE.
DMP
DMP
DMP
FWEEE
MAY I... OFFER YOU THIS?
TCH...
I AM IN YOUR DEBT.

Weird Flex

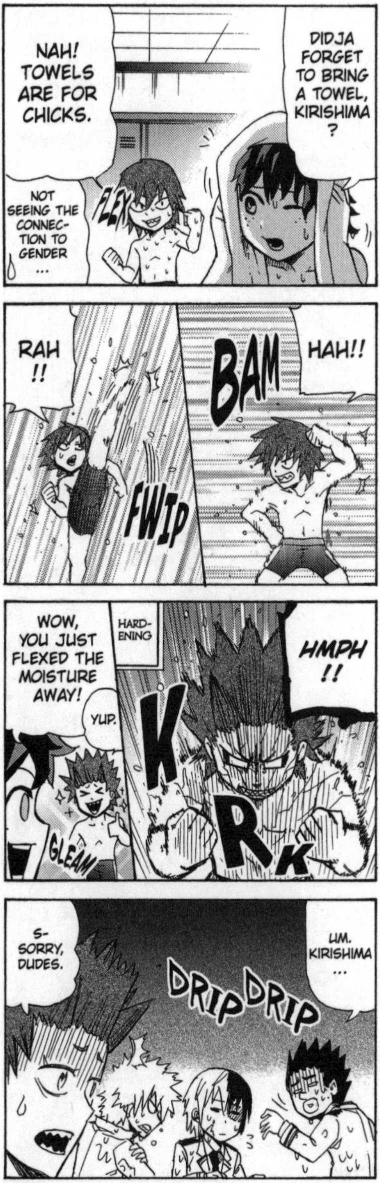
DIDJA FORGET TO BRING A TOWEL, KIRISHIMA?
NAH! TOWELS ARE FOR CHICKS.
FLEX
NOT SEEING THE CONNEC-TION TO GENDER...
HAH!!
BAM
RAH!!
FWIP
HMPH!!
HARD-ENING
KRK
WOW, YOU JUST FLEXED THE MOISTURE AWAY!
YUP.
GLEAM
UM. KIRISHIMA...
DRIP DRIP
S-SORRY, DUDES.

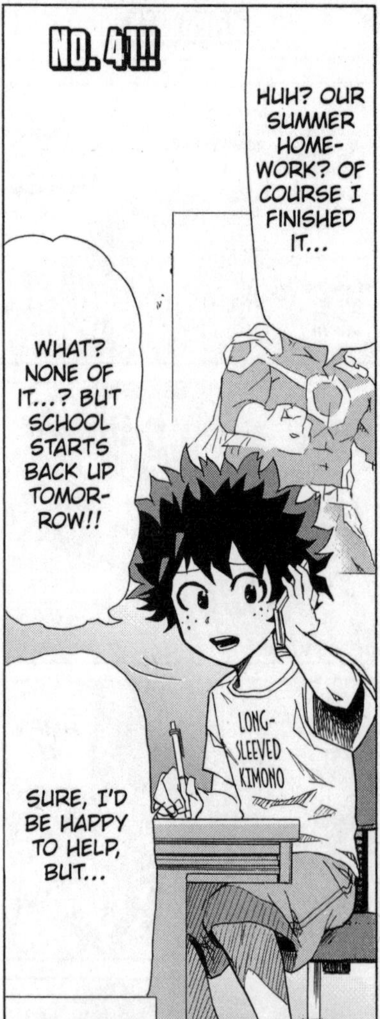
No. 41!!
HUH? OUR SUMMER HOME-WORK? OF COURSE I FINISHED IT...
WHAT? NONE OF IT...? BUT SCHOOL STARTS BACK UP TOMOR-ROW!!
LONG-SLEEVED KIMONO
SURE, I'D BE HAPPY TO HELP, BUT...
HOW ABOUT YOU? DID YOU REMEMBER TO DO ANY SUMMER ASSIGN-MENTS, DEAR READER?

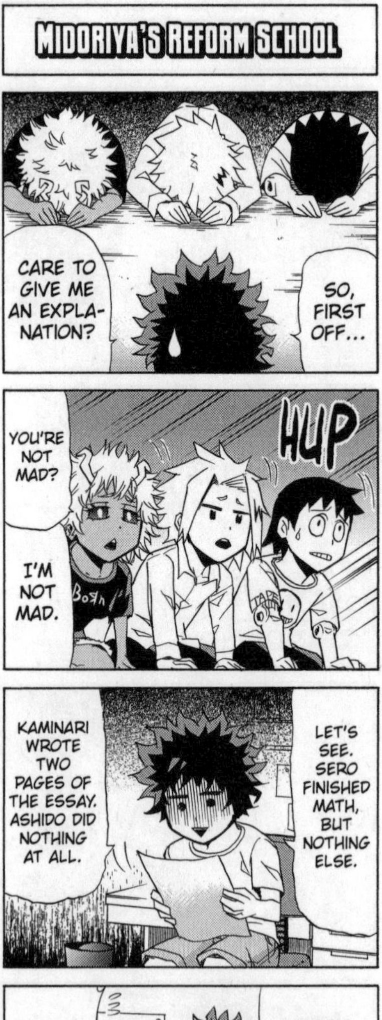
MIDORIYA'S REFORM SCHOOL
SO, FIRST OFF...
CARE TO GIVE ME AN EXPLA-NATION?
HUP
YOU'RE NOT MAD?
I'M NOT MAD.
LET'S SEE. SERO FINISHED MATH, BUT NOTHING ELSE.
KAMINARI WROTE TWO PAGES OF THE ESSAY. ASHIDO DID NOTHING AT ALL.
HERE'S OUR SCHEDULE FOR TODAY. THINK YOU'RE READY?
10:00-12:00
ASSICAL LITERATURE
12:00-2:00
BOOK REPORT
2:00-8:00
EPENDENT RESEARCH
8:00-10:00
ASSICAL JAPANESE
10:00-12:00
COOKING PROJECT
12:00-2:00
MATH
2:00-4:00
CHEMISTRY
YOU SAID YOU WEREN'T MAD!
BUT I'M NOT.

HOMEWORK BY ANY OTHER NAME

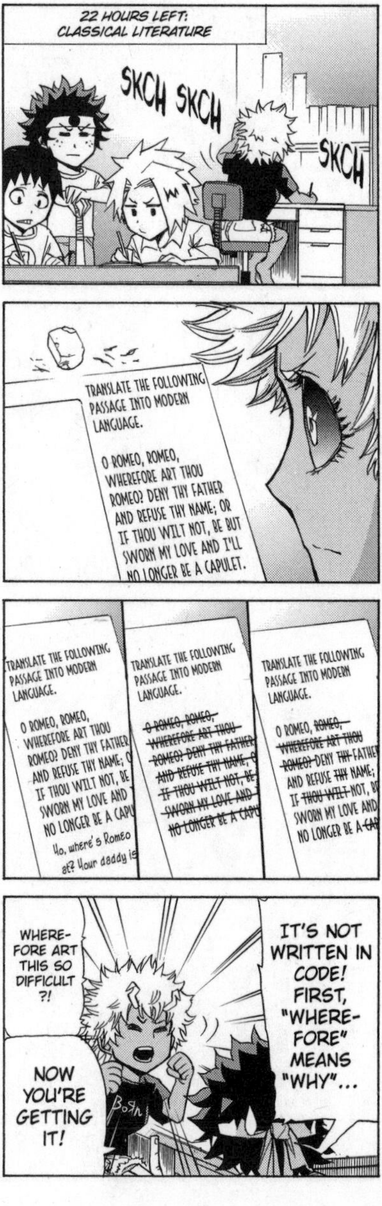
22 HOURS LEFT: CLASSICAL LITERATURE
SKCH SKCH
SKCH
TRANSLATE THE FOLLOWING PASSAGE INTO MODERN LANGUAGE.
O ROMEO, ROMEO, WHEREFORE ART THOU ROMEO? DENY THY FATHER AND REFUSE THY NAME; OR IF THOU WILT NOT, BE BUT SWORN MY LOVE AND I'LL NO LONGER BE A CAPULET.
TRANSLATE THE FOLLOWING PASSAGE INTO MODERN LANGUAGE.
O ROMEO, ROMEO, WHEREFORE ART THOU ROMEO? DENY THY FATHER AND REFUSE THY NAME; IF THOU WILT NOT, BE SWORN MY LOVE AND NO LONGER BE A CAP
TRANSLATE THE FOLLOWING PASSAGE INTO MODERN LANGUAGE.
O ROMEO, ROMEO, WHEREFORE ART THOU ROMEO? DENY THY FATHER AND REFUSE THY NAME; O IF THOU WILT NOT, BE SWORN MY LOVE AND NO LONGER BE A CAPU
TRANSLATE THE FOLLOWING PASSAGE INTO MODERN LANGUAGE.
O ROMEO, ROMEO, WHEREFORE ART THOU ROMEO? DENY THY FATHER AND REFUSE THY NAME; O IF THOU WILT NOT, BE SWORN MY LOVE AND NO LONGER BE A CAPUL
Yo, where's Romeo at? Your daddy is
IT'S NOT WRITTEN IN CODE! FIRST, "WHEREFORE" MEANS "WHY"...
WHEREFORE ART THIS SO DIFFICULT?!
NOW YOU'RE GETTING IT!

FOR LEARNING'S SAKE

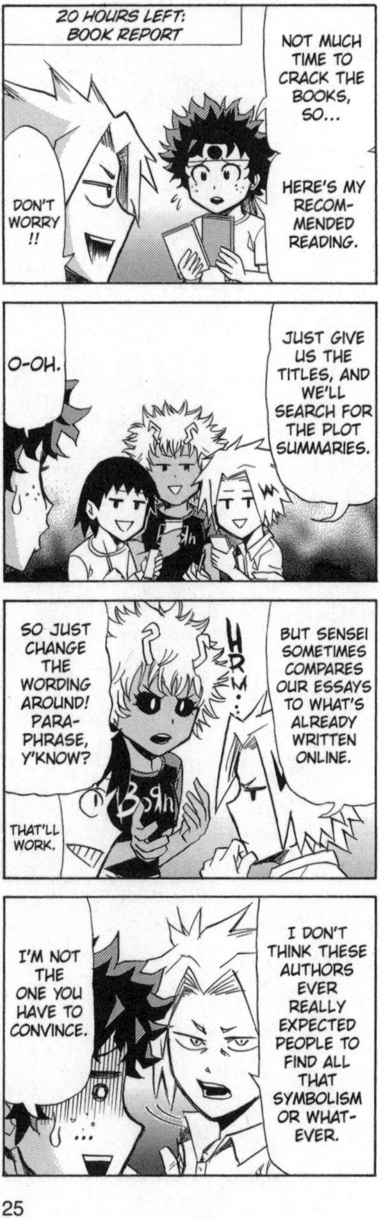
20 HOURS LEFT: BOOK REPORT
NOT MUCH TIME TO CRACK THE BOOKS, SO...
HERE'S MY RECOMMENDED READING.
DON'T WORRY!!
JUST GIVE US THE TITLES, AND WE'LL SEARCH FOR THE PLOT SUMMARIES.
O-OH.
BUT SENSEI SOMETIMES COMPARES OUR ESSAYS TO WHAT'S ALREADY WRITTEN ONLINE.
HRM...
SO JUST CHANGE THE WORDING AROUND! PARAPHRASE, Y'KNOW?
THAT'LL WORK.
I DON'T THINK THESE AUTHORS EVER REALLY EXPECTED PEOPLE TO FIND ALL THAT SYMBOLISM OR WHATEVER.
I'M NOT THE ONE YOU HAVE TO CONVINCE.
...

TEAMWORK

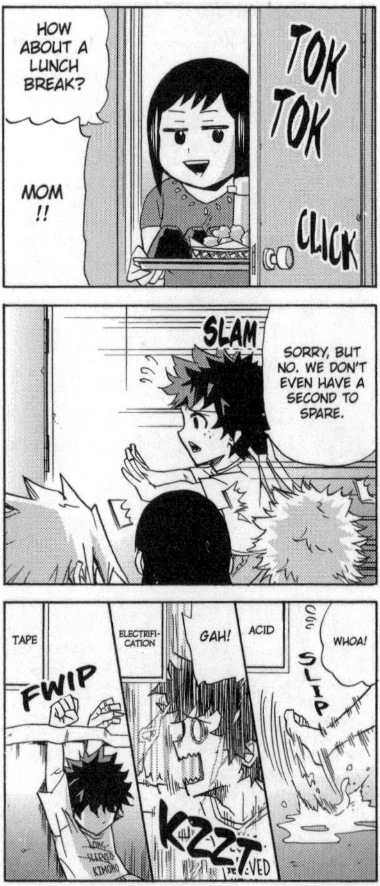
TOK TOK
HOW ABOUT A LUNCH BREAK?
CLICK
MOM!!
SORRY, BUT NO. WE DON'T EVEN HAVE A SECOND TO SPARE.
SLAM
WHOA!
SLIP
ACID
GAH!
ELECTRIFICATION
TAPE
FWIP
KZZT
YOU'RE TOO KIND, REALLY.
OH? BUT IZUKU SAID...
NAW, LOOK! HE'S GOT BOTH ARMS UP IN APPROVAL!
LONG-SLEEVED KIMONO

ALL PLAY AND NO WORK

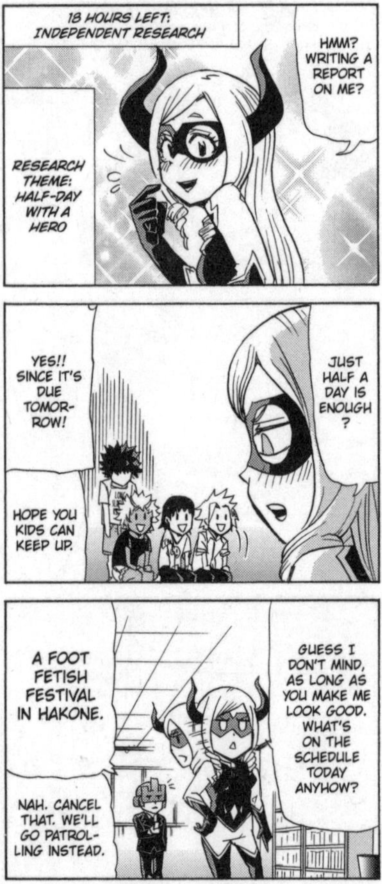
HMM? WRITING A REPORT ON ME?
18 HOURS LEFT: INDEPENDENT RESEARCH
RESEARCH THEME: HALF-DAY WITH A HERO
JUST HALF A DAY IS ENOUGH?
YES!! SINCE IT'S DUE TOMORROW!
HOPE YOU KIDS CAN KEEP UP.
GUESS I DON'T MIND, AS LONG AS YOU MAKE ME LOOK GOOD. WHAT'S ON THE SCHEDULE TODAY ANYHOW?
A FOOT FETISH FESTIVAL IN HAKONE.
NAH. CANCEL THAT. WE'LL GO PATROLLING INSTEAD.
I WOULDN'T MIND A TRIP TO HAKONE.
HOT SPRINGS! WOO!
WE'LL WRITE SOME GLOWING REPORTS ABOUT YOU.
I THOUGHT YOU KIDS HAD SCHOOL TOMORROW?

THE DEVIL WEARS SPANDEX

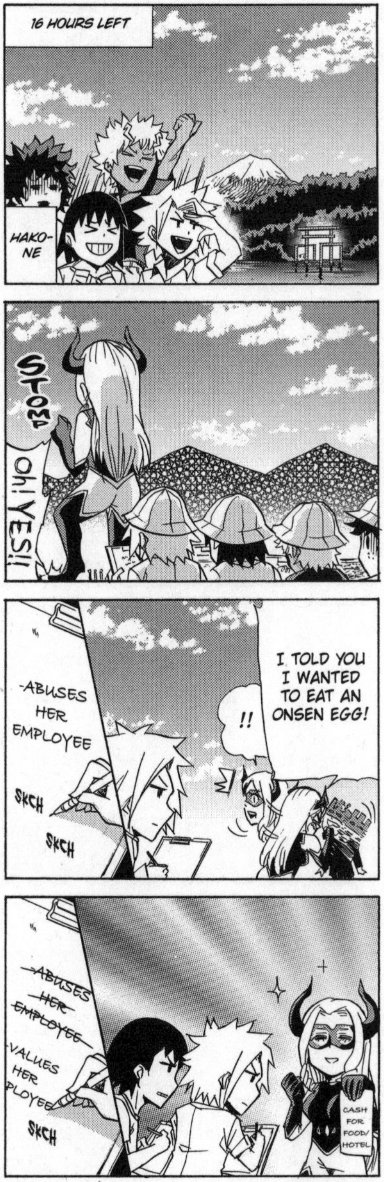
16 HOURS LEFT
HAKONE
STOMP
Oh! YES!!
I TOLD YOU I WANTED TO EAT AN ONSEN EGG!
!!
-ABUSES HER EMPLOYEE
SKCH
SKCH
CASH FOR FOOD/ HOTEL
ABUSES HER EMPLOYEE
-VALUES HER PLOYEE
SKCH

REST FOR THE WEARY

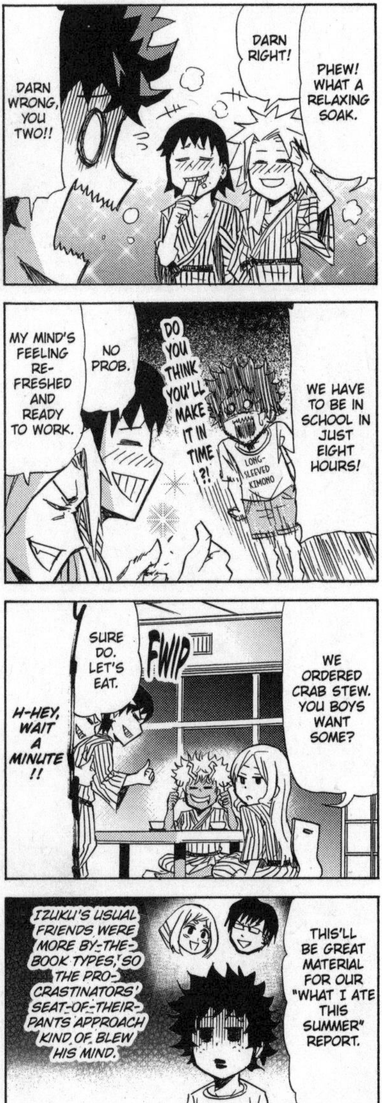
PHEW! WHAT A RELAXING SOAK.
DARN RIGHT!
DARN WRONG, YOU TWO!!
WE HAVE TO BE IN SCHOOL IN JUST EIGHT HOURS!
DO YOU THINK YOU'LL MAKE IT IN TIME ?!
LONG-SLEEVED KIMONO
NO PROB.
MY MIND'S FEELING RE-FRESHED AND READY TO WORK.
WE ORDERED CRAB STEW. YOU BOYS WANT SOME?
FWIP
SURE DO. LET'S EAT.
H-HEY, WAIT A MINUTE !!
THIS'LL BE GREAT MATERIAL FOR OUR "WHAT I ATE THIS SUMMER" REPORT.
YEAH, THAT!
IZUKU'S USUAL FRIENDS WERE MORE BY-THE-BOOK TYPES, SO THE PRO-CRASTINATORS' SEAT-OF-THEIR-PANTS APPROACH KIND OF BLEW HIS MIND.
LONG-SLEEVED KIMONO

Overachiever's Confusion

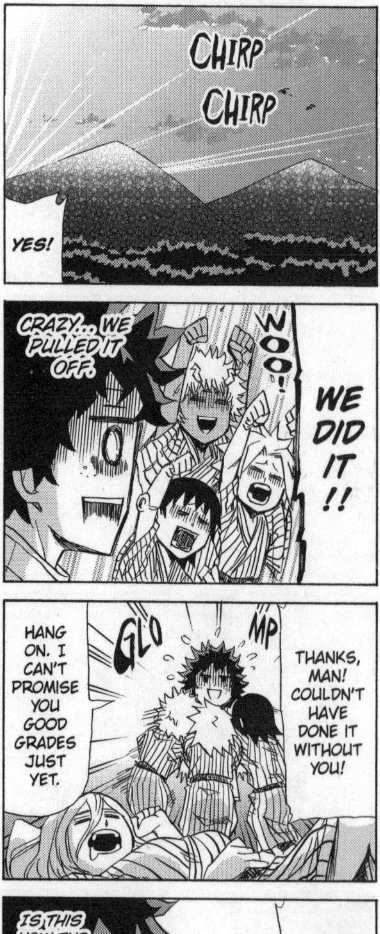
CHIRP
CHIRP
YES!
WOO!
WE DID IT!!
CRAZY... WE PULLED IT OFF.
THANKS, MAN! COULDN'T HAVE DONE IT WITHOUT YOU!
GLOMP
HANG ON. I CAN'T PROMISE YOU GOOD GRADES JUST YET.
GRADES?! WHO CARES! TURNING IN THE ASSIGNMENTS IS ALL THAT COUNTS.
IS THIS HOW THE BOTTOM OF THE CLASS LIVES THEIR LIVES?
PUMP

The Cautionary Tale of Deku

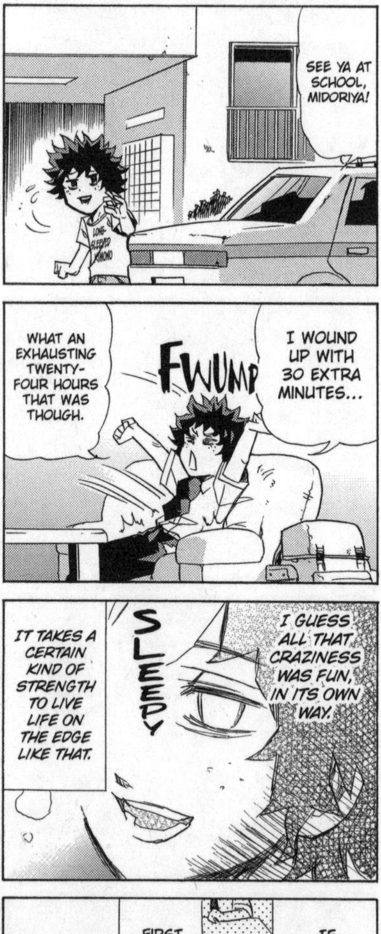
SEE YA AT SCHOOL, MIDORIYA!
I WOUND UP WITH 30 EXTRA MINUTES...
FWUMP
WHAT AN EXHAUSTING TWENTY-FOUR HOURS THAT WAS THOUGH.
I GUESS ALL THAT CRAZINESS WAS FUN, IN ITS OWN WAY.
SLEEPY
IT TAKES A CERTAIN KIND OF STRENGTH TO LIVE LIFE ON THE EDGE LIKE THAT.
IF NOTHING ELSE, THIS EXPERIENCE TAUGHT DEKU...
FIRST DAY BACK, AND MIDORIYA'S LATE?
...THE IMPORTANCE OF STICKING TO HOW HE DID THINGS.

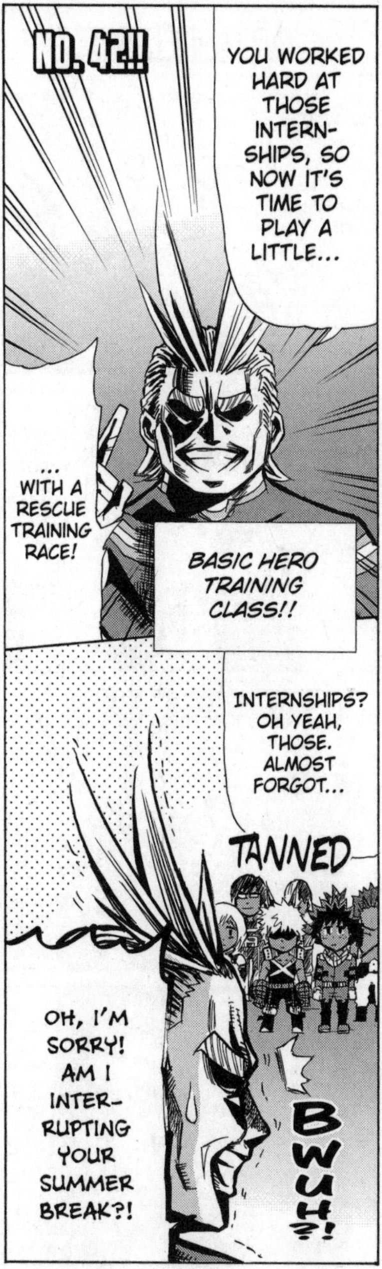
No. 42!!
YOU WORKED HARD AT THOSE INTERNSHIPS, SO NOW IT'S TIME TO PLAY A LITTLE...
...WITH A RESCUE TRAINING RACE!
BASIC HERO TRAINING CLASS!!
INTERNSHIPS? OH YEAH, THOSE. ALMOST FORGOT...
TANNED
BWUH?!
OH, I'M SORRY! AM I INTERRUPTING YOUR SUMMER BREAK?!

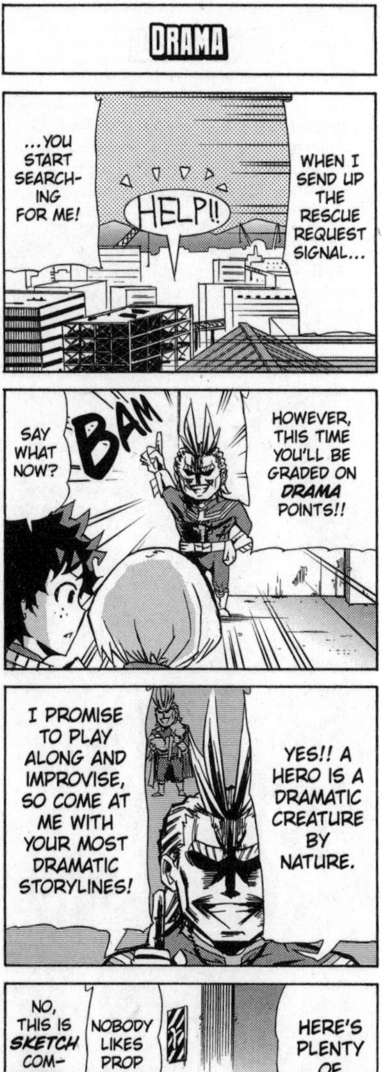
DRAMA
WHEN I SEND UP THE RESCUE REQUEST SIGNAL...
HELP!!
...YOU START SEARCHING FOR ME!
HOWEVER, THIS TIME YOU'LL BE GRADED ON DRAMA POINTS!!
BAM
SAY WHAT NOW?
YES!! A HERO IS A DRAMATIC CREATURE BY NATURE.
I PROMISE TO PLAY ALONG AND IMPROVISE, SO COME AT ME WITH YOUR MOST DRAMATIC STORYLINES!
HERE'S PLENTY OF PROPS TO USE AS YOU SEE FIT!
BAM
The heck is this?
NOBODY LIKES PROP COMEDY.
NO, THIS IS SKETCH COM— I MEAN, DRAMA!
SKETCH COMEDY. RIGHT. WE ALL HEARD THAT.

SMASHING

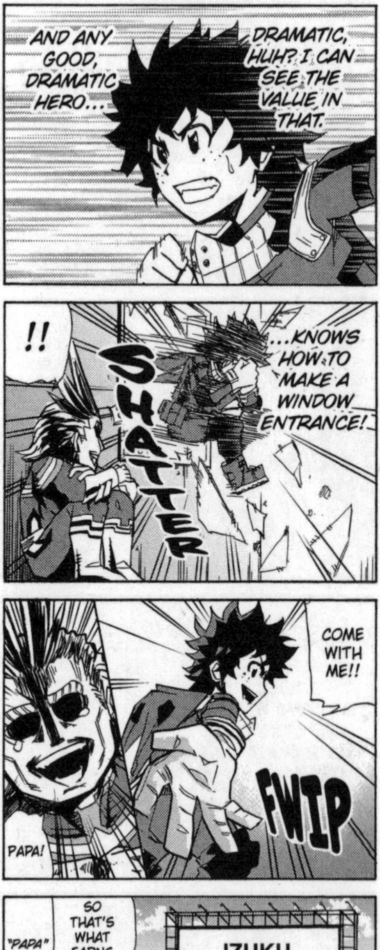
DRAMATIC, HUH? I CAN SEE THE VALUE IN THAT.
AND ANY GOOD, DRAMATIC HERO...
...KNOWS HOW TO MAKE A WINDOW ENTRANCE!
SHATTER
!!
COME WITH ME!!
FWIP
PAPA!
IZUKU MIDORIYA 70 POINTS
SO THAT'S WHAT EARNS 70 POINTS.
"PAPA"?
Booo!
OOOOH!

DARK-ISH KNIGHT

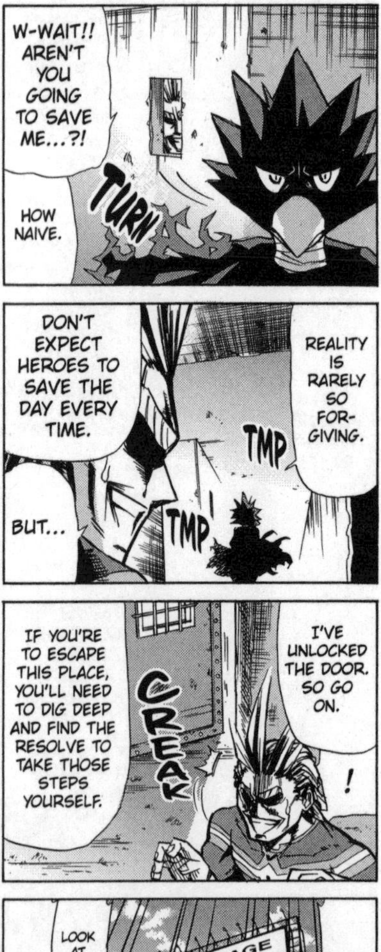
W-WAIT!! AREN'T YOU GOING TO SAVE ME...?!
TURN
HOW NAIVE.
DON'T EXPECT HEROES TO SAVE THE DAY EVERY TIME.
REALITY IS RARELY SO FOR-GIVING.
TMP
TMP
BUT...
I'VE UNLOCKED THE DOOR. SO GO ON.
IF YOU'RE TO ESCAPE THIS PLACE, YOU'LL NEED TO DIG DEEP AND FIND THE RESOLVE TO TAKE THOSE STEPS YOURSELF.
CREAK
!
FUMIKAGE TOKOYAMI 96 POINTS
HE WAS AN ANTI-HERO!!
LOOK AT THAT HIGH SCORE!!
TOO COOL!!
YEAAHH

Kirishima's Bizarre Adventure

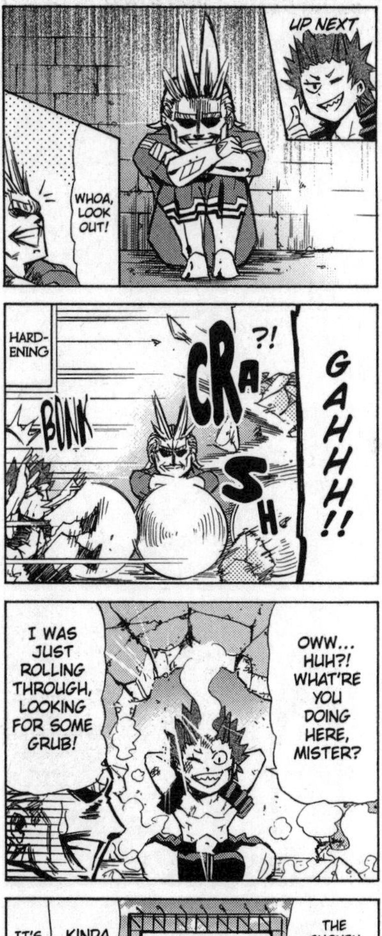
UP NEXT
WHOA, LOOK OUT!
GAHHHH!!
?!
CRASH
HARD-ENING
BONK
OWW... HUH?! WHAT'RE YOU DOING HERE, MISTER?
I WAS JUST ROLLING THROUGH, LOOKING FOR SOME GRUB!
THE SHONEN MANGA PRO-TAGONIST APPROACH. I LOVE IT!!
EIJIRO KIRISHIMA 52 POINTS
KINDA CLICHÉ.
IT'S BEEN DONE.
Huh? That was so good though.
Agreed.

Heeeere's Momoyao!

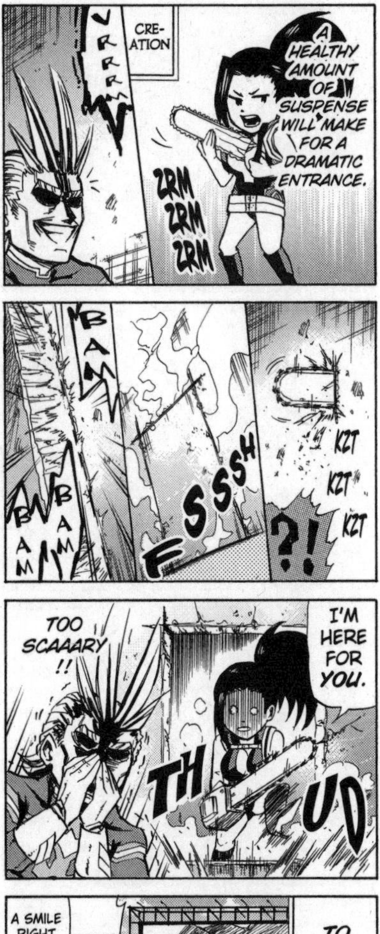
A HEALTHY AMOUNT OF SUSPENSE WILL MAKE FOR A DRAMATIC ENTRANCE.
CRE-ATION
VRRRM
ZRM ZRM ZRM
KZT KZT KZT
?!
BAM
FSSSH
BAM BAM
I'M HERE FOR YOU.
TOO SCAAARY!!
THUD
TO SAVE YOU.
GRIN
YIKES!
A SMILE RIGHT OUTTA A HORROR MOVIE!
30 POINTS
SHUDDER
THIS IS ACTUALLY WORKING FOR ME.

It's All Right, All Might

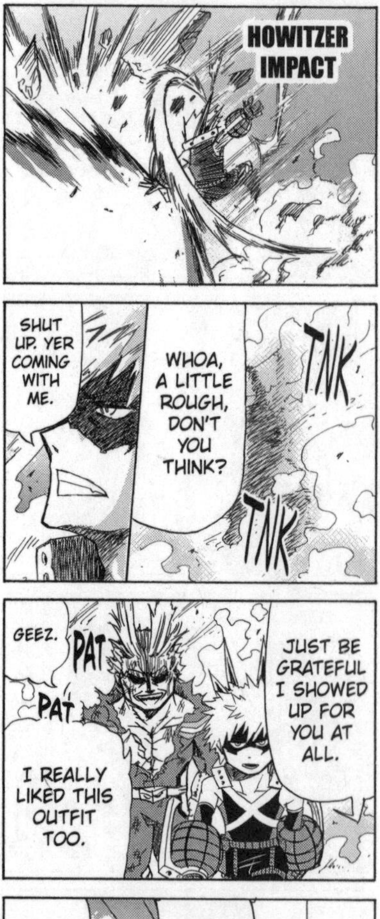
HOWITZER IMPACT
TNK
WHOA, A LITTLE ROUGH, DON'T YOU THINK?
SHUT UP. YER COMING WITH ME.
TNK
JUST BE GRATEFUL I SHOWED UP FOR YOU AT ALL.
PAT
GEEZ.
PAT
I REALLY LIKED THIS OUTFIT TOO.
93 POINTS
EH ?!
BUT THAT WOULDA KILLED AN ORDINARY CIVILIAN!
I GOT TO FLESH OUT MY CHAR-ACTER THOUGH.
NOT THE POINT!

Soapy

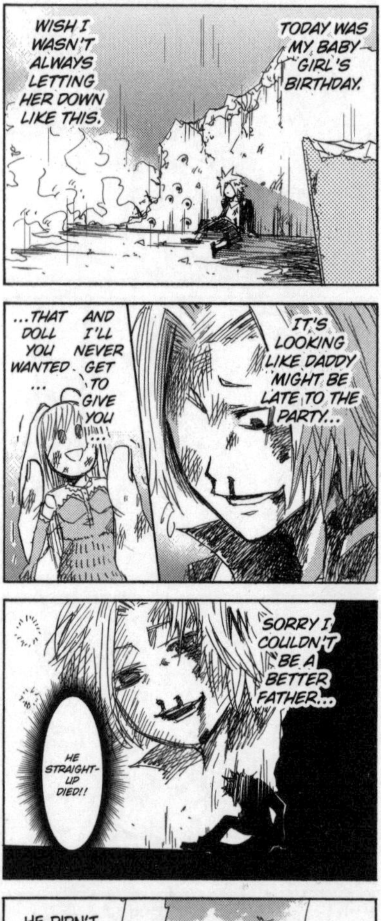
TODAY WAS MY BABY GIRL'S BIRTHDAY.
WISH I WASN'T ALWAYS LETTING HER DOWN LIKE THIS.
IT'S LOOKING LIKE DADDY MIGHT BE LATE TO THE PARTY...
AND I'LL NEVER GET TO GIVE YOU...
...THAT DOLL YOU WANTED...
SORRY I COULDN'T BE A BETTER FATHER...
HE STRAIGHT-UP DIED!!
OHH. SO DRAMATIC.
DENKI KAMINARI 100 POINTS
THE HELL ?!
HE DIDN'T EVEN BOTHER WITH THE RESCUE PART!
BOOOOO!!

MEGA MINETA X

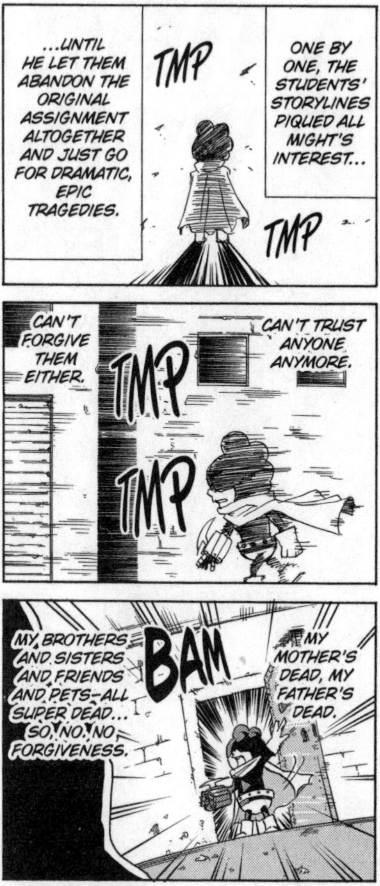
ONE BY ONE, THE STUDENTS' STORYLINES PIQUED ALL MIGHT'S INTEREST...
TMP
...UNTIL HE LET THEM ABANDON THE ORIGINAL ASSIGNMENT ALTOGETHER AND JUST GO FOR DRAMATIC, EPIC TRAGEDIES.
TMP
CAN'T TRUST ANYONE ANYMORE.
TMP
CAN'T FORGIVE THEM EITHER.
TMP
MY MOTHER'S DEAD, MY FATHER'S DEAD.
BAM
MY BROTHERS AND SISTERS AND FRIENDS AND PETS—ALL SUPER DEAD... SO, NO. NO FORGIVENESS.
YOU ARE...
...BEYOND REDEMPTION.

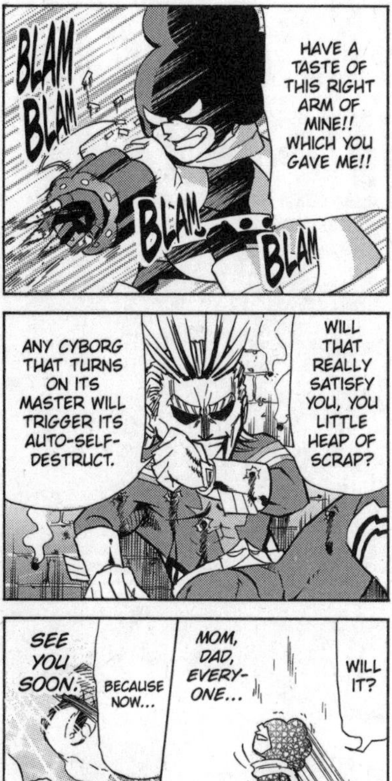
HAVE A TASTE OF THIS RIGHT ARM OF MINE!! WHICH YOU GAVE ME!!
BLAM
BLAM
BLAM
BLAM
WILL THAT REALLY SATISFY YOU, YOU LITTLE HEAP OF SCRAP?
ANY CYBORG THAT TURNS ON ITS MASTER WILL TRIGGER ITS AUTO-SELF-DESTRUCT.
WILL IT?
MOM, DAD, EVERYONE...
YEAH. I'M OKAY WITH THAT.
BECAUSE NOW...
SEE YOU SOON.
...I CAN KNOW PEACE.
MINORU MINETA 120 POINTS
KABOOM
ALL THOSE PLOT HOLES, EVERYONE DIED, AND HE STILL GOT EXTRA CREDIT?!

MY HERO ACADEMIA: SMASH!!

CHARACTER PROFILES!!

VOLUME 3 ALREADY?
HOW'D THAT HAPPEN?!
STILL ENDEAVORING TO BRING YOU
THAT SAME OLD *SMASH!!* QUALITY,
TIME AFTER TIME!!

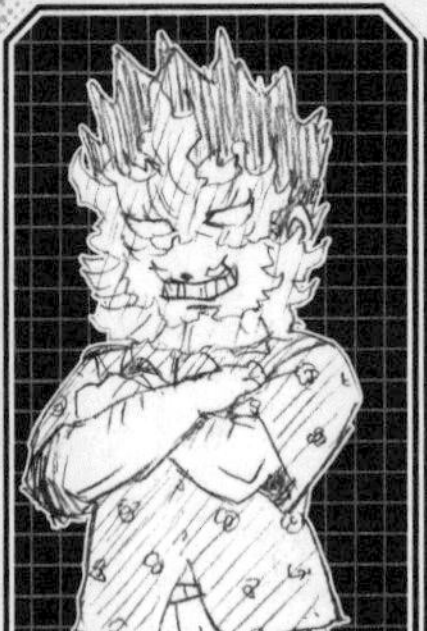

ENDEAVOR

SHOTO TODOROKI'S DAD AND THE CURRENT NUMBER TWO HERO!! WHEN HE REALIZED THAT HE COULD NEVER SURPASS ALL MIGHT WITH EFFORT ALONE, HE TRIED USING EUGENICS AND BRUTAL EDUCATIONAL METHODS TO TURN HIS OWN PROGENY INTO THE NEXT TOP HEROES. IN *SMASH!!*, THOUGH, HE CAN'T QUITE HIDE HIS DOTING-PARENT SIDE.

BASICALLY A SELFISH, PRATFALL-PRONE SITCOM DAD!!

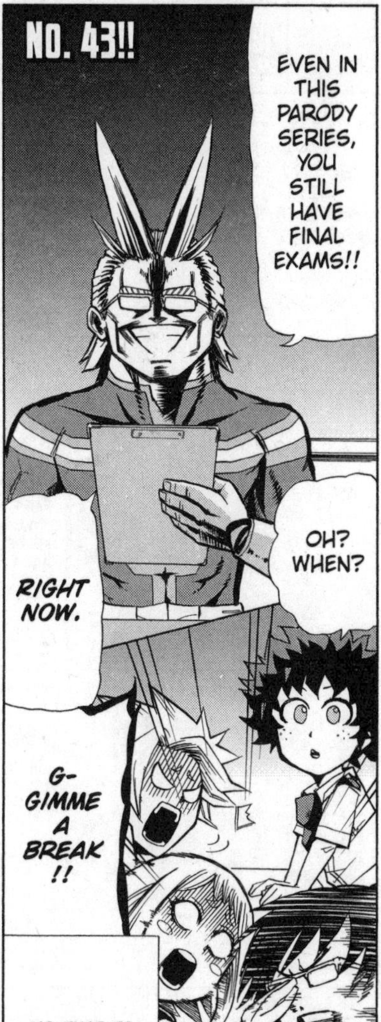
NO. 43!!
EVEN IN THIS PARODY SERIES, YOU STILL HAVE FINAL EXAMS!!
OH? WHEN?
RIGHT NOW.
G-GIMME A BREAK!!
NO TIME TO STUDY? TOO BAD! WE'RE DIVING RIGHT INTO THE FINAL EXAM ARC!
CLATTER

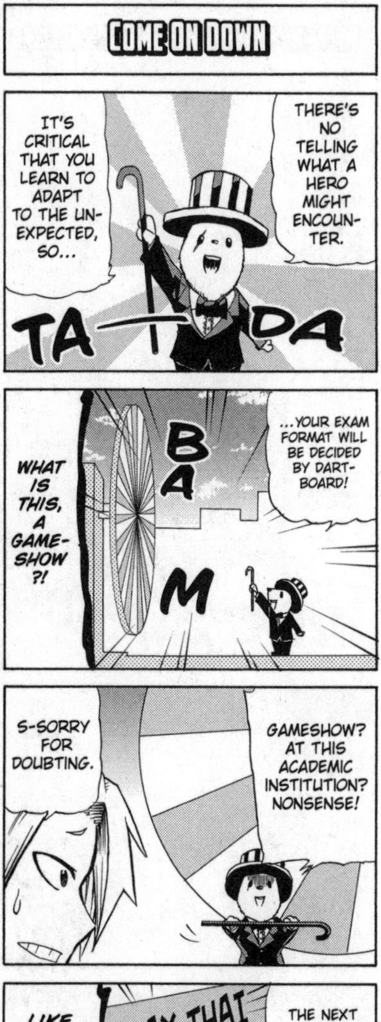
COME ON DOWN
THERE'S NO TELLING WHAT A HERO MIGHT ENCOUNTER.
IT'S CRITICAL THAT YOU LEARN TO ADAPT TO THE UNEXPECTED, SO...
TA-DA
...YOUR EXAM FORMAT WILL BE DECIDED BY DARTBOARD!
BAM
WHAT IS THIS, A GAMESHOW?!
GAMESHOW? AT THIS ACADEMIC INSTITUTION? NONSENSE!
S-SORRY FOR DOUBTING.
THE NEXT PERSON TO MAKE FUN OF THE PROCESS GOES TEN ROUNDS WITH A MUAY THAI FIGHTER!!
MUAY THAI
MARATHON
LIKE WE SAID, A GAMESHOW!!

Where We're Going, We Don't Need Muscles

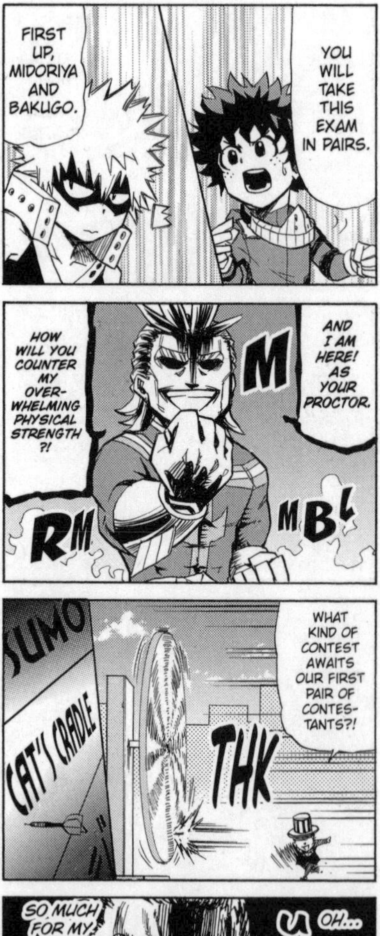
YOU WILL TAKE THIS EXAM IN PAIRS.
FIRST UP, MIDORIYA AND BAKUGO.
AND I AM HERE! AS YOUR PROCTOR.
M
HOW WILL YOU COUNTER MY OVER-WHELMING PHYSICAL STRENGTH?!
RM
MB
WHAT KIND OF CONTEST AWAITS OUR FIRST PAIR OF CONTES-TANTS?!
SUMO
THK
CAT'S CRADLE
OH...
SO MUCH FOR MY PHYSICAL STRENGTH.

Higher Education

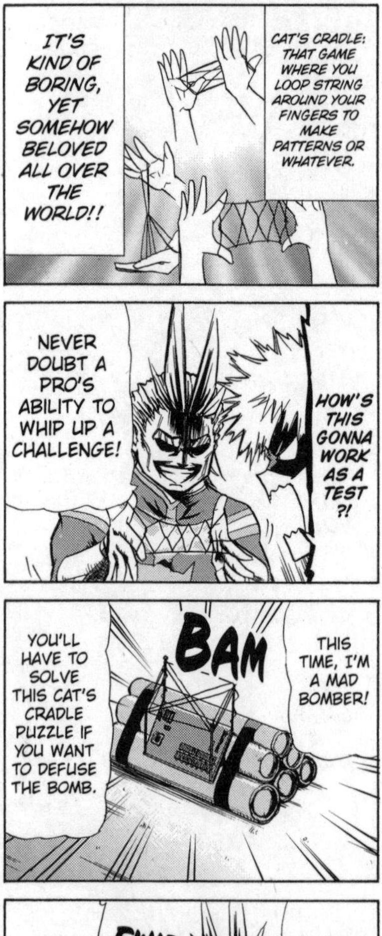
CAT'S CRADLE: THAT GAME WHERE YOU LOOP STRING AROUND YOUR FINGERS TO MAKE PATTERNS OR WHATEVER.
IT'S KIND OF BORING, YET SOMEHOW BELOVED ALL OVER THE WORLD!!
HOW'S THIS GONNA WORK AS A TEST?!
NEVER DOUBT A PRO'S ABILITY TO WHIP UP A CHALLENGE!
THIS TIME, I'M A MAD BOMBER!
BAM
YOU'LL HAVE TO SOLVE THIS CAT'S CRADLE PUZZLE IF YOU WANT TO DEFUSE THE BOMB.
TAKE ME ON IF YOU DARE!!
FWIP
I WANT MY TUITION BACK!!

DIDN'T GET OUT MUCH

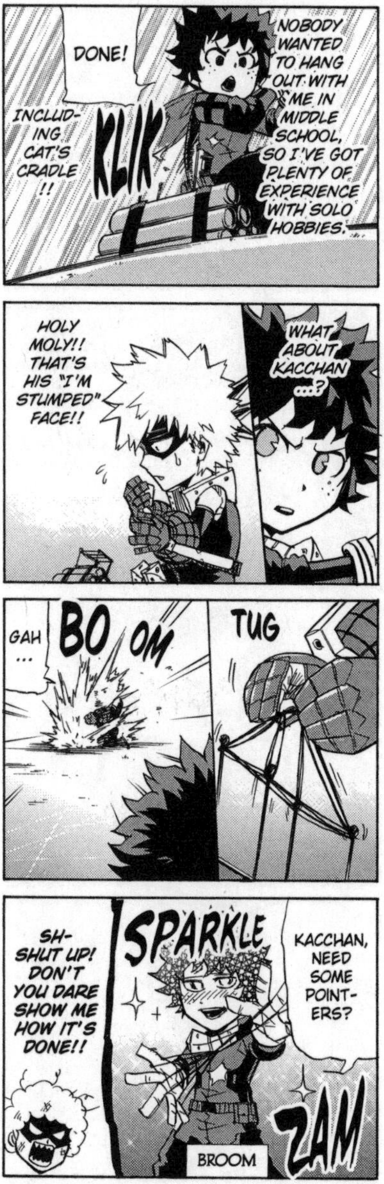
NOBODY WANTED TO HANG OUT WITH ME IN MIDDLE SCHOOL, SO I'VE GOT PLENTY OF EXPERIENCE WITH SOLO HOBBIES.
DONE!
KLIK
INCLUDING CAT'S CRADLE!!
WHAT ABOUT KACCHAN...?
HOLY MOLY!! THAT'S HIS "I'M STUMPED" FACE!!
TUG
BOOM
GAH...
KACCHAN, NEED SOME POINTERS?
SPARKLE
SH-SHUT UP! DON'T YOU DARE SHOW ME HOW IT'S DONE!!
ZAM
BROOM

THE STRINGS THAT BIND

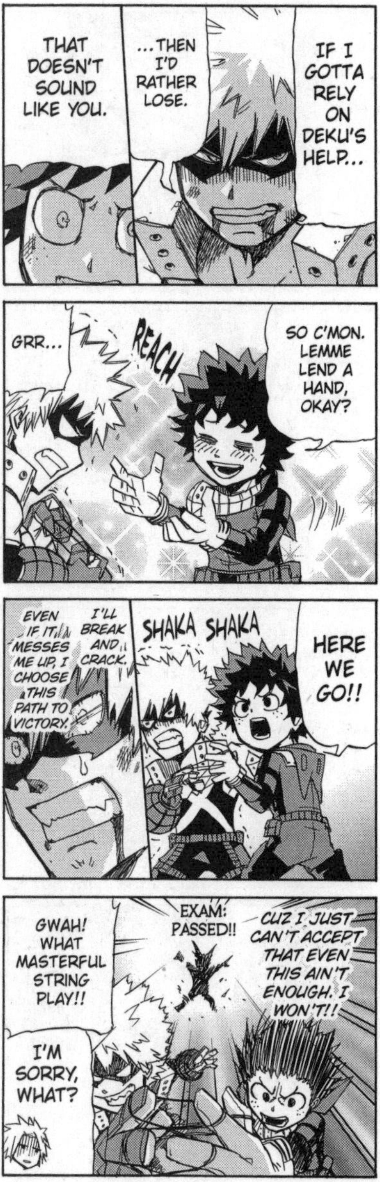
IF I GOTTA RELY ON DEKU'S HELP...
...THEN I'D RATHER LOSE.
THAT DOESN'T SOUND LIKE YOU.
SO C'MON. LEMME LEND A HAND, OKAY?
REACH
GRR...
HERE WE GO!!
SHAKA SHAKA
I'LL BREAK AND CRACK.
EVEN IF IT MESSES ME UP, I CHOOSE THIS PATH TO VICTORY.
CUZ I JUST CAN'T ACCEPT THAT EVEN THIS AIN'T ENOUGH. I WON'T!!
EXAM: PASSED!!
GWAH! WHAT MASTERFUL STRING PLAY!!
I'M SORRY, WHAT?

ERASER MOTIVATOR

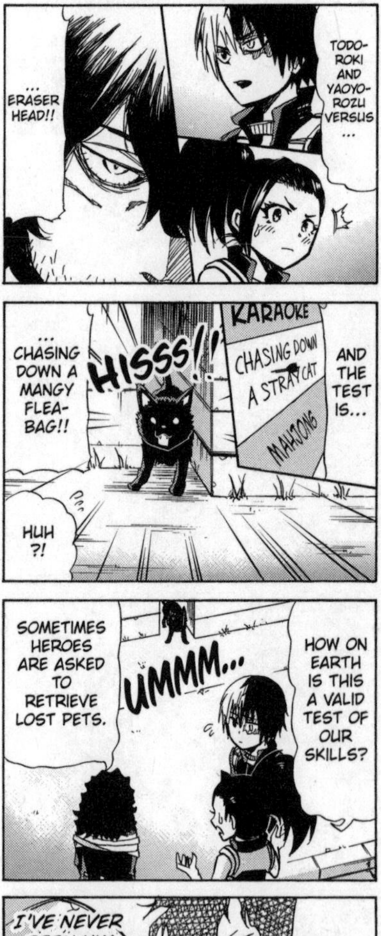
TODOROKI AND YAOYOROZU VERSUS...
...ERASER HEAD!!
AND THE TEST IS...
KARAOKE
CHASING DOWN A STRAY CAT
MAHJONG
HISSS!!
...CHASING DOWN A MANGY FLEABAG!!
HUH ?!
HOW ON EARTH IS THIS A VALID TEST OF OUR SKILLS?
UMMM...
SOMETIMES HEROES ARE ASKED TO RETRIEVE LOST PETS.
BUT ENOUGH WHINING. LET US BEGIN.
I'VE NEVER SEEN HIM THIS WIDE AWAKE BEFORE.
CAT PERSON
FWIP

THE PRICE OF PRIVILEGE

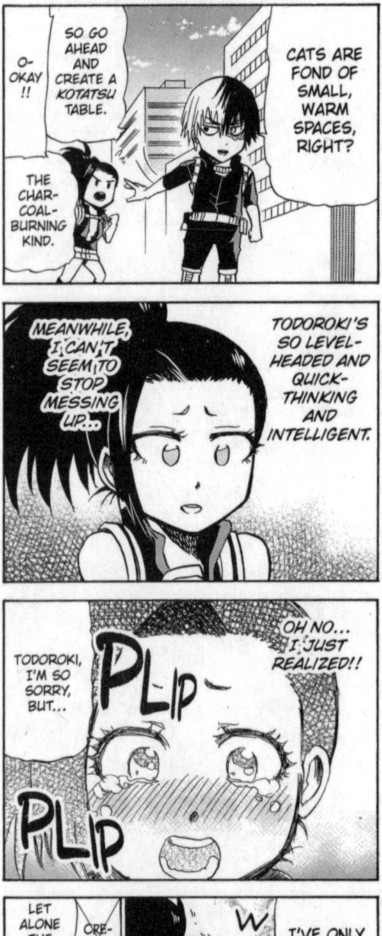
CATS ARE FOND OF SMALL, WARM SPACES, RIGHT?
SO GO AHEAD AND CREATE A KOTATSU TABLE.
O-OKAY!!
THE CHARCOAL-BURNING KIND.
TODOROKI'S SO LEVEL-HEADED AND QUICK-THINKING AND INTELLIGENT.
MEANWHILE, I CAN'T SEEM TO STOP MESSING UP...
OH NO... I JUST REALIZED!!
PLIP
TODOROKI, I'M SO SORRY, BUT...
PLIP
I'VE ONLY EVER SEEN A KOTATSU ON THE TELEVISION... I DON'T KNOW HOW TO CREATE ONE.
WAHHH!
CREATION
LET ALONE THE CHARCOAL-BURNING VARIETY!
NO BIG DEAL. HOW ABOUT A FIREPLACE?
I CAN DO THAT.

MOMOYAO RISING

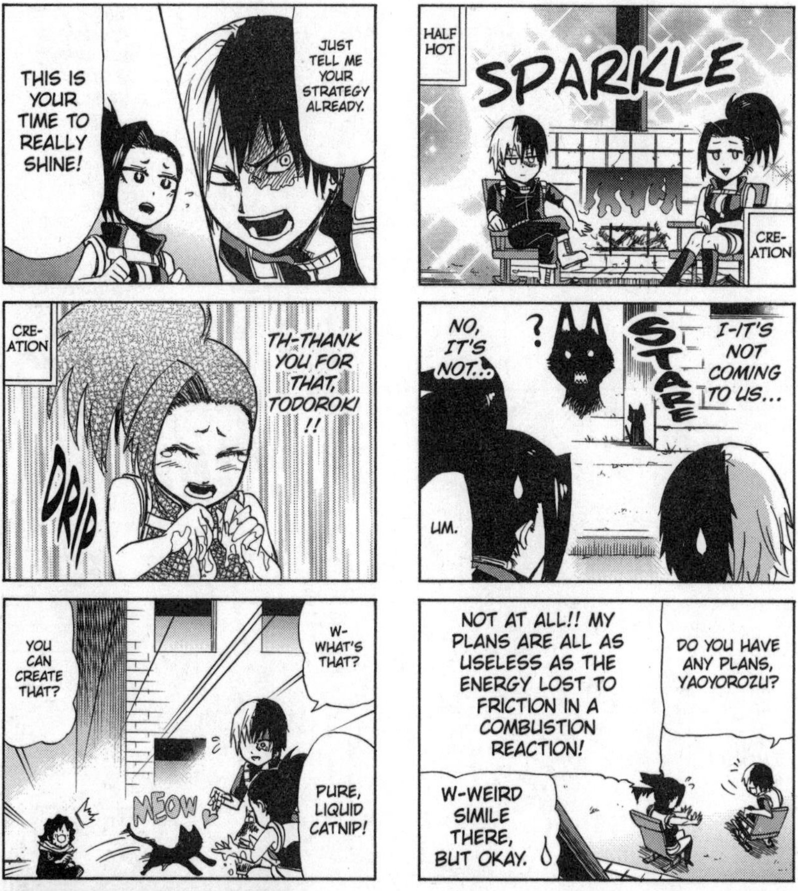

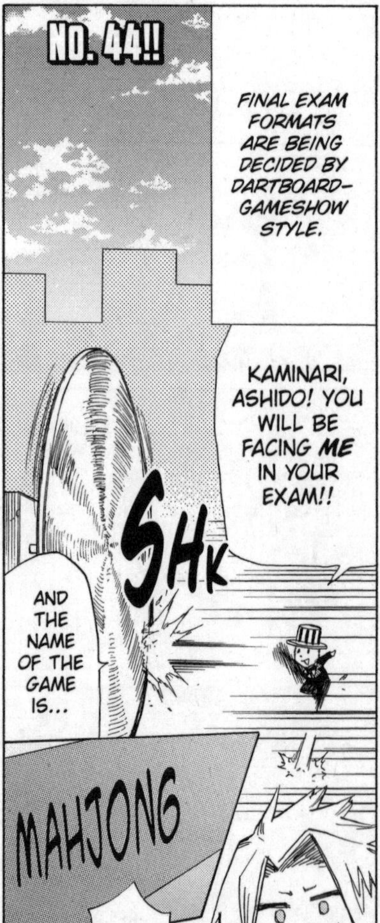
NO. 44!!
FINAL EXAM FORMATS ARE BEING DECIDED BY DARTBOARD-GAMESHOW STYLE.
KAMINARI, ASHIDO! YOU WILL BE FACING ME IN YOUR EXAM!!
SHK
AND THE NAME OF THE GAME IS...
MAHJONG
...MAH-JONG!!
MAH...JONG?

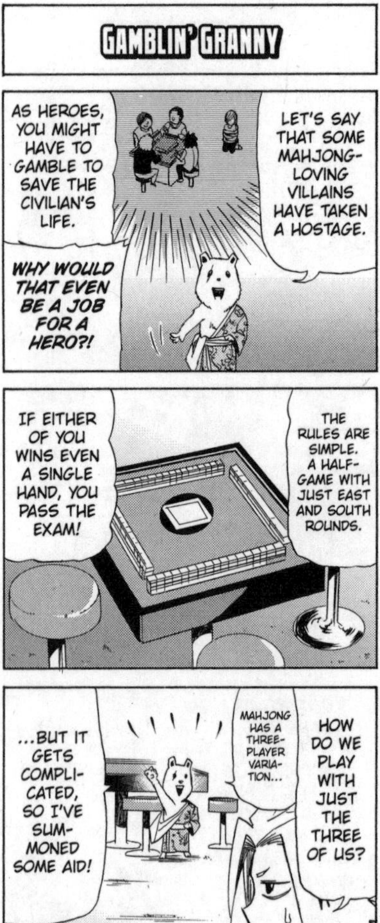
GAMBLIN' GRANNY
LET'S SAY THAT SOME MAHJONG-LOVING VILLAINS HAVE TAKEN A HOSTAGE.
AS HEROES, YOU MIGHT HAVE TO GAMBLE TO SAVE THE CIVILIAN'S LIFE.
WHY WOULD THAT EVEN BE A JOB FOR A HERO?!
THE RULES ARE SIMPLE. A HALF-GAME WITH JUST EAST AND SOUTH ROUNDS.
IF EITHER OF YOU WINS EVEN A SINGLE HAND, YOU PASS THE EXAM!
HOW DO WE PLAY WITH JUST THE THREE OF US?
MAHJONG HAS A THREE-PLAYER VARIATION...
...BUT IT GETS COMPLICATED, SO I'VE SUMMONED SOME AID!
VETERAN GAMBLER: RECOVERY GIRL!!
WE PLAYIN' BY THE KUITAN APPENDIX RULES OR WHAT?
SHE PLAYS FOR KEEPS!!
KASLAM

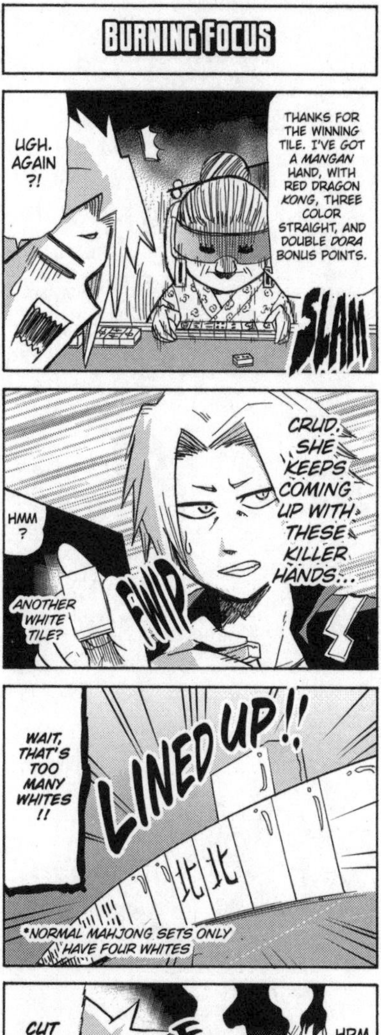
BURNING FOCUS
THANKS FOR THE WINNING TILE. I'VE GOT A MANGAN HAND, WITH RED DRAGON KONG, THREE COLOR STRAIGHT, AND DOUBLE DORA BONUS POINTS.
UGH. AGAIN?!
SLAM
CRUD. SHE KEEPS COMING UP WITH THESE KILLER HANDS...
FWIP
HMM?
ANOTHER WHITE TILE?
LINED UP!!
WAIT, THAT'S TOO MANY WHITES!!
北 北
*NORMAL MAHJONG SETS ONLY HAVE FOUR WHITES
HRM...
FSSSSH
CUT THAT OUT!! YOU'RE BURNING THE WRITING CLEAN OFF!!
ACID

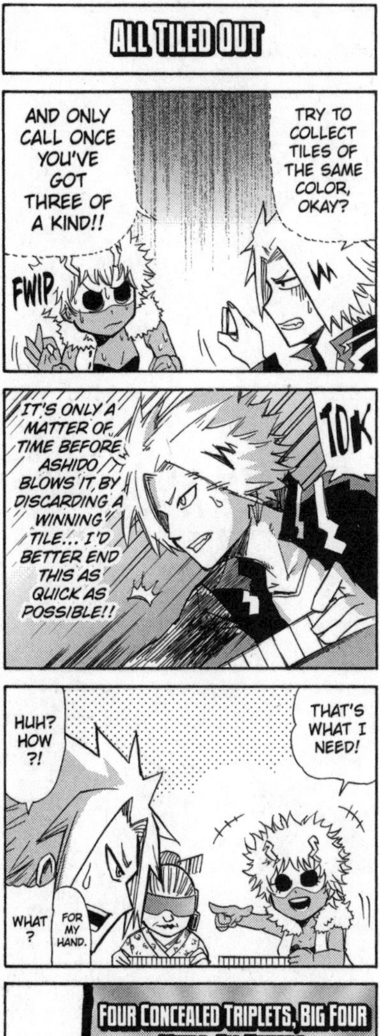
ALL TILED OUT
TRY TO COLLECT TILES OF THE SAME COLOR, OKAY?
AND ONLY CALL ONCE YOU'VE GOT THREE OF A KIND!!
FWIP
TOK
IT'S ONLY A MATTER OF TIME BEFORE ASHIDO BLOWS IT, BY DISCARDING A WINNING TILE... I'D BETTER END THIS AS QUICK AS POSSIBLE!!
THAT'S WHAT I NEED!
HUH? HOW?!
FOR MY HAND.
WHAT?
FOUR CONCEALED TRIPLETS, BIG FOUR WINDS, ALL HONORS
西 西 南 南 南 北 北 北 東 東 東
EXAM ENDED, THANKS TO KAMINARI'S DISCARDED TILE!!
I DISCARDED THE WINNING TILE?

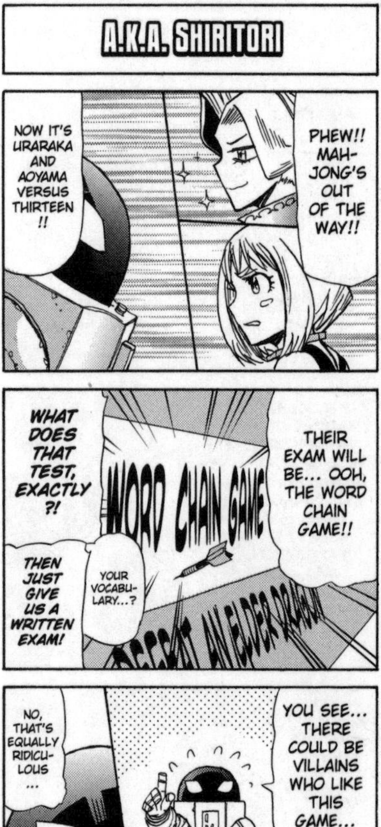
A.K.A. SHIRITORI
PHEW!! MAH-JONG'S OUT OF THE WAY!!
NOW IT'S URARAKA AND AOYAMA VERSUS THIRTEEN !!
THEIR EXAM WILL BE... OOH, THE WORD CHAIN GAME!!
WORD CHAIN GAME
WHAT DOES THAT TEST, EXACTLY ?!
YOUR VOCABULARY...?
THEN JUST GIVE US A WRITTEN EXAM!
YOU SEE... THERE COULD BE VILLAINS WHO LIKE THIS GAME...
OR, UM, RAPPER VILLAINS WHO LOVE WORDPLAY ...
NO, THAT'S EQUALLY RIDICULOUS ...
UMM...
I'VE GOT NOTHING ...
SLUMP
THAT'S OKAY, REALLY. LET'S GET THIS OVER WITH?
THANK YOU.

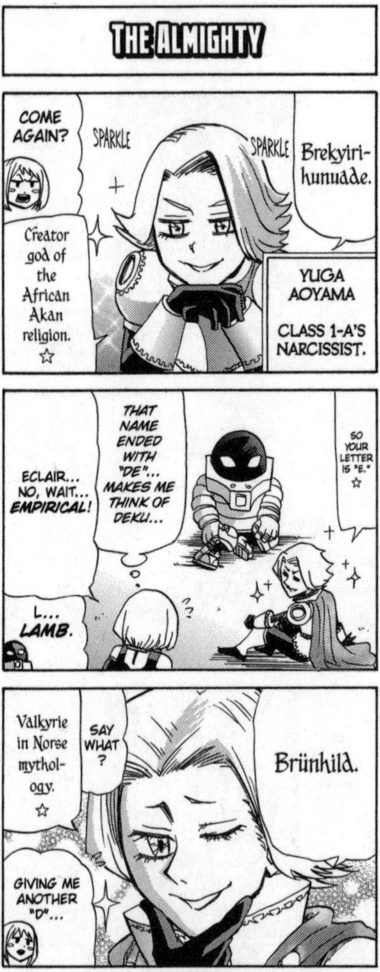
THE ALMIGHTY
Brekyiri-hunuade.
SPARKLE
SPARKLE
COME AGAIN?
Creator god of the African Akan religion. ☆
YUGA AOYAMA
CLASS 1-A'S NARCISSIST.
SO YOUR LETTER IS "E." ☆
THAT NAME ENDED WITH "DE"... MAKES ME THINK OF DEKU...
ECLAIR... NO, WAIT... EMPIRICAL!
L... LAMB.
Brünhild.
SAY WHAT ?
Valkyrie in Norse mythol-ogy. ☆
GIVING ME ANOTHER "D"...
UMM.
HEY.
NO. CAN'T SAY DEKU...
You were just thinking of Izuku Midoriya, weren't you?
BADUM
HUHH ?!

What the Ura-Rock is Cooking

You like him, don't you?
WHAT ...
CUT THAT OUT! I KNOW YOU'VE BEEN MESSING WITH ME.
Amour is a beautiful thing. ☆
STEAM
YOUR LETTER IS "D," URARAKA ...
STEAM
What do you find attractive about him, pray tell?
POW
THIS IS STILL AN EXAM, YOU TWO, SO SAVE THE ROMANCE GOSSIP FOR LATER. YOUR LETTER IS "D"...
I'M TELLING YOU, THAT'S NOT HOW IT IS!
WHO SAID ANYTHING ABOUT ROMANCE? ARRRGH!
D.D.T.*
TOTALLY SORRY!!
EXAM: PASSED!!

*A PRO-WRESTLING MOVE THAT CAN KILL A PERSON IF PERFORMED ON A HARD SURFACE

Staring Down the Opponent

NEXT IS TOKOYAMI AND ASUI VERSUS ECTO-PLASM!!
THEIR TEST WILL BE...
A STARING CONTEST !!
BAM
STARING ~~KONTEST~~ CONTES
WITHOUT LAUGHING
THIS IS GETTING RIDICU-LOUS!
BOXING
AND A SPELLING MISTAKE? REALLY?
I ADMIT THAT I NEEDED A FEW SPACE-FILLERS.
BUT I NEVER THOUGHT THE GAG ONES WOULD KEEP COMING UP...
THEN WHY INCLUDE THEM AT ALL?
I'VE NEVER LOST A STARING CON-TEST.
I DON'T REMEM-BER THE LAST TIME I BLINKED.
EXPRESSIONLESS CHARACTER SHOWDOWN
THIS IS THE FAIREST MATCHUP YET...
NEITHER HAVE I.

The Mouse Will Play

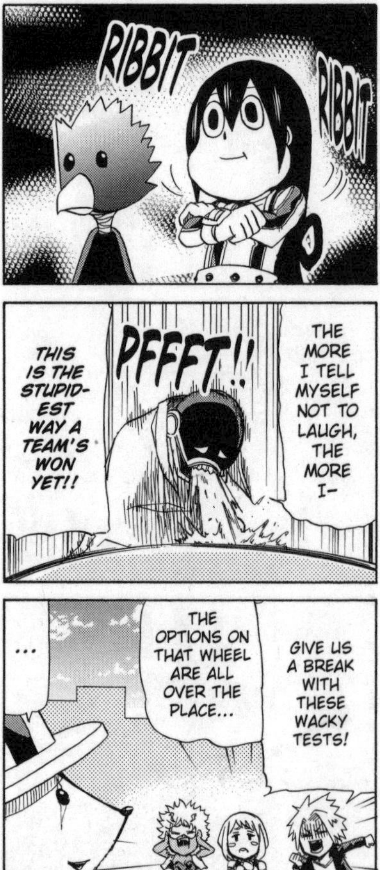
RIBBIT
RIBBIT
THE MORE I TELL MYSELF NOT TO LAUGH, THE MORE I—
PFFFT!!
THIS IS THE STUPIDEST WAY A TEAM'S WON YET!!
GIVE US A BREAK WITH THESE WACKY TESTS!
THE OPTIONS ON THAT WHEEL ARE ALL OVER THE PLACE...
...
HONESTLY, I FELT THIS WHOLE THING FALLING APART HALFWAY THROUGH.
GOT THE FLOP SWEATS REAL BAD, IN FACT.
TRY PLANNING BETTER NEXT TIME!!

Lawsuit Waiting to Happen

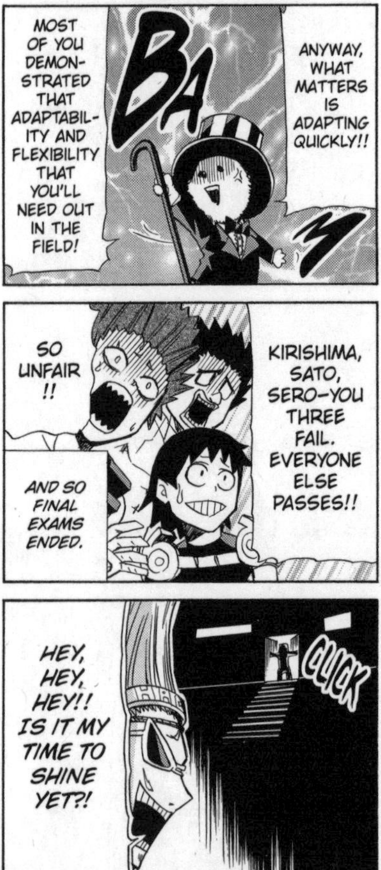
ANYWAY, WHAT MATTERS IS ADAPTING QUICKLY!!
BAM
MOST OF YOU DEMONSTRATED THAT ADAPTABILITY AND FLEXIBILITY THAT YOU'LL NEED OUT IN THE FIELD!
KIRISHIMA, SATO, SERO—YOU THREE FAIL. EVERYONE ELSE PASSES!!
SO UNFAIR!!
AND SO FINAL EXAMS ENDED.
CLICK
HEY, HEY, HEY!! IS IT MY TIME TO SHINE YET?!
NOPE. WE WRAPPED UP THE EXAMS EARLY, SO YOU CAN HEAD HOME.
MUAY THAI
BUT I DIDN'T GET TO DO ANYTHING!

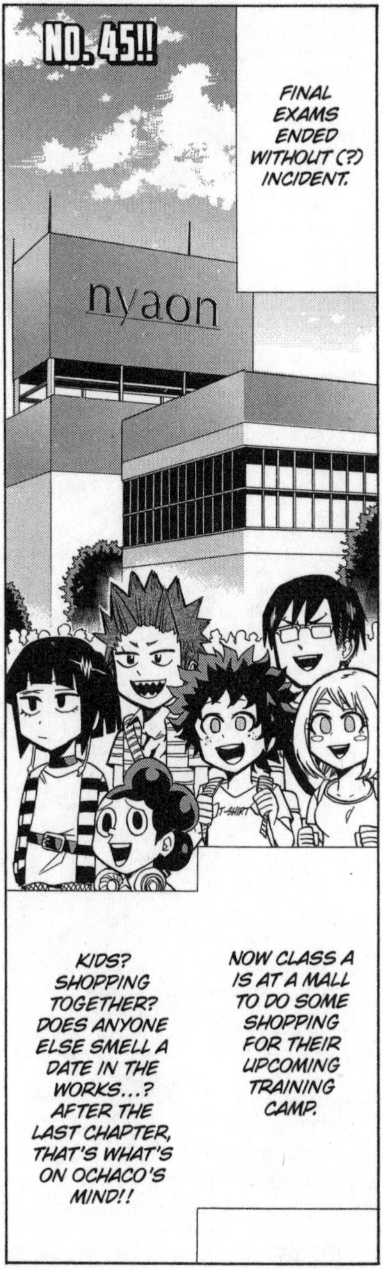
No. 45!!
FINAL EXAMS ENDED WITHOUT (?) INCIDENT.
nyaon
T-SHIRT
NOW CLASS A IS AT A MALL TO DO SOME SHOPPING FOR THEIR UPCOMING TRAINING CAMP.
KIDS? SHOPPING TOGETHER? DOES ANYONE ELSE SMELL A DATE IN THE WORKS...? AFTER THE LAST CHAPTER, THAT'S WHAT'S ON OCHACO'S MIND!!

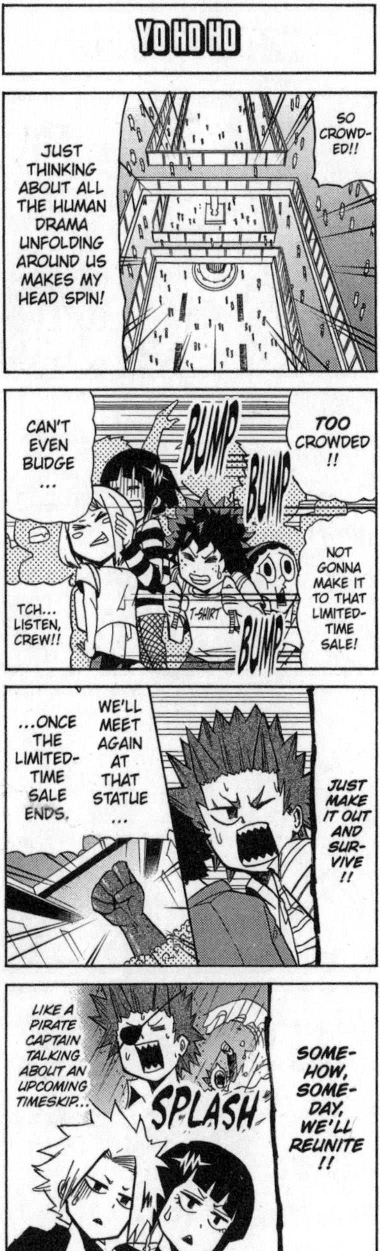
Yo Ho Ho
SO CROWDED!!
JUST THINKING ABOUT ALL THE HUMAN DRAMA UNFOLDING AROUND US MAKES MY HEAD SPIN!
T-SHIRT
TOO CROWDED!!
BUMP
BUMP
CAN'T EVEN BUDGE...
NOT GONNA MAKE IT TO THAT LIMITED-TIME SALE!
BUMP
T-SHIRT
TCH... LISTEN, CREW!!
JUST MAKE IT OUT AND SURVIVE!!
WE'LL MEET AGAIN AT THAT STATUE...
...ONCE THE LIMITED-TIME SALE ENDS.
SOME-HOW, SOME-DAY, WE'LL REUNITE!!
SPLASH
LIKE A PIRATE CAPTAIN TALKING ABOUT AN UPCOMING TIMESKIP...

Missed Opportunity

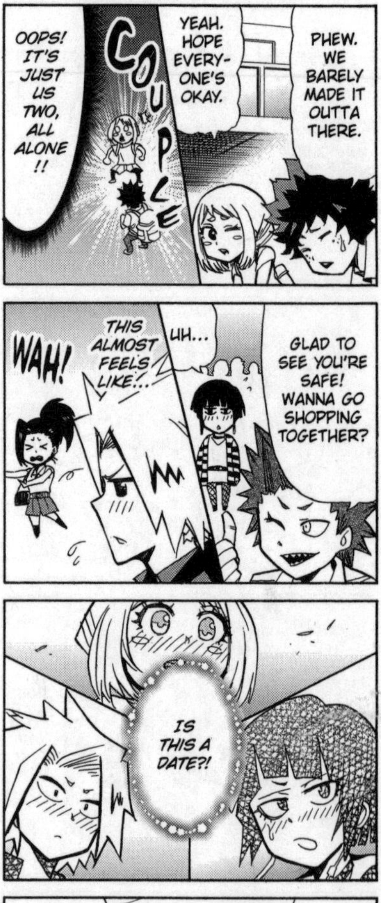
PHEW. WE BARELY MADE IT OUTTA THERE.
YEAH. HOPE EVERY-ONE'S OKAY.
COUPLE
OOPS! IT'S JUST US TWO, ALL ALONE!!
GLAD TO SEE YOU'RE SAFE! WANNA GO SHOPPING TOGETHER?
UH...
THIS ALMOST FEELS LIKE...
WAH!
IS THIS A DATE?!
WHY THE ODD EXPRES-SION, MINETA?
MY GRAPE SENSE IS TINGLING...
LIKE THE ROAD FORKED, AND I TOOK THE PATH LESS BODACIOUS... OR SOMETHING.

Gaga for Merch

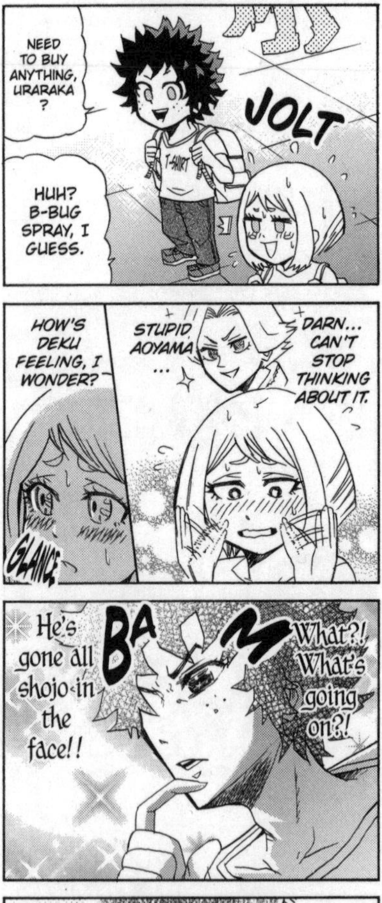
NEED TO BUY ANYTHING, URARAKA?
JOLT
HUH? B-BUG SPRAY, I GUESS.
DARN... CAN'T STOP THINKING ABOUT IT.
STUPID AOYAMA...
HOW'S DEKU FEELING, I WONDER?
GLANCE
What?! What's going on?!
BAM
He's gone all shojo in the face!!
THE COLORING ON THIS FIGURE... ALMOST LOOKS LIKE AN INTENTIONAL RARE VARIANT...
MUTTER MUTTER MUTTER MUTTER MUTTER
OF COURSE THAT'S ALL IT WAS. YEESH, WHAT'S WITH ME TODAY?

No Offense

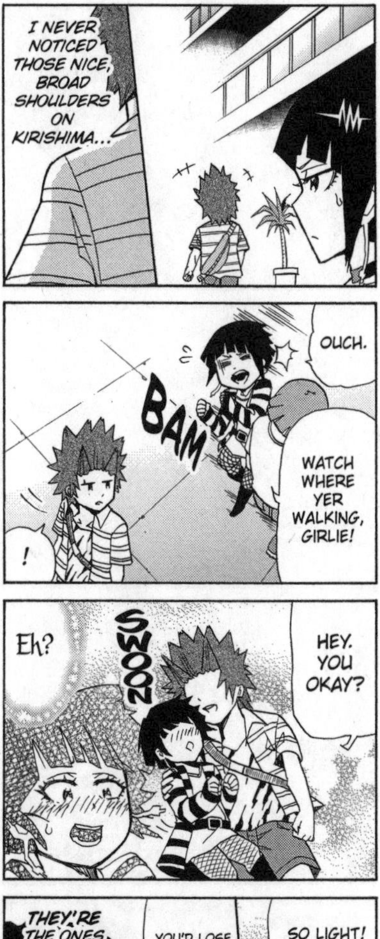
I NEVER NOTICED THOSE NICE, BROAD SHOULDERS ON KIRISHIMA...
OUCH.
BAM
WATCH WHERE YER WALKING, GIRLIE!
!
HEY. YOU OKAY?
SWOON
Eh?
SO LIGHT! ARE ALL GALS AS LIGHT AS YOU?!
TMP
YOU'D LOSE TO IDA AND SATO AT A WEIGH-IN, FOR SURE!
THEY'RE THE ONES WHO SPRING TO MIND?
HUH ...
FWIP

How the Other Half Lives

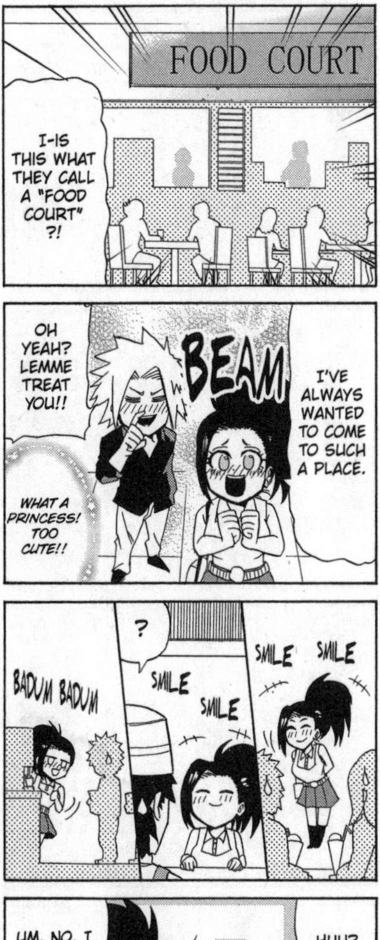
FOOD COURT
I-IS THIS WHAT THEY CALL A "FOOD COURT"?!
I'VE ALWAYS WANTED TO COME TO SUCH A PLACE.
BEAM
OH YEAH? LEMME TREAT YOU!!
WHAT A PRINCESS! TOO CUTE!!
SMILE
SMILE
SMILE
SMILE
?
BADUM BADUM
HUH? NOT HUNGRY?
UM, NO. I WAS JUST HERE TO OBSERVE. GOSH.
LIKE AT A ZOO OR SOMETHING?!

HUNTSMAN IDA

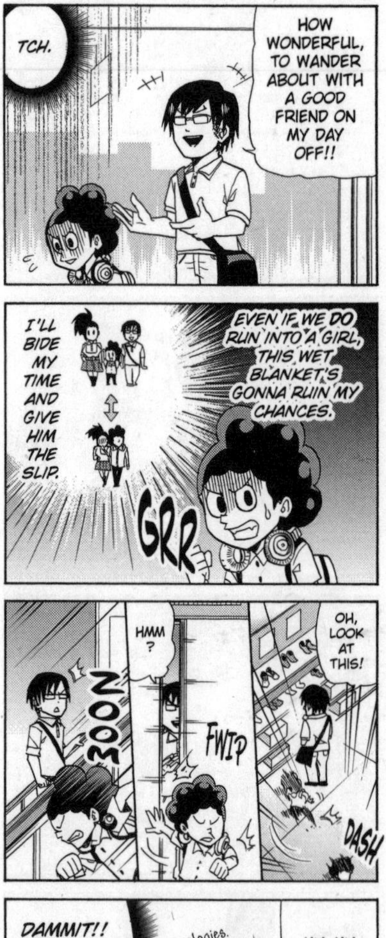
HOW WONDERFUL, TO WANDER ABOUT WITH A GOOD FRIEND ON MY DAY OFF!!
TCH.
EVEN IF WE DO RUN INTO A GIRL, THIS WET BLANKET'S GONNA RUIN MY CHANCES.
I'LL BIDE MY TIME AND GIVE HIM THE SLIP.
GRR
OH, LOOK AT THIS!
HMM?
ZOOM
FWIP
DASH
MY, MY, I NEARLY LOST YOU AGAIN.
Apologies.
DAMMIT!! HE JUST HAD TO BE THE QUICKEST DUDE IN CLASS!
SLAM

NO OFFENSE, PART 2

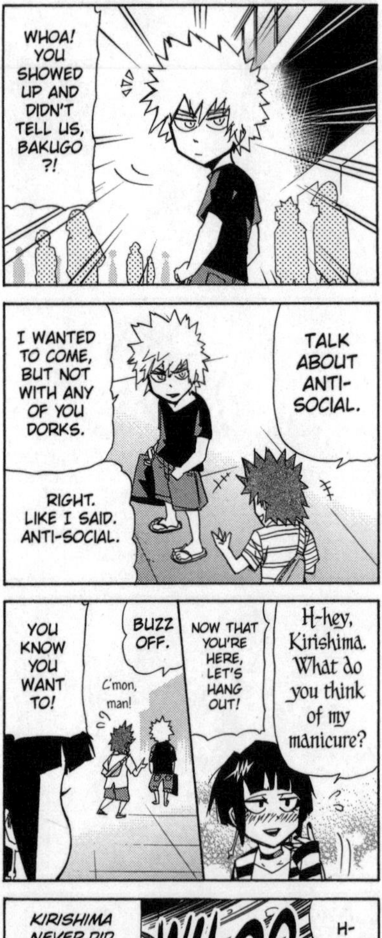
WHOA! YOU SHOWED UP AND DIDN'T TELL US, BAKUGO?!
TALK ABOUT ANTI-SOCIAL.
I WANTED TO COME, BUT NOT WITH ANY OF YOU DORKS.
RIGHT. LIKE I SAID. ANTI-SOCIAL.
H-hey, Kirishima. What do you think of my manicure?
NOW THAT YOU'RE HERE, LET'S HANG OUT!
BUZZ OFF.
YOU KNOW YOU WANT TO!
C'mon, man!
H-HEY.
WHOOSH
KIRISHIMA NEVER DID FIGURE OUT WHY JIRO REFUSED TO SPEAK TO HIM FOR THE NEXT THREE DAYS.
GAB
GAB

AW, CREPE

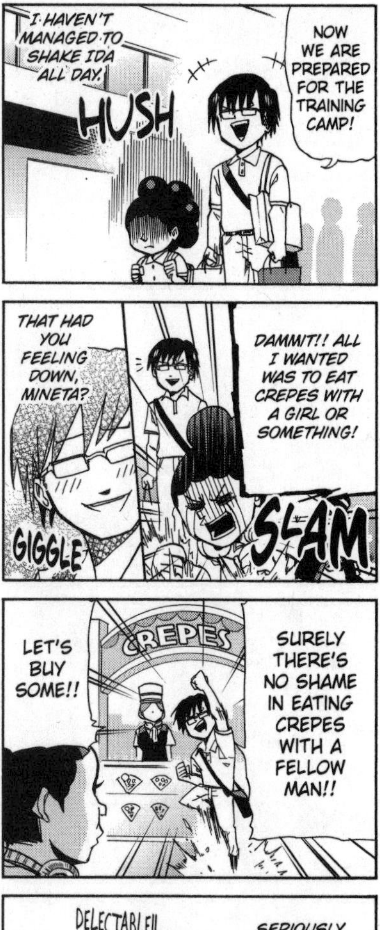
NOW WE ARE PREPARED FOR THE TRAINING CAMP!
I HAVEN'T MANAGED TO SHAKE IDA ALL DAY.
HUSH
DAMMIT!! ALL I WANTED WAS TO EAT CREPES WITH A GIRL OR SOMETHING!
THAT HAD YOU FEELING DOWN, MINETA?
SLAM
GIGGLE
SURELY THERE'S NO SHAME IN EATING CREPES WITH A FELLOW MAN!!
CREPES
LET'S BUY SOME!!
SERIOUSLY MISSING THE POINT...
DELECTABLE!!
MINETA'S CREPE WOUND UP WELL-SALTED.

TWO TYPES OF PEOPLE IN THIS WORLD

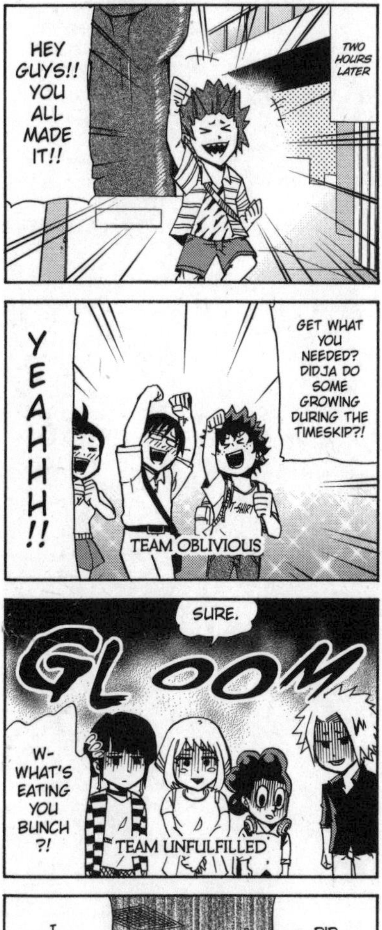
TWO HOURS LATER
HEY GUYS!! YOU ALL MADE IT!!
GET WHAT YOU NEEDED? DIDJA DO SOME GROWING DURING THE TIMESKIP?!
T-SHIRT
YEAHHHH!!
TEAM OBLIVIOUS
SURE.
GLOOM
W-WHAT'S EATING YOU BUNCH?!
TEAM UNFULFILLED
DID SOMETHING HAPPEN TO THEM?
I THINK THE CROWDS JUST TIRED THEM OUT.

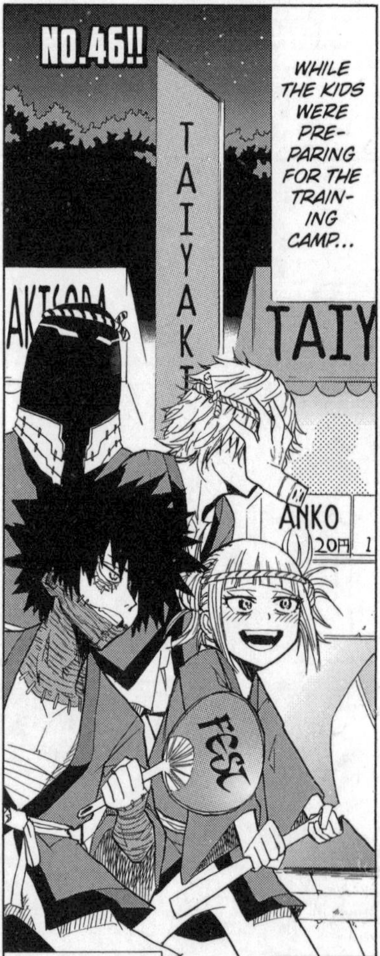
NO.46!!
WHILE THE KIDS WERE PREPARING FOR THE TRAINING CAMP...
TAIYAKI
TAIY
ANKO
20円
FeST
...THE VILLAINS WERE PLOTTING.
PLOTTING HOW TO WELCOME THEIR NEWEST MEMBERS INTO THE FOLD, THAT IS!!
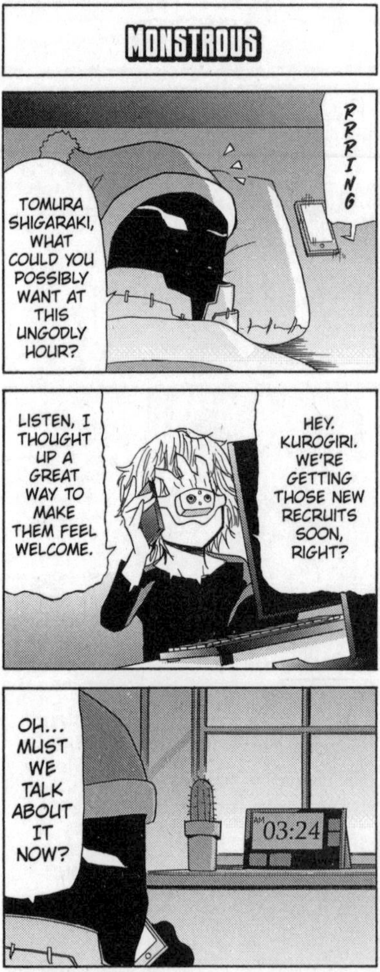
MONSTROUS
RRRING
TOMURA SHIGARAKI, WHAT COULD YOU POSSIBLY WANT AT THIS UNGODLY HOUR?
HEY. KUROGIRI. WE'RE GETTING THOSE NEW RECRUITS SOON, RIGHT?
LISTEN, I THOUGHT UP A GREAT WAY TO MAKE THEM FEEL WELCOME.
OH... MUST WE TALK ABOUT IT NOW?
AM 03:24
YEAH. NOW IS PERFECT.
VERY WELL. I'LL OPEN UP THE BAR.
TOMURA SHIGARAKI
A MONSTER CREATED BY MODERN SOCIETY.

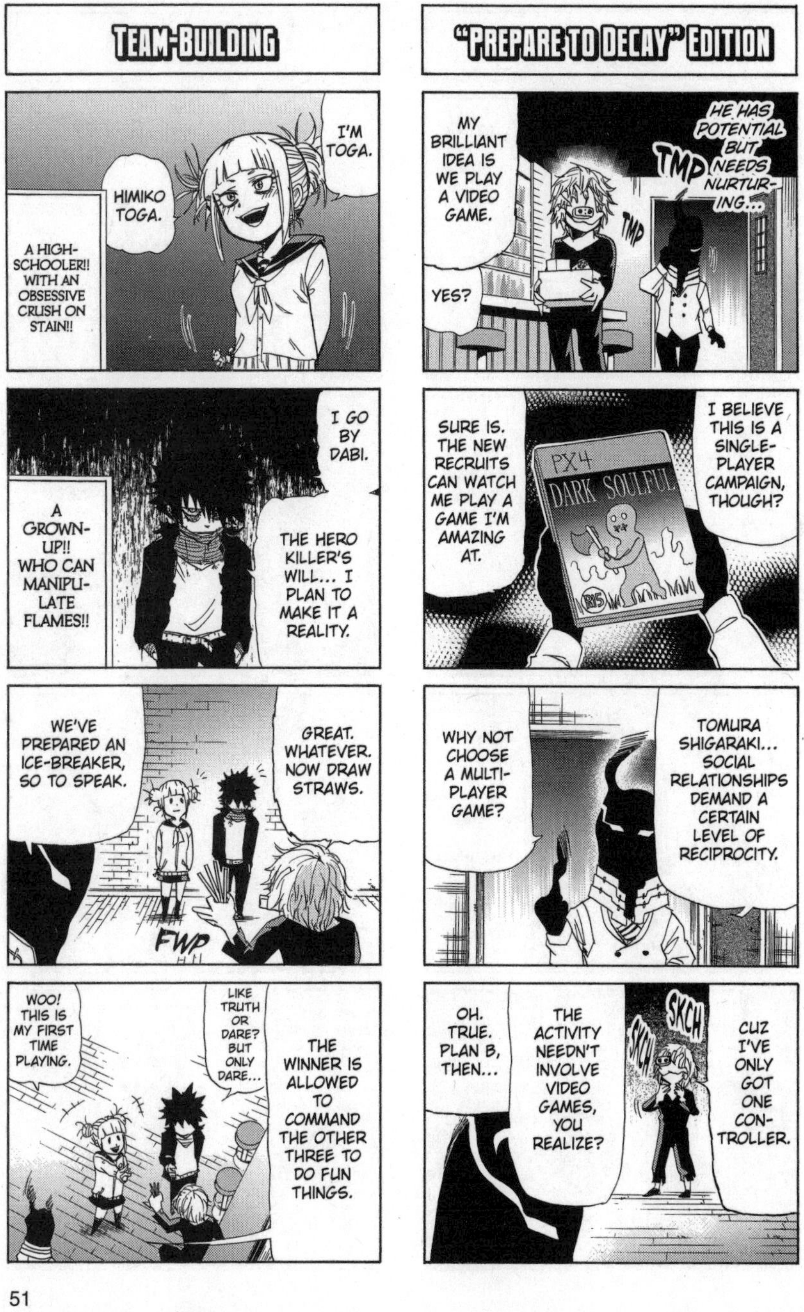
TEAM-BUILDING
"PREPARE TO DECAY" EDITION
I'M TOGA.
HIMIKO TOGA.
A HIGH-SCHOOLER!! WITH AN OBSESSIVE CRUSH ON STAIN!!
I GO BY DABI.
THE HERO KILLER'S WILL... I PLAN TO MAKE IT A REALITY.
A GROWN-UP!! WHO CAN MANIPULATE FLAMES!!
WE'VE PREPARED AN ICE-BREAKER, SO TO SPEAK.
GREAT. WHATEVER. NOW DRAW STRAWS.
FWP
THE WINNER IS ALLOWED TO COMMAND THE OTHER THREE TO DO FUN THINGS.
LIKE TRUTH OR DARE? BUT ONLY DARE...
WOO! THIS IS MY FIRST TIME PLAYING.
HE HAS POTENTIAL BUT NEEDS NURTURING...
TMP
TMP
MY BRILLIANT IDEA IS WE PLAY A VIDEO GAME.
YES?
I BELIEVE THIS IS A SINGLE-PLAYER CAMPAIGN, THOUGH?
PX4
DARK SOULFUL
R15
SURE IS. THE NEW RECRUITS CAN WATCH ME PLAY A GAME I'M AMAZING AT.
TOMURA SHIGARAKI... SOCIAL RELATIONSHIPS DEMAND A CERTAIN LEVEL OF RECIPROCITY.
WHY NOT CHOOSE A MULTIPLAYER GAME?
CUZ I'VE ONLY GOT ONE CONTROLLER.
SKCH
SKCH
THE ACTIVITY NEEDN'T INVOLVE VIDEO GAMES, YOU REALIZE?
OH. TRUE. PLAN B, THEN...

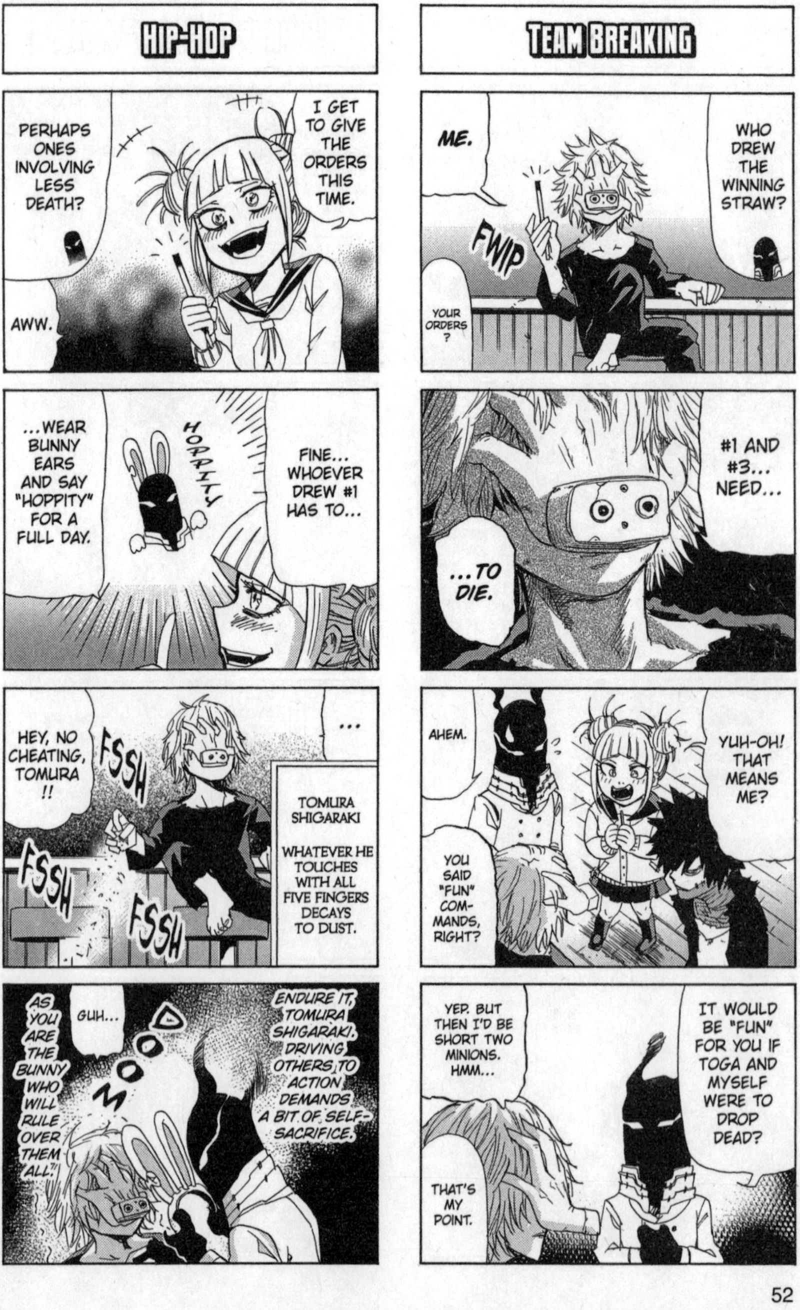
TEAM BREAKING
WHO DREW THE WINNING STRAW?
ME.
FWIP
YOUR ORDERS ?
#1 AND #3... NEED...
...TO DIE.
YUH-OH! THAT MEANS ME?
AHEM.
YOU SAID "FUN" COMMANDS, RIGHT?
IT WOULD BE "FUN" FOR YOU IF TOGA AND MYSELF WERE TO DROP DEAD?
YEP. BUT THEN I'D BE SHORT TWO MINIONS. HMM...
THAT'S MY POINT.
HIP-HOP
I GET TO GIVE THE ORDERS THIS TIME.
PERHAPS ONES INVOLVING LESS DEATH?
AWW.
FINE... WHOEVER DREW #1 HAS TO...
HOPPITY
...WEAR BUNNY EARS AND SAY "HOPPITY" FOR A FULL DAY.
...
TOMURA SHIGARAKI
WHATEVER HE TOUCHES WITH ALL FIVE FINGERS DECAYS TO DUST.
FSSH
HEY, NO CHEATING, TOMURA !!
FSSH
FSSH
ENDURE IT, TOMURA SHIGARAKI. DRIVING OTHERS TO ACTION DEMANDS A BIT OF SELF-SACRIFICE.
DOOM
GUH...
AS YOU ARE THE BUNNY WHO WILL RULE OVER THEM ALL.

Hang in There, Kurogiri

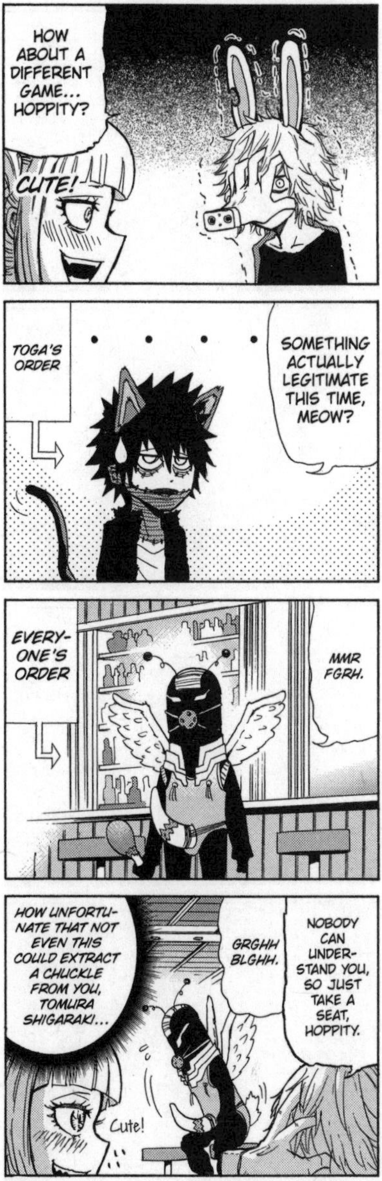
HOW ABOUT A DIFFERENT GAME... HOPPITY?
CUTE!
SOMETHING ACTUALLY LEGITIMATE THIS TIME, MEOW?
. . . .
TOGA'S ORDER
MMR FGRH.
EVERY-ONE'S ORDER
NOBODY CAN UNDER-STAND YOU, SO JUST TAKE A SEAT, HOPPITY.
GRGHH BLGHH.
HOW UNFORTU-NATE THAT NOT EVEN THIS COULD EXTRACT A CHUCKLE FROM YOU, TOMURA SHIGARAKI...
Cute!

Gag Order

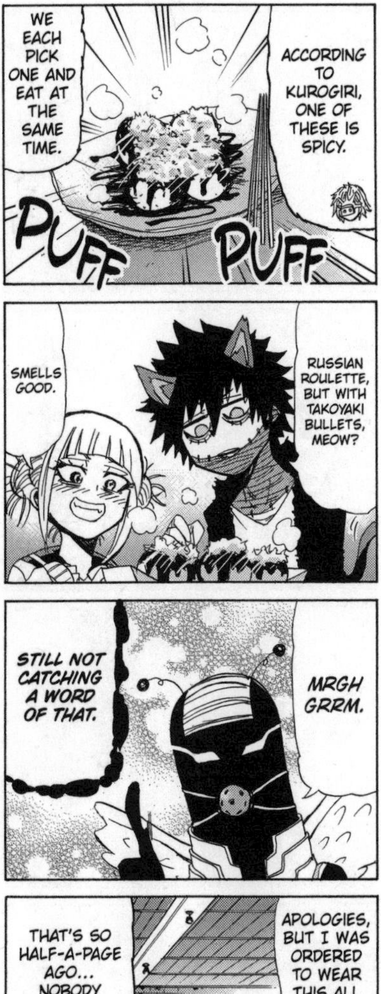
ACCORDING TO KUROGIRI, ONE OF THESE IS SPICY.
WE EACH PICK ONE AND EAT AT THE SAME TIME.
PUFF
PUFF
RUSSIAN ROULETTE, BUT WITH TAKOYAKI BULLETS, MEOW?
SMELLS GOOD.
MRGH GRRM.
STILL NOT CATCHING A WORD OF THAT.
APOLOGIES, BUT I WAS ORDERED TO WEAR THIS ALL DAY.
THAT'S SO HALF-A-PAGE AGO... NOBODY EXPECTS CONSISTENCY IN THESE GAGS.
OH.

READ THE ROOM

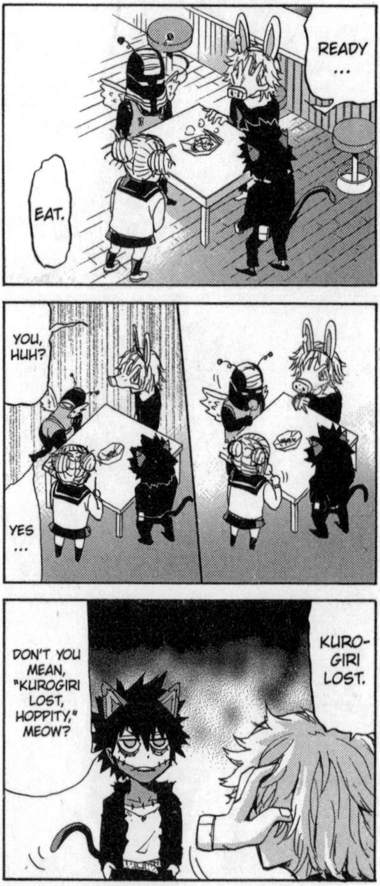
READY ...
EAT.
YOU, HUH?
YES ...
KURO-GIRI LOST.
DON'T YOU MEAN, "KUROGIRI LOST, HOPPITY," MEOW?
LISTEN, THAT JOKE'S ALREADY STALE.
JUST SEEMS LIKE DOUBLE STAN-DARDS TO ME-OW.
THIS RUNNING GAG HAS RUN AWAY...
SHAKA
SHAKA
SHAKA

1 PENDING INVITE FROM TOMURA SHIGARAKI

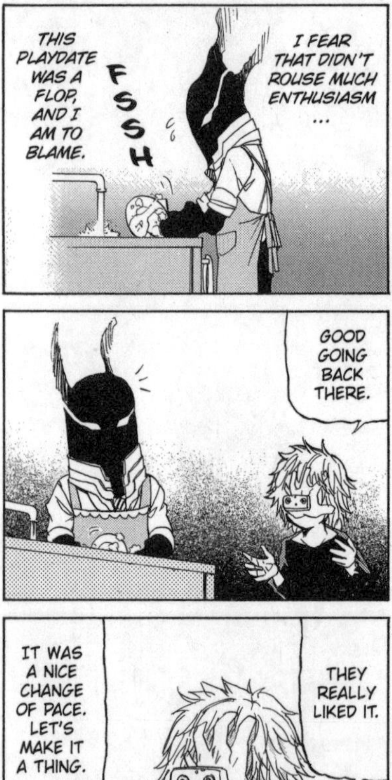
I FEAR THAT DIDN'T ROUSE MUCH ENTHUSIASM ...
FSSH
THIS PLAYDATE WAS A FLOP, AND I AM TO BLAME.
GOOD GOING BACK THERE.
THEY REALLY LIKED IT.
IT WAS A NICE CHANGE OF PACE. LET'S MAKE IT A THING.
DO YOU REALLY BELIEVE IT WENT WELL?
WIPE
WIPE
I ALREADY GOT A GROUP CHAT ABOUT OUR NEXT EVENT...
OH ...
I SUPPOSE IT TAKES A FEW HACKS WITH A DEADLY PICK TO BREAK THROUGH ICE.

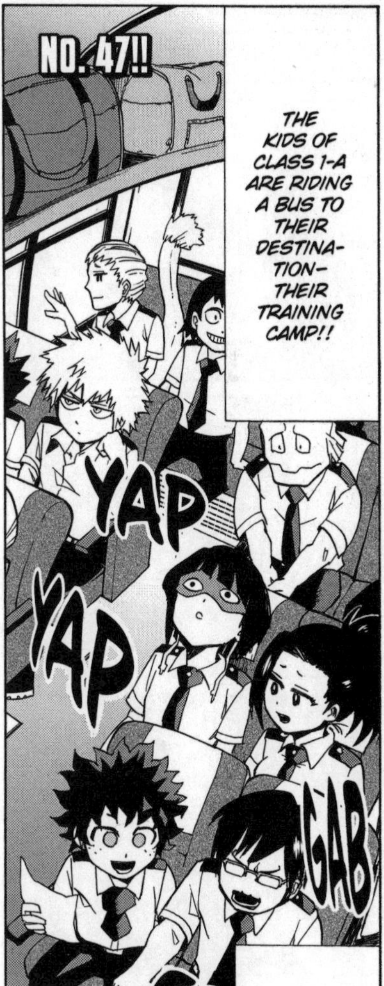
No. 47!!
THE KIDS OF CLASS 1-A ARE RIDING A BUS TO THEIR DESTINATION—THEIR TRAINING CAMP!!
YAP
YAP
GAB
GAB
SMASH!! IS GONNA ZOOM IN ON THE BUS RIDE IN PARTICULAR!!
LET'S TAKE A PEEK!!

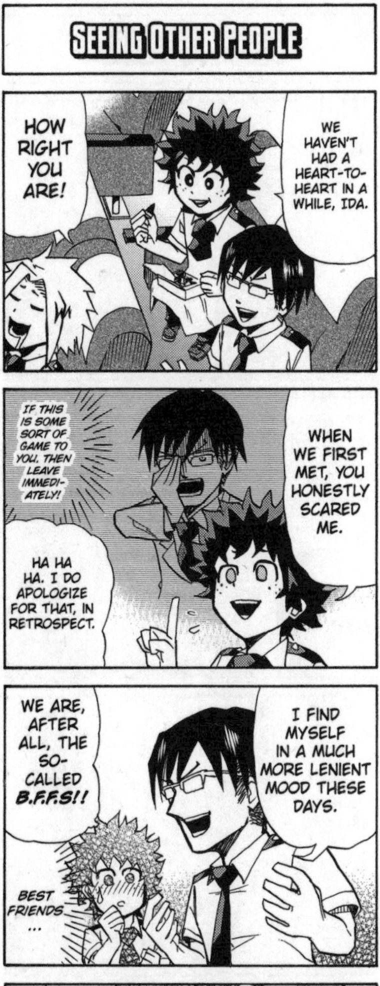
SEEING OTHER PEOPLE
WE HAVEN'T HAD A HEART-TO-HEART IN A WHILE, IDA.
HOW RIGHT YOU ARE!
WHEN WE FIRST MET, YOU HONESTLY SCARED ME.
IF THIS IS SOME SORT OF GAME TO YOU, THEN LEAVE IMMEDIATELY!
HA HA HA. I DO APOLOGIZE FOR THAT, IN RETROSPECT.
I FIND MYSELF IN A MUCH MORE LENIENT MOOD THESE DAYS.
WE ARE, AFTER ALL, THE SO-CALLED B.F.F.S!!
BEST FRIENDS...
SORRY, KACCHAN. I'VE... MOVED ON.
SWOON
WHAT.
SIGH.
WHAT?!

COMMON INTERESTS

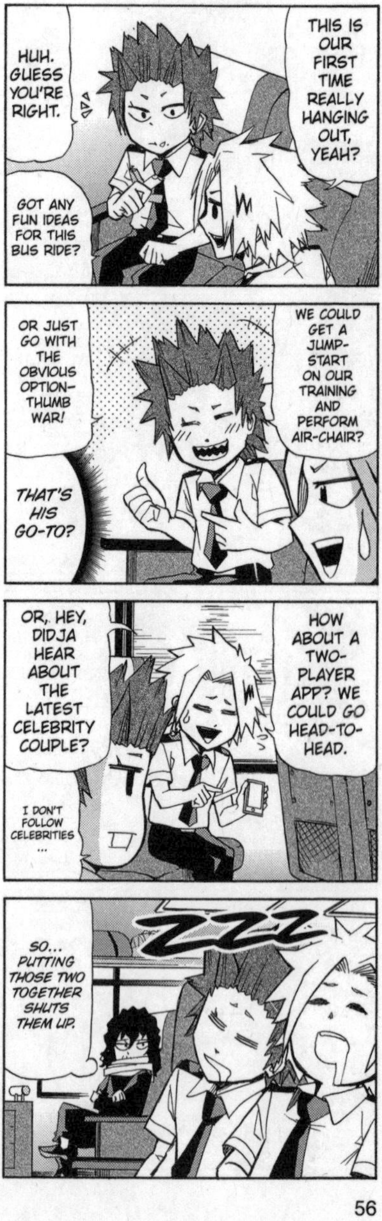
THIS IS OUR FIRST TIME REALLY HANGING OUT, YEAH?
HUH. GUESS YOU'RE RIGHT.
GOT ANY FUN IDEAS FOR THIS BUS RIDE?
WE COULD GET A JUMP-START ON OUR TRAINING AND PERFORM AIR-CHAIR?
OR JUST GO WITH THE OBVIOUS OPTION—THUMB WAR!
THAT'S HIS GO-TO?
HOW ABOUT A TWO-PLAYER APP? WE COULD GO HEAD-TO-HEAD.
OR, HEY, DIDJA HEAR ABOUT THE LATEST CELEBRITY COUPLE?
I DON'T FOLLOW CELEBRITIES ...
ZZZ
SO... PUTTING THOSE TWO TOGETHER SHUTS THEM UP.

RIDING COACH

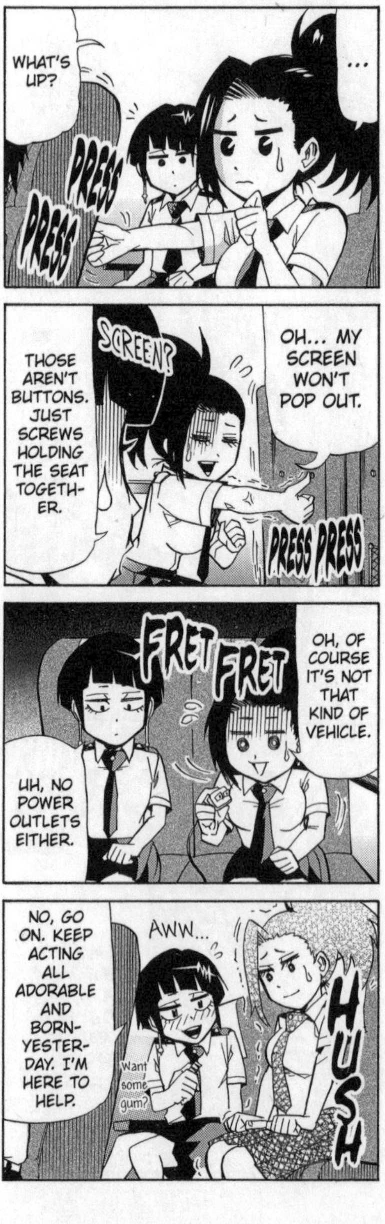
...
WHAT'S UP?
PRESS
PRESS
OH... MY SCREEN WON'T POP OUT.
SCREEN?
THOSE AREN'T BUTTONS. JUST SCREWS HOLDING THE SEAT TOGETHER.
PRESS PRESS
OH, OF COURSE IT'S NOT THAT KIND OF VEHICLE.
FRET FRET
UH, NO POWER OUTLETS EITHER.
HUSH
AWW...
NO, GO ON. KEEP ACTING ALL ADORABLE AND BORN-YESTERDAY. I'M HERE TO HELP.
Want some gum?

BIRDS OF A FEATHER

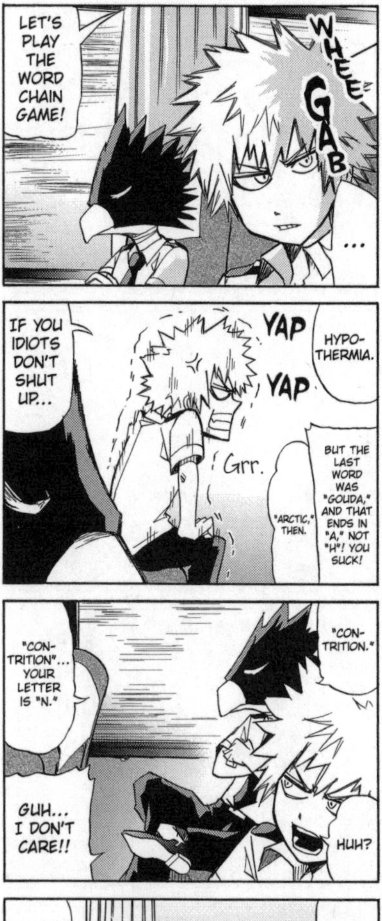
WHEE
GAB
LET'S PLAY THE WORD CHAIN GAME!
...
HYPO-THERMIA.
YAP
YAP
IF YOU IDIOTS DON'T SHUT UP...
BUT THE LAST WORD WAS "GOUDA," AND THAT ENDS IN "A," NOT "H"! YOU SUCK!
"ARCTIC," THEN.
Grr.
"CON-TRITION."
"CON-TRITION"... YOUR LETTER IS "N."
HUH?
GUH... I DON'T CARE!!
"NA-PALM."
"MOURN."
YOU'RE DIFFER-ENT THAN THEM.
YES. YES I AM.

MISCOMMUNICATION

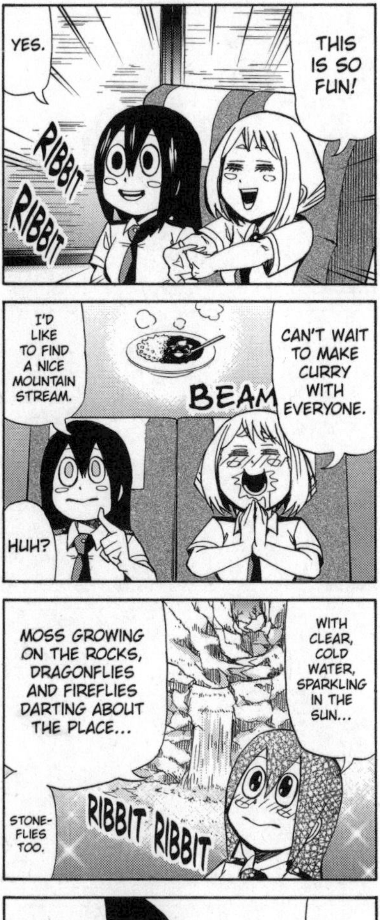
THIS IS SO FUN!
YES.
RIBBIT
RIBBIT
CAN'T WAIT TO MAKE CURRY WITH EVERYONE.
BEAM
I'D LIKE TO FIND A NICE MOUNTAIN STREAM.
HUH?
WITH CLEAR, COLD WATER, SPARKLING IN THE SUN...
MOSS GROWING ON THE ROCKS, DRAGONFLIES AND FIREFLIES DARTING ABOUT THE PLACE...
STONE-FLIES TOO.
RIBBIT RIBBIT
A-ALL TASTY TREATS, HUH?
THAT WASN'T A MENU. I JUST LIKE NATURE.

Key to a Man's Heart

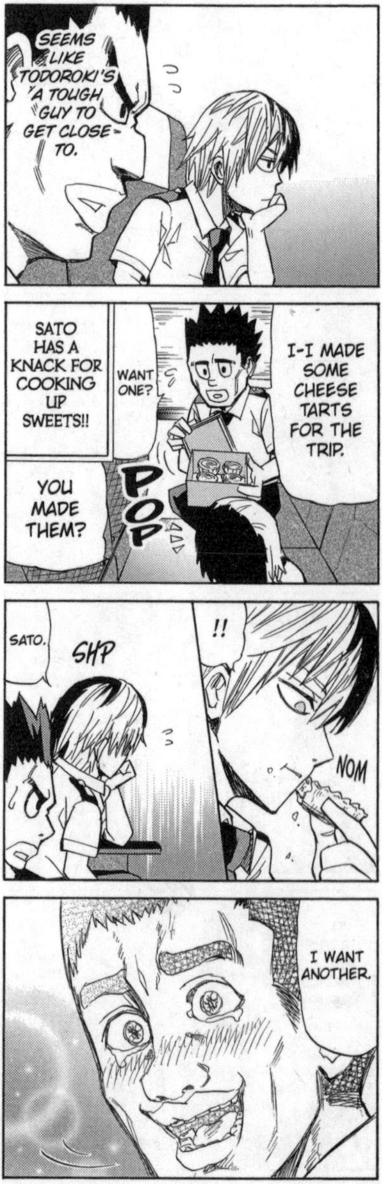
SEEMS LIKE TODOROKI'S A TOUGH GUY TO GET CLOSE TO.
I-I MADE SOME CHEESE TARTS FOR THE TRIP.
WANT ONE?
SATO HAS A KNACK FOR COOKING UP SWEETS!!
POP
YOU MADE THEM?
!!
SHP
SATO.
NOM
I WANT ANOTHER.

Transparent Moves

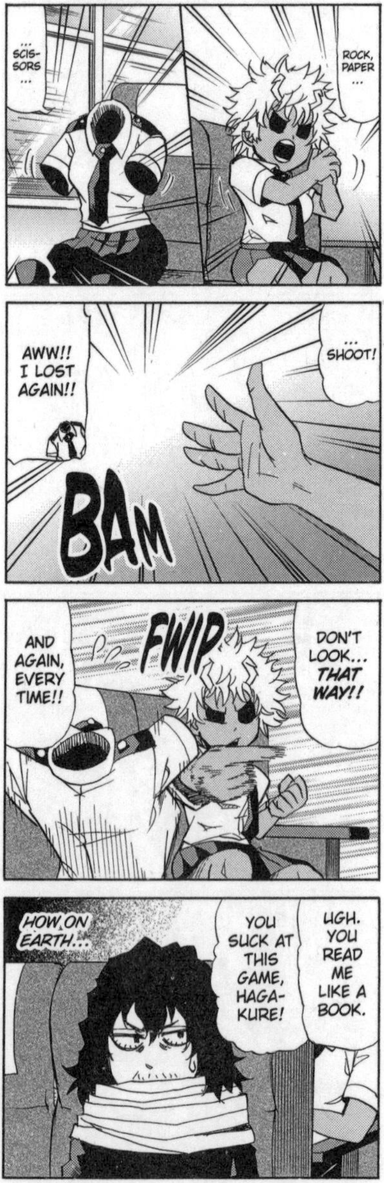
ROCK, PAPER ...
... SCIS-SORS ...
... SHOOT!
AWW!! I LOST AGAIN!!
BAM
DON'T LOOK... THAT WAY!!
FWIP
AND AGAIN, EVERY TIME!!
UGH. YOU READ ME LIKE A BOOK.
YOU SUCK AT THIS GAME, HAGAKURE!
HOW ON EARTH...

DARK SAVIOR

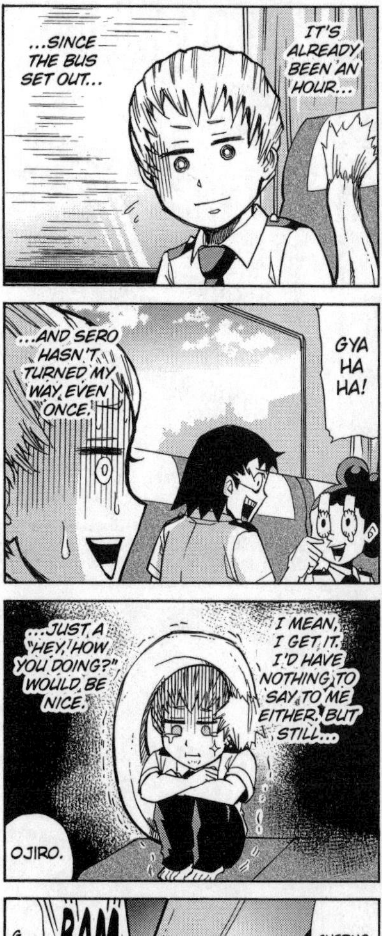
IT'S ALREADY BEEN AN HOUR...
...SINCE THE BUS SET OUT...
GYA HA HA HA!
...AND SERO HASN'T TURNED MY WAY EVEN ONCE.
I MEAN, I GET IT. I'D HAVE NOTHING TO SAY TO ME EITHER, BUT STILL...
...JUST A "HEY, HOW YOU DOING?" WOULD BE NICE.
OJIRO.
CHERNO-BOG... YOUR LETTER IS "G."
BAM
G...
GRATE-FUL !!

COMPARTMENTALIZING

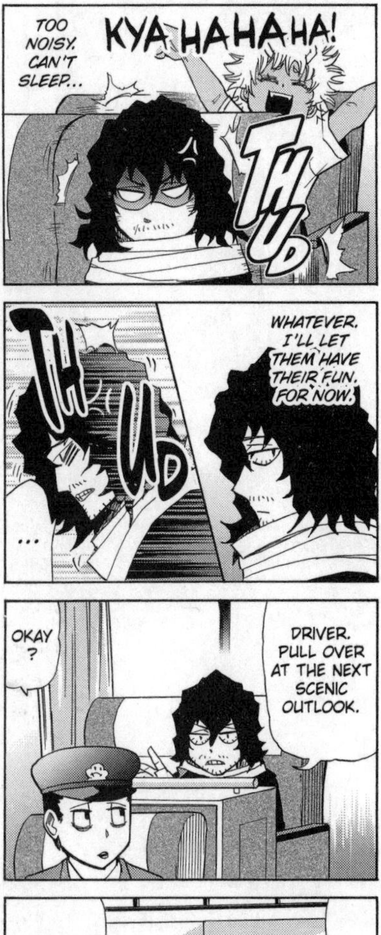
KYA HAHAHA!
TOO NOISY. CAN'T SLEEP...
THUD
WHATEVER. I'LL LET THEM HAVE THEIR FUN. FOR NOW.
THUD
...
DRIVER. PULL OVER AT THE NEXT SCENIC OUTLOOK.
OKAY ?
ARE YOU QUITE SURE ?
WAKE ME UP WHEN WE GET THERE.

DENKI KAMINARI

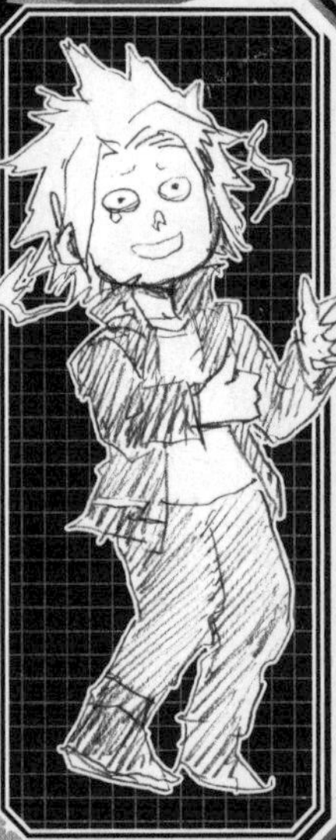

A DUMB CHARACTER!!

THAT SAID, THE FUN HAD AT HIS EXPENSE IS PRETTY MILD, AND MOST OF THE TIME HE CAN ACTUALLY READ THE ROOM WHILE DELIVERING INSIGHTFUL COMMENTARY!! HE'S ALSO THE ONLY ONE IN *SMASH!!* WHO TOLERATES MINETA, WHICH IS A VERY IMPORTANT ROLE. WITHOUT KAMINARI, MINETA COULDN'T SHINE BRIGHT!!

BE GRATEFUL FOR THIS GUY, MINETA!

HANTA SERO

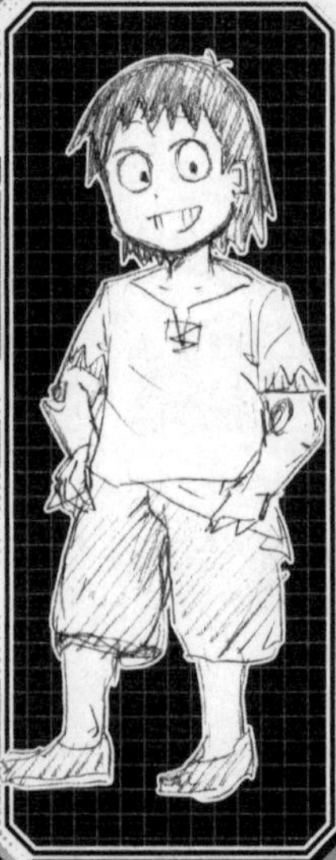

CLASS 1-A'S "BALANCER."

HE CAN SERVE AS A SPACE FILLER IN BASICALLY ANY OF THE CLIQUES! WOW!! THAT MAKES IT RELATIVELY TOUGH FOR HIM TO STAND OUT, BUT WHOEVER HAS SERO ON THEIR SIDE USUALLY TRIUMPHS. HIS REACTIONS CARRY A LOT OF SWAYING POWER!!

EVERYONE'S SORT OF A WEIRD CARICATURE OF THEMSELVES IN *SMASH!!*, AND SERO CAN POINT OUT HOW THEY'RE BEING WEIRD!

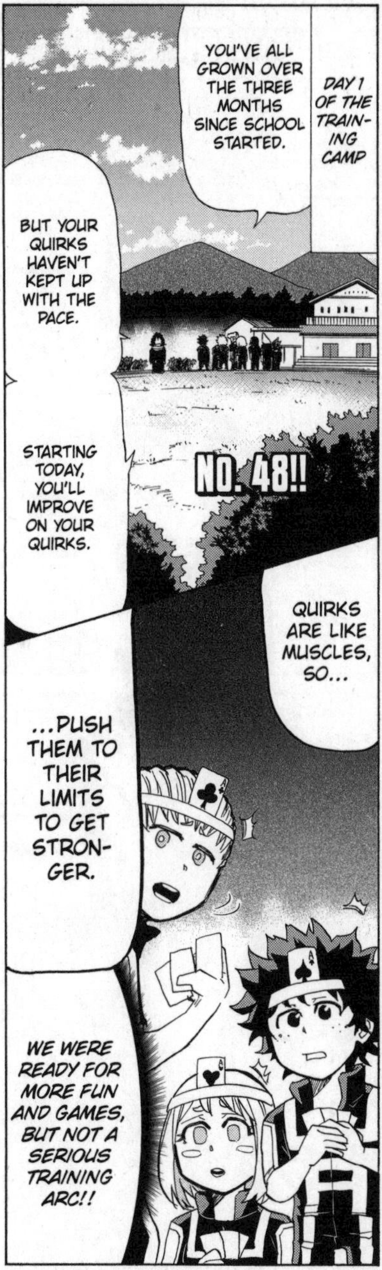
DAY 1 OF THE TRAIN-ING CAMP
YOU'VE ALL GROWN OVER THE THREE MONTHS SINCE SCHOOL STARTED.
BUT YOUR QUIRKS HAVEN'T KEPT UP WITH THE PACE.
STARTING TODAY, YOU'LL IMPROVE ON YOUR QUIRKS.
NO. 48!!
QUIRKS ARE LIKE MUSCLES, SO...
...PUSH THEM TO THEIR LIMITS TO GET STRON-GER.
WE WERE READY FOR MORE FUN AND GAMES, BUT NOT A SERIOUS TRAINING ARC!!

BE CAREFUL WHAT YOU WISH FOR

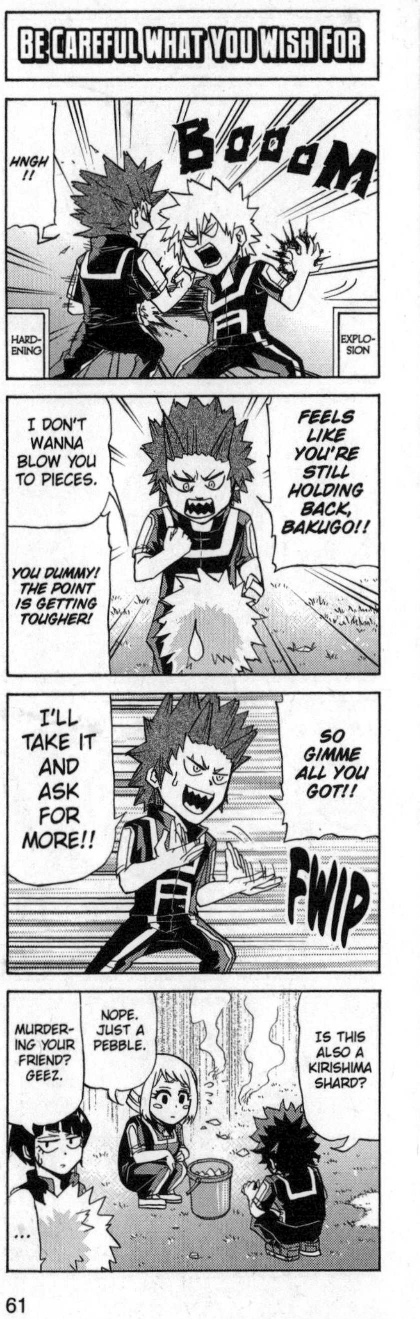
BOOOM
HNGH !!
HARD-ENING
EXPLO-SION
FEELS LIKE YOU'RE STILL HOLDING BACK, BAKUGO!!
I DON'T WANNA BLOW YOU TO PIECES.
YOU DUMMY! THE POINT IS GETTING TOUGHER!
SO GIMME ALL YOU GOT!!
FWIP
I'LL TAKE IT AND ASK FOR MORE!!
IS THIS ALSO A KIRISHIMA SHARD?
NOPE. JUST A PEBBLE.
MURDER-ING YOUR FRIEND? GEEZ.
...

WOODEN

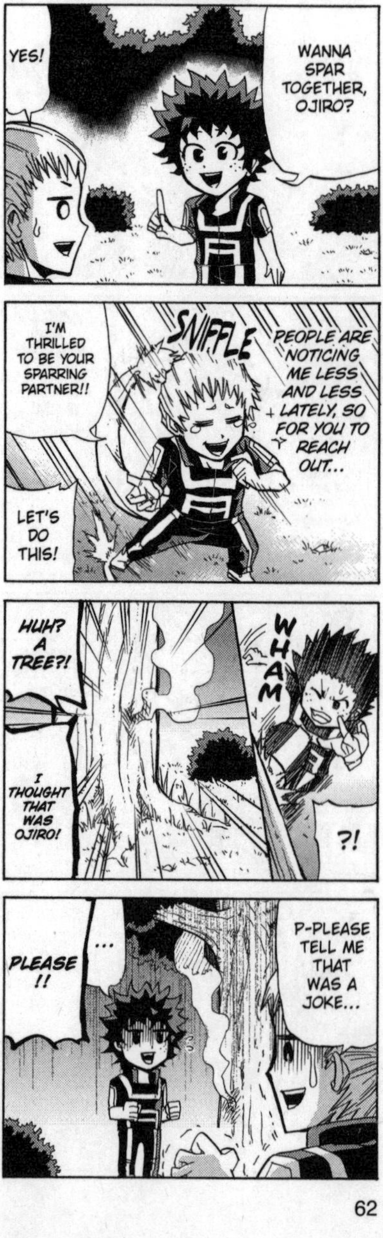

WANNA SPAR TOGETHER, OJIRO?
YES!
PEOPLE ARE NOTICING ME LESS AND LESS LATELY, SO FOR YOU TO REACH OUT...
SNIFFLE
I'M THRILLED TO BE YOUR SPARRING PARTNER!!
LET'S DO THIS!
WHAM
HUH? A TREE?!
?!
I THOUGHT THAT WAS OJIRO!
P-PLEASE TELL ME THAT WAS A JOKE...
...
PLEASE!!

YAOYOROMAZON.COM

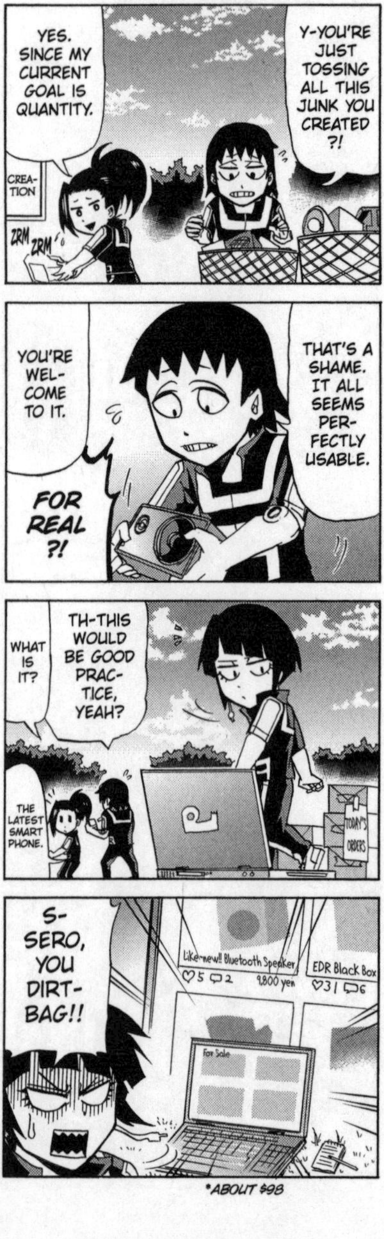

Y-YOU'RE JUST TOSSING ALL THIS JUNK YOU CREATED?!
YES. SINCE MY CURRENT GOAL IS QUANTITY.
CREATION
ZRM ZRM
THAT'S A SHAME. IT ALL SEEMS PERFECTLY USABLE.
YOU'RE WELCOME TO IT.
FOR REAL?!
TODAY'S ORDERS
TH-THIS WOULD BE GOOD PRACTICE, YEAH?
WHAT IS IT?
THE LATEST SMARTPHONE.
EDR Black Box ♡31 6
Like-new!! Bluetooth Speaker ♡5 2 9,800 yen
S-SERO, YOU DIRT-BAG!!
For Sale

*ABOUT $98

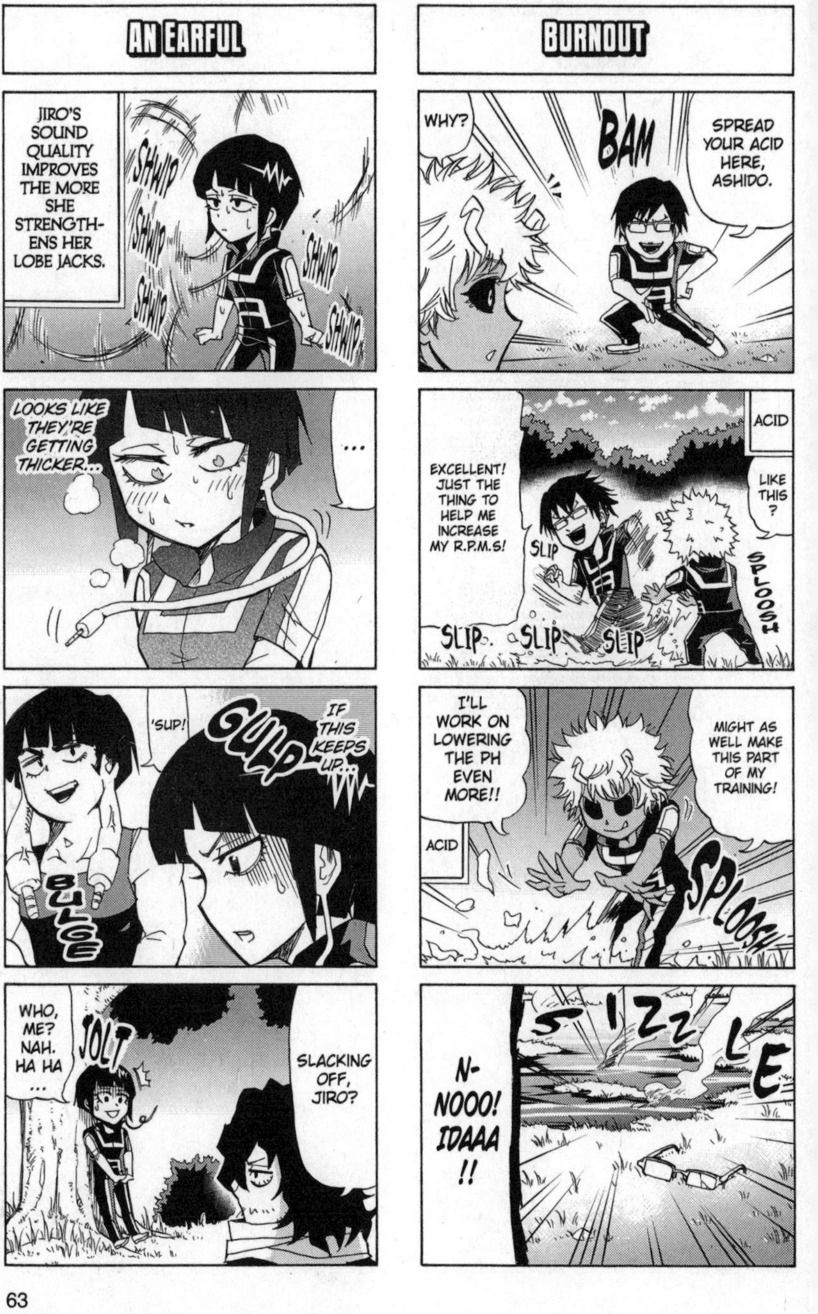
BURNOUT
SPREAD YOUR ACID HERE, ASHIDO.
BAM
WHY?
ACID
LIKE THIS?
SPLOOSH
EXCELLENT! JUST THE THING TO HELP ME INCREASE MY R.P.M.S!
SLIP
SLIP SLIP SLIP
MIGHT AS WELL MAKE THIS PART OF MY TRAINING!
I'LL WORK ON LOWERING THE PH EVEN MORE!!
ACID
SPLOOSH
SIZZLE
N-NOOO! IDAAA!!
AN EARFUL
SHWIP SHWIP
SHWIP SHWIP SHWIP SHWIP
JIRO'S SOUND QUALITY IMPROVES THE MORE SHE STRENGTH-ENS HER LOBE JACKS.
...
LOOKS LIKE THEY'RE GETTING THICKER...
IF THIS KEEPS UP...
GULP
'SUP!
BULGE
SLACKING OFF, JIRO?
JOLT
WHO, ME? NAH. HA HA ...

QUEEN OF THE JUNGLE

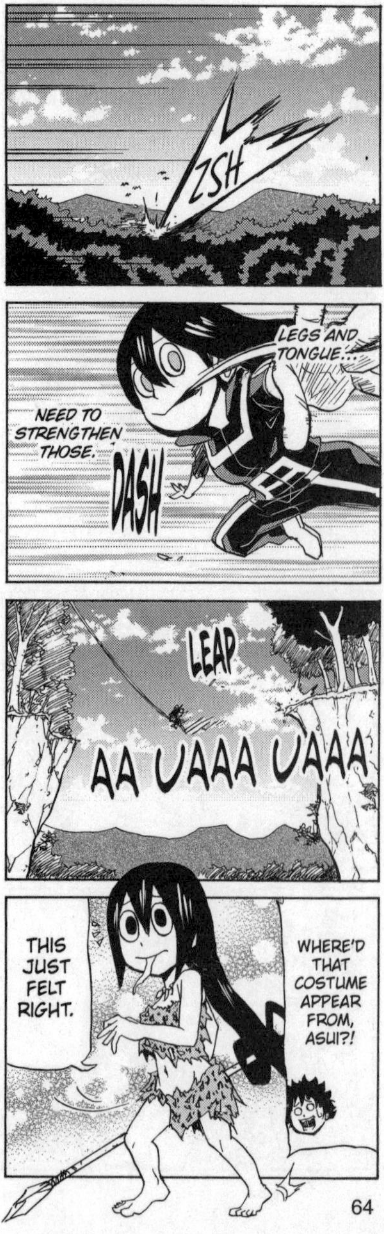
ZSH
LEGS AND TONGUE...
NEED TO STRENGTHEN THOSE.
DASH
LEAP
AA UAAA UAAA
WHERE'D THAT COSTUME APPEAR FROM, ASUI?!
THIS JUST FELT RIGHT.

SKETCHY

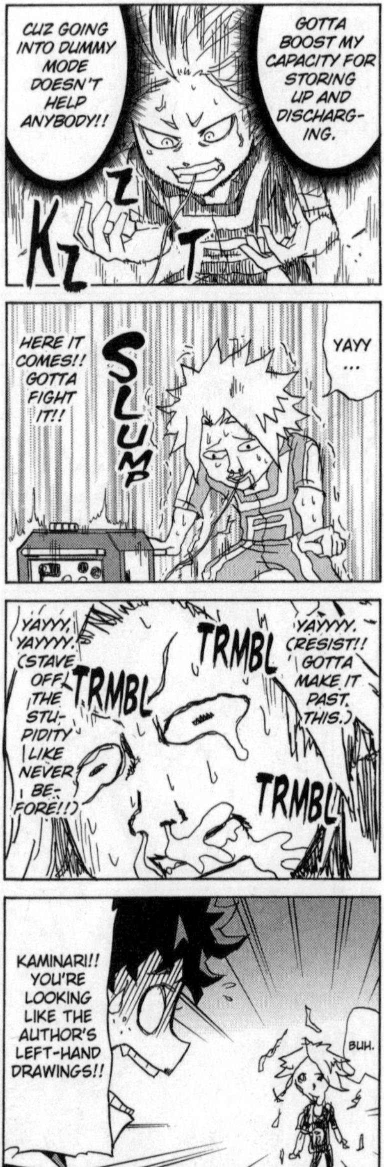
GOTTA BOOST MY CAPACITY FOR STORING UP AND DISCHARG-ING.
CUZ GOING INTO DUMMY MODE DOESN'T HELP ANYBODY!!
KZZT
YAYY ...
SLUMP
HERE IT COMES!! GOTTA FIGHT IT!!
YAYYYY. (RESIST!! GOTTA MAKE IT PAST THIS.)
TRMBL
YAYYY, YAYYYY. (STAVE OFF THE STU-PIDITY LIKE NEVER BE-FORE!!)
TRMBL
TRMBL
BUH.
KAMINARI!! YOU'RE LOOKING LIKE THE AUTHOR'S LEFT-HAND DRAWINGS!!

Sticky Situation

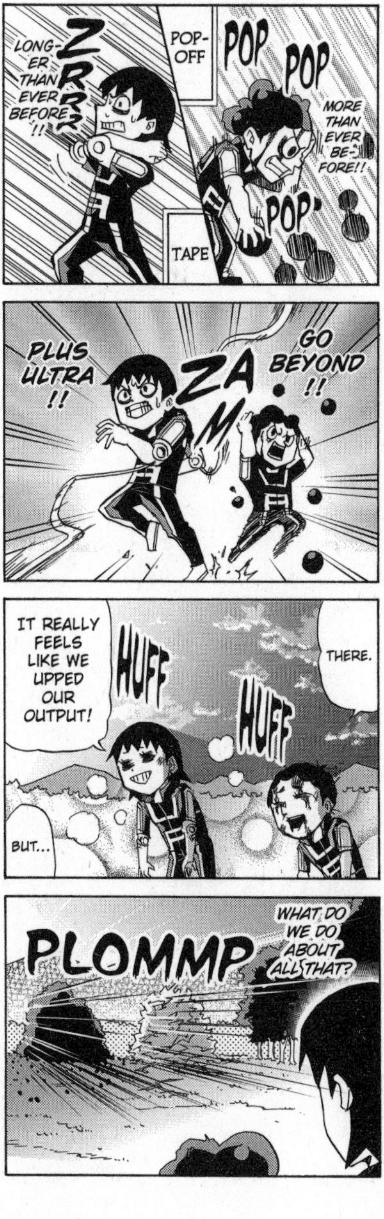

POP POP
POP-OFF
MORE THAN EVER BEFORE!!
ZRRRR
LONGER THAN EVER BEFORE!!
POP
TAPE
GO BEYOND!!
ZAM
PLUS ULTRA!!
THERE.
HUFF
HUFF
IT REALLY FEELS LIKE WE UPPED OUR OUTPUT!
BUT...
WHAT DO WE DO ABOUT ALL THAT?
PLOMMP

Ochachuck

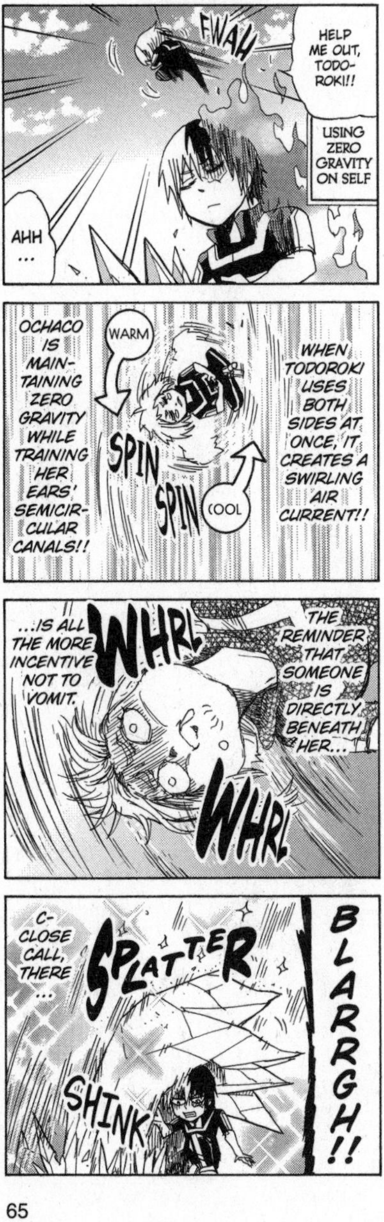

HELP ME OUT, TODOROKI!!
FWAH
USING ZERO GRAVITY ON SELF
AHH...
WHEN TODOROKI USES BOTH SIDES AT ONCE, IT CREATES A SWIRLING AIR CURRENT!!
COOL
WARM
SPIN
SPIN
OCHACO IS MAINTAINING ZERO GRAVITY WHILE TRAINING HER EARS' SEMICIRCULAR CANALS!!
THE REMINDER THAT SOMEONE IS DIRECTLY BENEATH HER...
WHRL
...IS ALL THE MORE INCENTIVE NOT TO VOMIT.
WHRL
BLARRGH!!
SPLATTER
C-CLOSE CALL, THERE...
SHINK

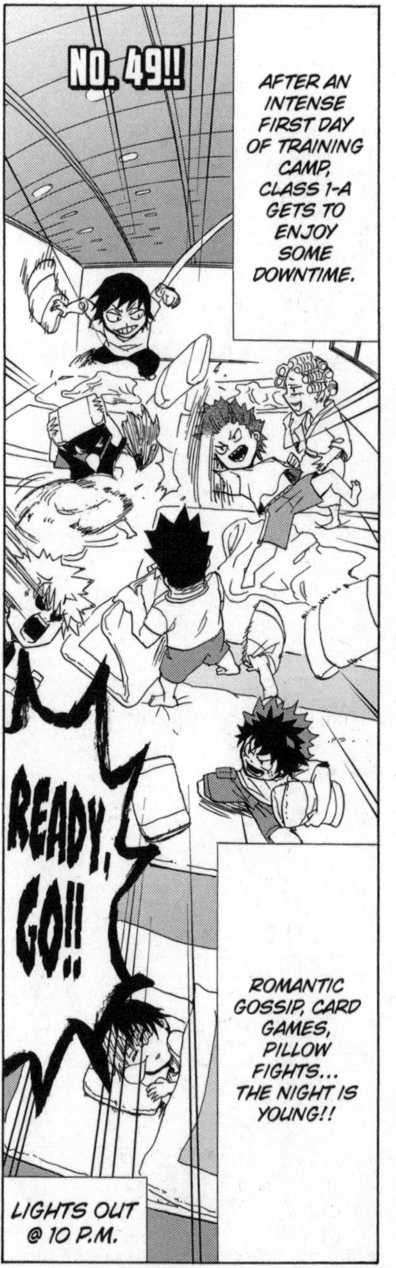
NO. 49!!
AFTER AN INTENSE FIRST DAY OF TRAINING CAMP, CLASS 1-A GETS TO ENJOY SOME DOWNTIME.
READY, GO!!
ROMANTIC GOSSIP, CARD GAMES, PILLOW FIGHTS... THE NIGHT IS YOUNG!!
LIGHTS OUT @ 10 P.M.

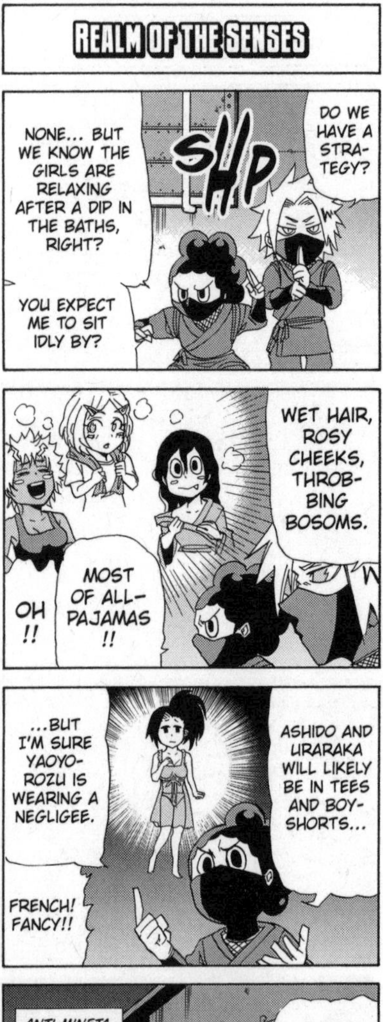
REALM OF THE SENSES
DO WE HAVE A STRATEGY?
SHP
NONE... BUT WE KNOW THE GIRLS ARE RELAXING AFTER A DIP IN THE BATHS, RIGHT?
YOU EXPECT ME TO SIT IDLY BY?
WET HAIR, ROSY CHEEKS, THROBBING BOSOMS.
MOST OF ALL— PAJAMAS!!
OH!!
ASHIDO AND URARAKA WILL LIKELY BE IN TEES AND BOY-SHORTS...
...BUT I'M SURE YAOYOROZU IS WEARING A NEGLIGEE.
FRENCH! FANCY!!
AN ENTIRE WORLD OF PAJAMAS AWAITS BEYOND THIS WALL.
ANTI-MINETA MEASURE BY YAOYOROZU
SIGH
INDEED. JUST THINKING ABOUT IT IS A BUFFET FOR THE MIND.
SOMEHOW IT WAS STILL TIME WELL SPENT FOR THESE TWO?

Seeking Solace

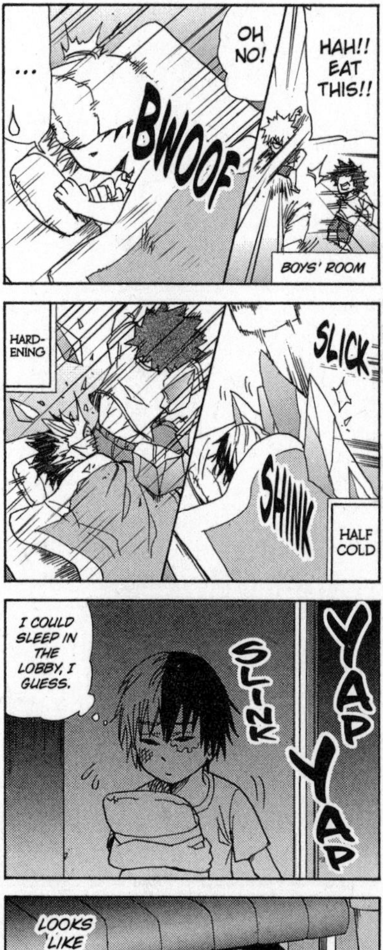
HAH!! EAT THIS!!
OH NO!
BWOOF
...
BOYS' ROOM
SLICK
HARD-ENING
SHINK
HALF COLD
YAP YAP
YAP YAP
SLINK
I COULD SLEEP IN THE LOBBY, I GUESS.
LOOKS LIKE SOMEONE BEAT ME TO IT.

Stopgap

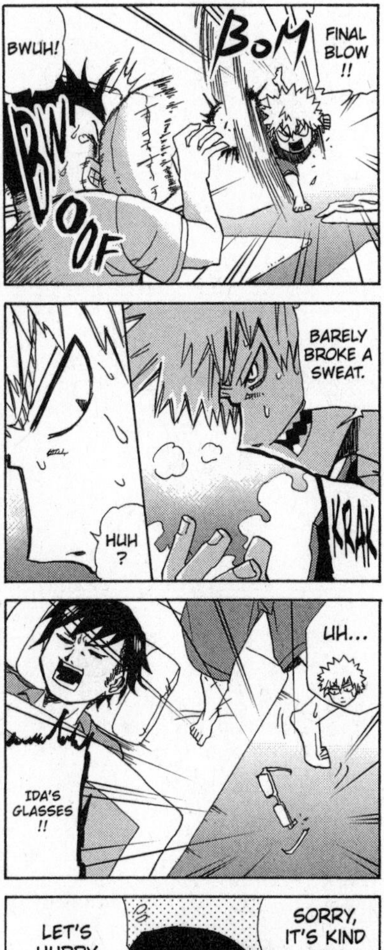
FINAL BLOW !!
BOM
BWUH!
BWOOF
BARELY BROKE A SWEAT.
KRAK
HUH ?
UH...
IDA'S GLASSES !!
SORRY, IT'S KIND OF A SHABBY FIX-IT JOB.
TAPE
LET'S HURRY AND GET YAOYO-ROZU.

HER TELL

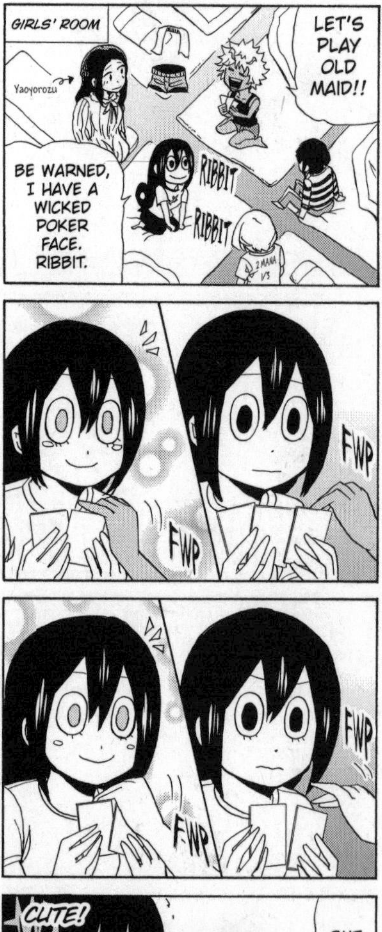
LET'S PLAY OLD MAID!!
GIRLS' ROOM
Yaoyorozu
RIBBIT
RIBBIT
BE WARNED, I HAVE A WICKED POKER FACE. RIBBIT.
2 MANA 1/3
FWP
FWP
FWP
FWP
BUT HOW?
I am?
CUTE!
KEEP UP THAT POKER FACE. YOU'RE DOING GREAT.

HEARTSTRINGS

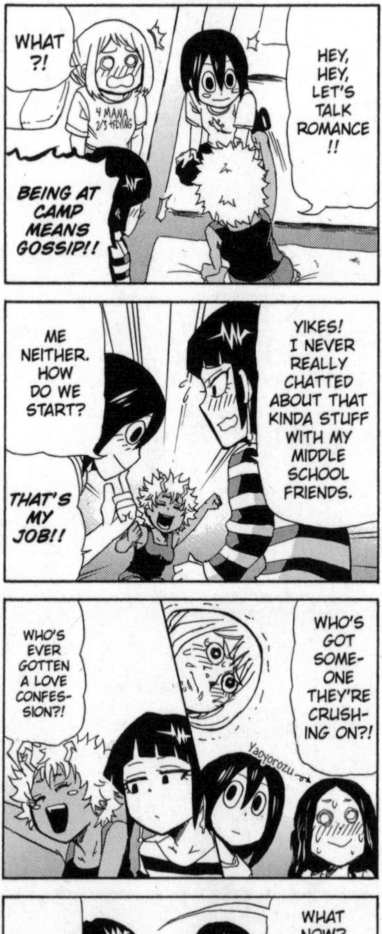
HEY, HEY, LET'S TALK ROMANCE!!
WHAT?!
4 MANA 2/3 +FLYING
BEING AT CAMP MEANS GOSSIP!!
YIKES! I NEVER REALLY CHATTED ABOUT THAT KINDA STUFF WITH MY MIDDLE SCHOOL FRIENDS.
ME NEITHER. HOW DO WE START?
THAT'S MY JOB!!
WHO'S GOT SOME-ONE THEY'RE CRUSH-ING ON?!
Yaoyorozu
WHO'S EVER GOTTEN A LOVE CONFES-SION?!
WHAT NOW? ASHIDO'S ALL TUCKERED OUT.
ANOTHER CARD GAME?

In the Closet

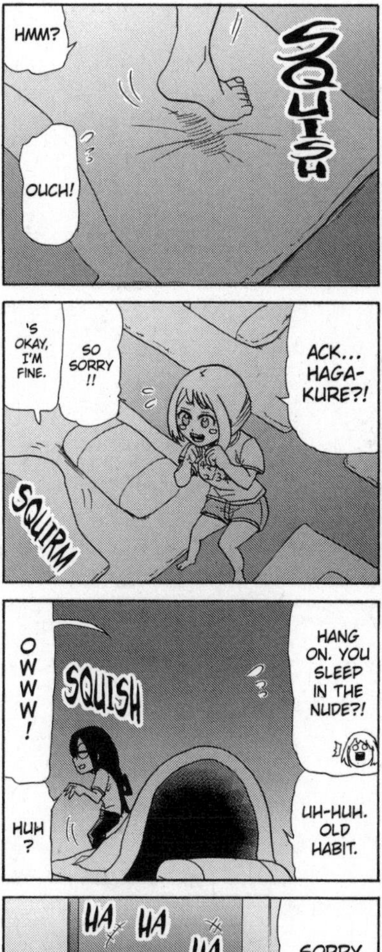
SQUISH
HMM?
OUCH!
ACK... HAGAKURE?!
SO SORRY!!
'S OKAY, I'M FINE.
SQUIRM
HANG ON. YOU SLEEP IN THE NUDE?!
SQUISH
OWWW!
UH-HUH. OLD HABIT.
HUH?
SORRY, REALLY...
HA HA HA
IT'S OKAY! JUST THINK OF ME AS A CARTOON ANIMAL!

Bright Idea

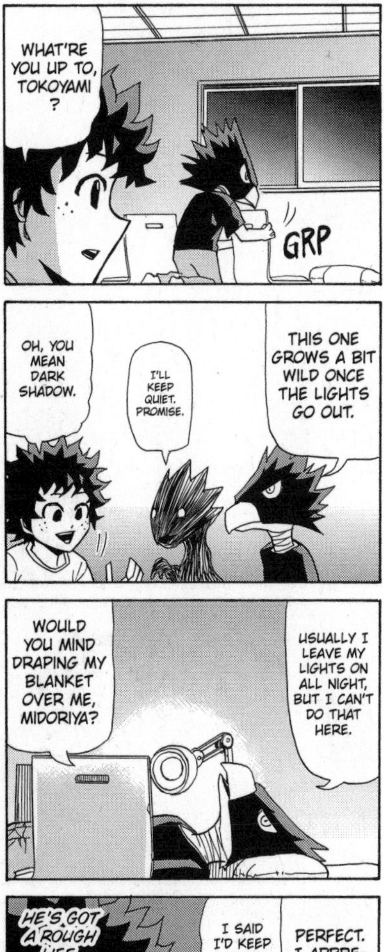
WHAT'RE YOU UP TO, TOKOYAMI?
GRP
THIS ONE GROWS A BIT WILD ONCE THE LIGHTS GO OUT.
I'LL KEEP QUIET. PROMISE.
OH, YOU MEAN DARK SHADOW.
USUALLY I LEAVE MY LIGHTS ON ALL NIGHT, BUT I CAN'T DO THAT HERE.
WOULD YOU MIND DRAPING MY BLANKET OVER ME, MIDORIYA?
PERFECT. I APPRECIATE IT.
I SAID I'D KEEP QUIET.
HE'S GOT A ROUGH LIFE.

PRINCESS AND THE PEA-BRAINS

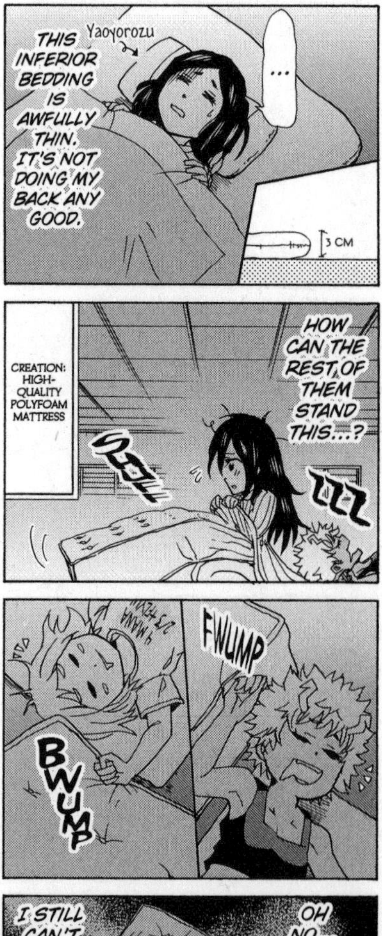
...
Yaoyorozu
THIS INFERIOR BEDDING IS AWFULLY THIN. IT'S NOT DOING MY BACK ANY GOOD.
3 CM
HOW CAN THE REST OF THEM STAND THIS...?
CREATION: HIGH-QUALITY POLYFOAM MATTRESS
ZZZ
FWUMP
BWUMP
OH NO...
I STILL CAN'T SLEEP.
GRIND GRIND
SQUIRM SQUIRM

SEEKING SOLACE, PART 2

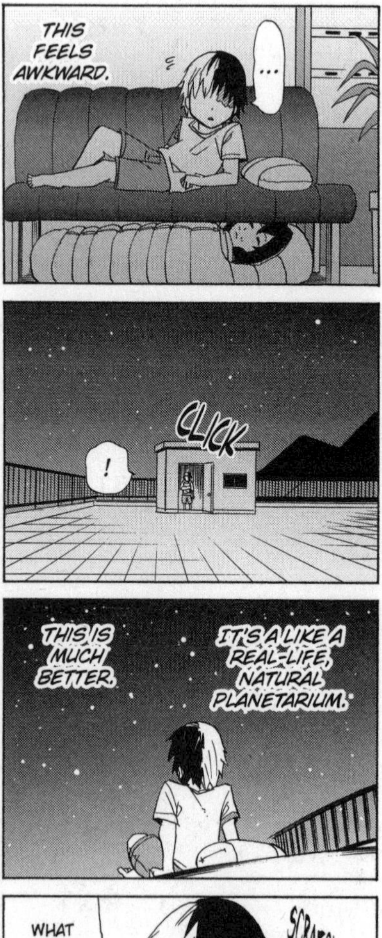
...
THIS FEELS AWKWARD.
CLICK
!
IT'S A LIKE A REAL-LIFE, NATURAL PLANETARIUM.
THIS IS MUCH BETTER.
SCRATCH SCRATCH
WHAT HAPPENED TO TODO-ROKI?!
S-SO MANY MOSQUI-TOES...

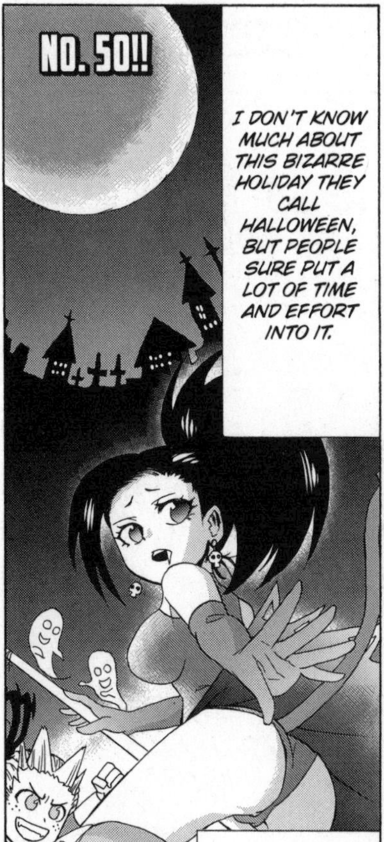
No. 50!!
I DON'T KNOW MUCH ABOUT THIS BIZARRE HOLIDAY THEY CALL HALLOWEEN, BUT PEOPLE SURE PUT A LOT OF TIME AND EFFORT INTO IT.
OUTTA NOWHERE, THE KIDS OF 1-A ARE HEADING TO SPOOKY SHIBUYA–THE TOKYO NEIGHBORHOOD WHERE YOU'RE GUARANTEED TO FIND PEOPLE IN COSTUME ON HALLOWEEN.

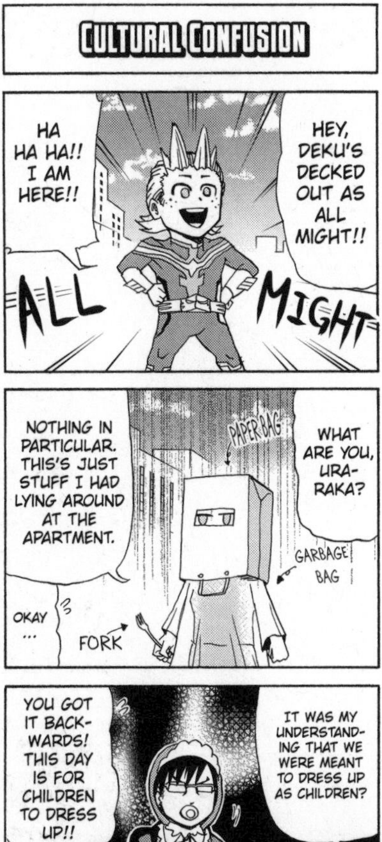
CULTURAL CONFUSION
HEY, DEKU'S DECKED OUT AS ALL MIGHT!!
HA HA HA!! I AM HERE!!
ALL MIGHT
WHAT ARE YOU, URARAKA?
PAPER BAG
NOTHING IN PARTICULAR. THIS'S JUST STUFF I HAD LYING AROUND AT THE APARTMENT.
GARBAGE BAG
OKAY ...
FORK
IT WAS MY UNDERSTANDING THAT WE WERE MEANT TO DRESS UP AS CHILDREN?
YOU GOT IT BACKWARDS! THIS DAY IS FOR CHILDREN TO DRESS UP!!
W-WHAT?!
WEIRDLY ENOUGH, THAT MAKES YOU LOOK LIKE THE ***WRONG SORT*** OF ADULT.
OH DEAR!!
YEP. YOU'D GET ARRESTED ON ANY OTHER DAY OF THE YEAR.
BULGE
YOU TOO, GIRL.

RED RIOT HOOD

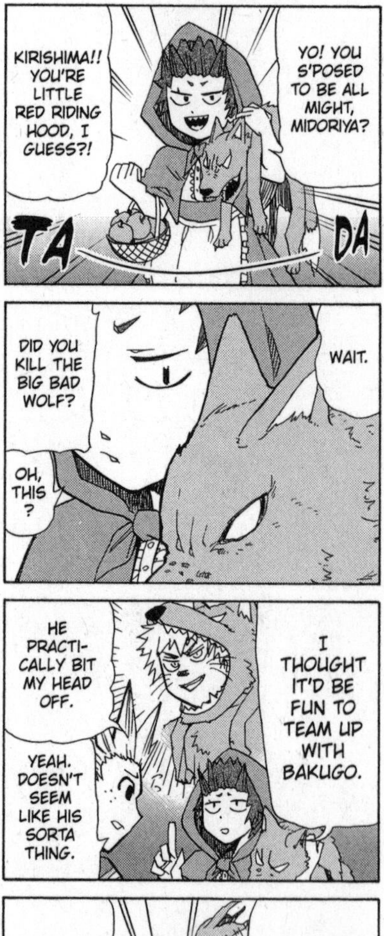
YO! YOU S'POSED TO BE ALL MIGHT, MIDORIYA?
KIRISHIMA!! YOU'RE LITTLE RED RIDING HOOD, I GUESS?!
TA DA
WAIT.
DID YOU KILL THE BIG BAD WOLF?
OH, THIS?
I THOUGHT IT'D BE FUN TO TEAM UP WITH BAKUGO.
HE PRACTI-CALLY BIT MY HEAD OFF.
YEAH. DOESN'T SEEM LIKE HIS SORTA THING.
BUT THAT'S NOT A BAD TAKE ON THE CHARACTER? YOU'RE BIG BAD RED RIDING HOOD.
'ZACTLY! I'M KINDA INTO IT.
SWING

MISSING THE MARK

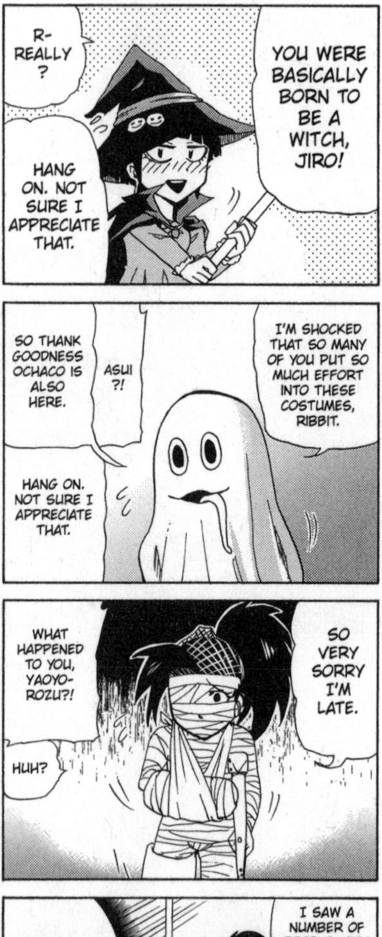
YOU WERE BASICALLY BORN TO BE A WITCH, JIRO!
R-REALLY?
HANG ON. NOT SURE I APPRECIATE THAT.
I'M SHOCKED THAT SO MANY OF YOU PUT SO MUCH EFFORT INTO THESE COSTUMES, RIBBIT.
ASUI?!
SO THANK GOODNESS OCHACO IS ALSO HERE.
HANG ON. NOT SURE I APPRECIATE THAT.
SO VERY SORRY I'M LATE.
WHAT HAPPENED TO YOU, YAOYO-ROZU?!
HUH?
I SAW A NUMBER OF PEOPLE WITH FAKE FLESH WOUNDS, OR WRAPPED HEAD TO TOE IN BANDAGES, SO THIS SEEMED APPRO-PRIATE.
PHEW.
HONESTLY LOOKS LIKE SHE GOT HIT BY A BUS.

Under the Veil of Night, From the Mouth of the Abyss, Molded by Darkness, Etc.

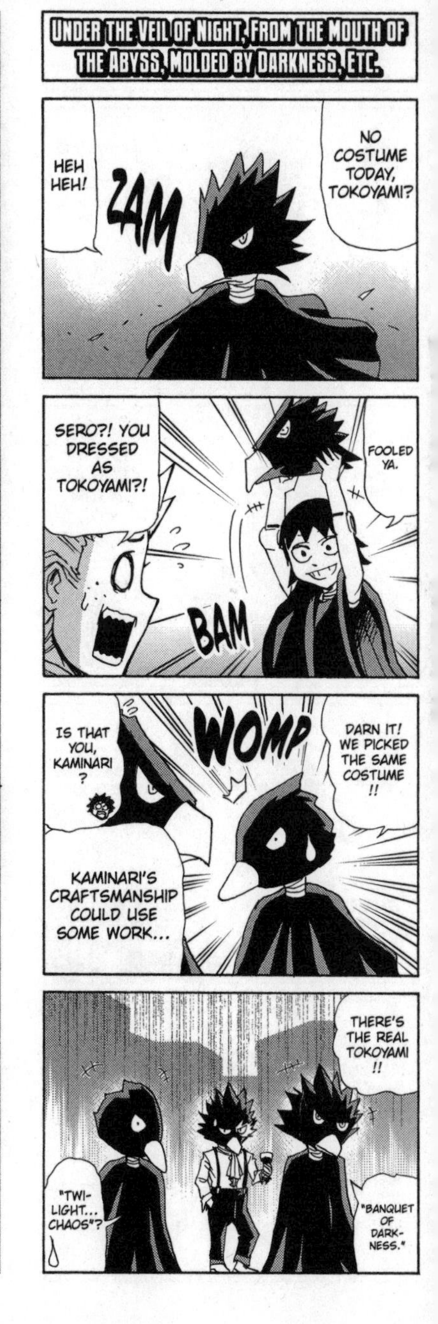
NO COSTUME TODAY, TOKOYAMI?
ZAM
HEH HEH!
FOOLED YA.
SERO?! YOU DRESSED AS TOKOYAMI?!
BAM
DARN IT! WE PICKED THE SAME COSTUME!!
WOMP
IS THAT YOU, KAMINARI?
KAMINARI'S CRAFTSMANSHIP COULD USE SOME WORK...
THERE'S THE REAL TOKOYAMI!!
"BANQUET OF DARK-NESS."
"TWI-LIGHT... CHAOS"?

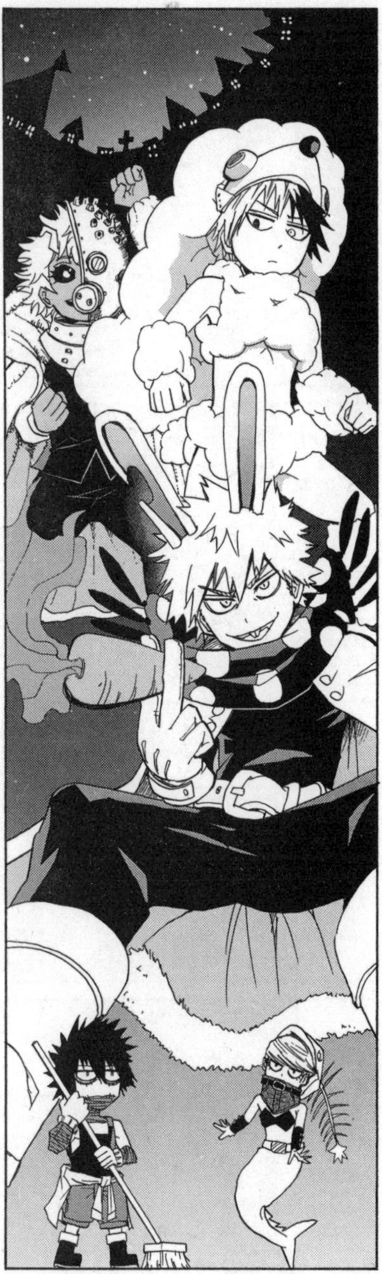

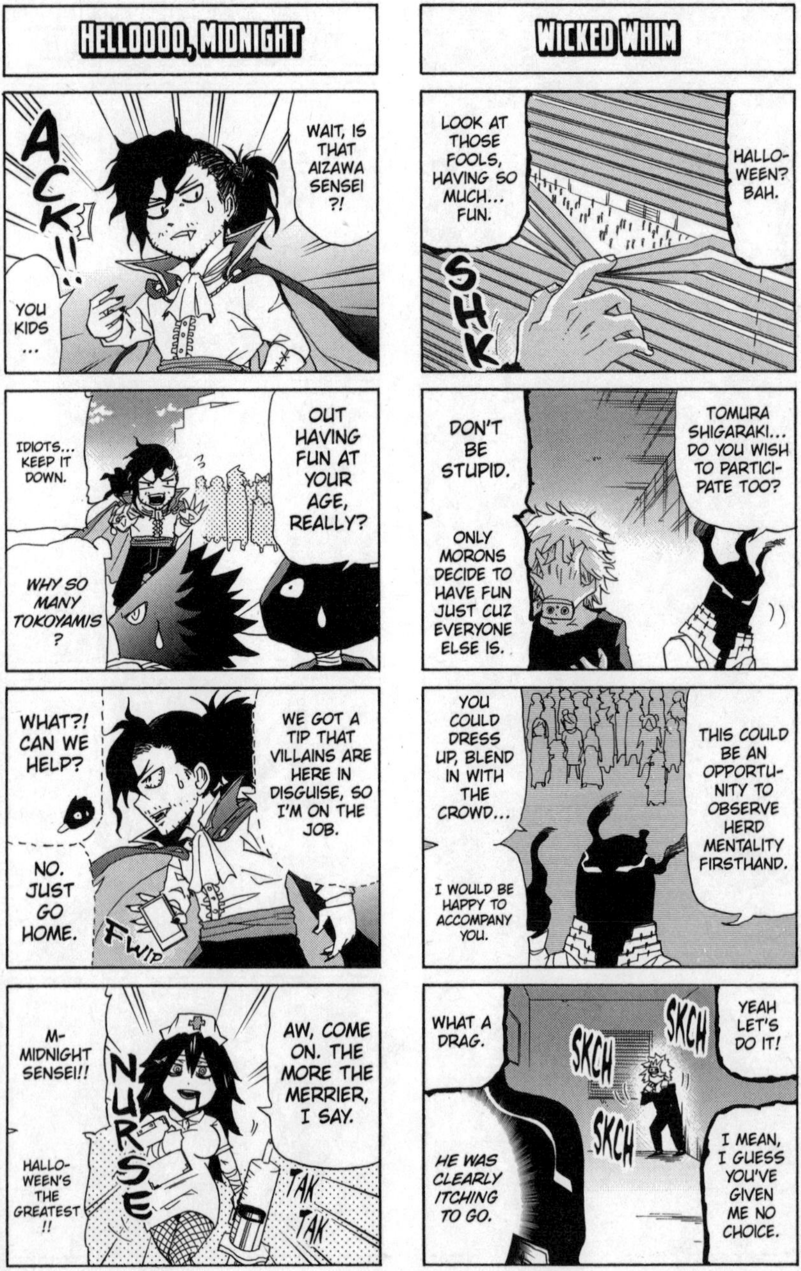
WICKED WHIM
HALLO-WEEN? BAH.
LOOK AT THOSE FOOLS, HAVING SO MUCH... FUN.
SHK
TOMURA SHIGARAKI... DO YOU WISH TO PARTICI-PATE TOO?
DON'T BE STUPID.
ONLY MORONS DECIDE TO HAVE FUN JUST CUZ EVERYONE ELSE IS.
THIS COULD BE AN OPPORTU-NITY TO OBSERVE HERD MENTALITY FIRSTHAND.
YOU COULD DRESS UP, BLEND IN WITH THE CROWD...
I WOULD BE HAPPY TO ACCOMPANY YOU.
YEAH LET'S DO IT!
SKCH
WHAT A DRAG.
SKCH
SKCH
I MEAN, I GUESS YOU'VE GIVEN ME NO CHOICE.
HE WAS CLEARLY ITCHING TO GO.
HELLOOOO, MIDNIGHT
WAIT, IS THAT AIZAWA SENSEI ?!
ACK!!
YOU KIDS ...
OUT HAVING FUN AT YOUR AGE, REALLY?
IDIOTS... KEEP IT DOWN.
WHY SO MANY TOKOYAMIS ?
WE GOT A TIP THAT VILLAINS ARE HERE IN DISGUISE, SO I'M ON THE JOB.
WHAT?! CAN WE HELP?
NO. JUST GO HOME.
FWIP
AW, COME ON. THE MORE THE MERRIER, I SAY.
NURSE
M-MIDNIGHT SENSEI!!
HALLO-WEEN'S THE GREATEST !!
TAK
TAK

STAINED REPUTATION

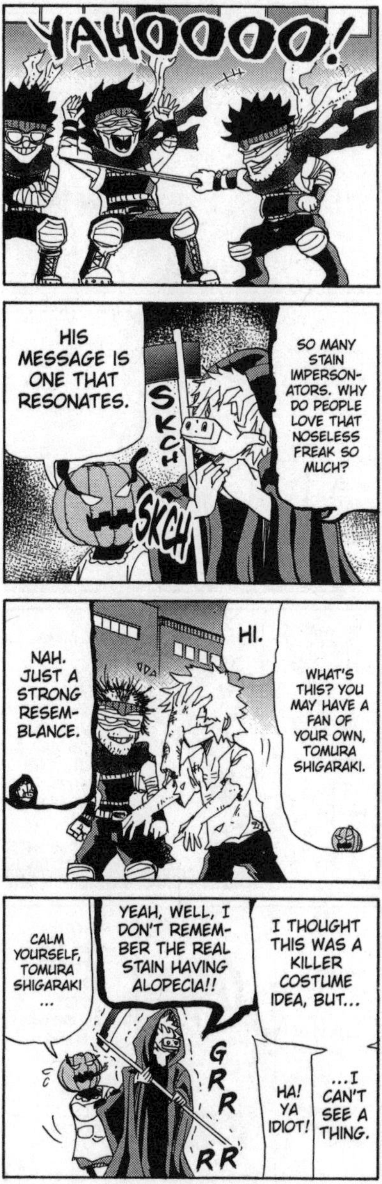
YAHOOOO!
SO MANY STAIN IMPERSON-ATORS. WHY DO PEOPLE LOVE THAT NOSELESS FREAK SO MUCH?
SKCH
HIS MESSAGE IS ONE THAT RESONATES.
SKCH
HI.
WHAT'S THIS? YOU MAY HAVE A FAN OF YOUR OWN, TOMURA SHIGARAKI.
NAH. JUST A STRONG RESEM-BLANCE.
I THOUGHT THIS WAS A KILLER COSTUME IDEA, BUT...
YEAH, WELL, I DON'T REMEM-BER THE REAL STAIN HAVING ALOPECIA!!
CALM YOURSELF, TOMURA SHIGARAKI ...
...I CAN'T SEE A THING.
HA! YA IDIOT!
GRRRR

REPRESENTATION

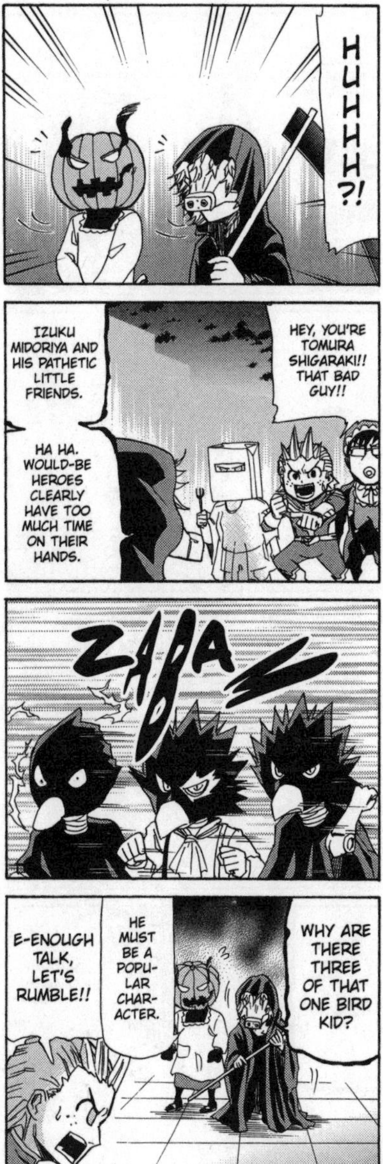
HUHHHH?!
HEY, YOU'RE TOMURA SHIGARAKI!! THAT BAD GUY!!
IZUKU MIDORIYA AND HIS PATHETIC LITTLE FRIENDS.
HA HA. WOULD-BE HEROES CLEARLY HAVE TOO MUCH TIME ON THEIR HANDS.
ZABA
WHY ARE THERE THREE OF THAT ONE BIRD KID?
HE MUST BE A POPU-LAR CHAR-ACTER.
E-ENOUGH TALK, LET'S RUMBLE!!

Commodification Culture

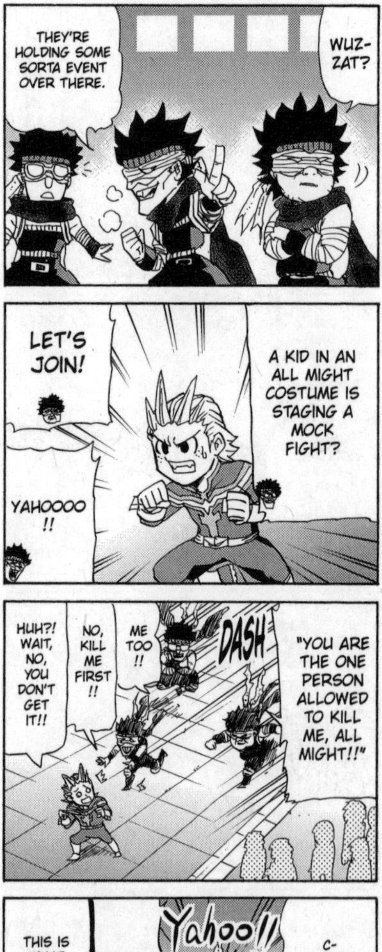
WUZ-ZAT?
THEY'RE HOLDING SOME SORTA EVENT OVER THERE.
A KID IN AN ALL MIGHT COSTUME IS STAGING A MOCK FIGHT?
LET'S JOIN!
YAHOOOO !!
DASH
"YOU ARE THE ONE PERSON ALLOWED TO KILL ME, ALL MIGHT!!"
ME TOO !!
NO, KILL ME FIRST !!
HUH?! WAIT, NO, YOU DON'T GET IT!!
C-CAROLINA SMASH?
Yahoo!!
PERFECT! JUST LIKE THAT!!
THIS IS WHAT SOCIETY'S BEEN REDUCED TO.
IT IS A BIT PITIFUL ...

Go Big or Go Home

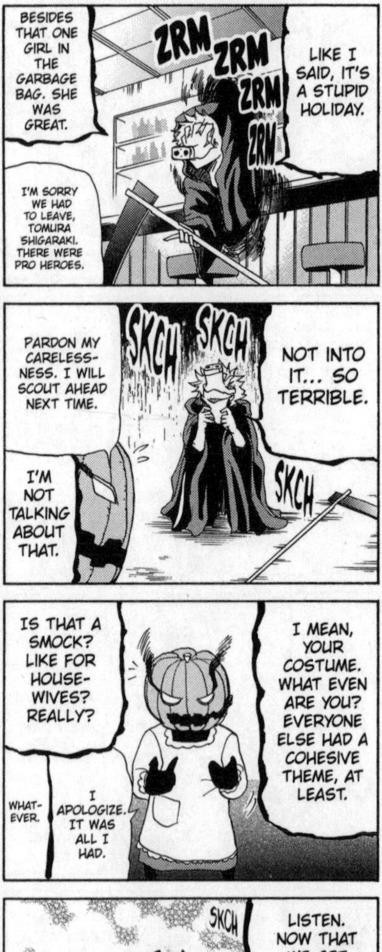
LIKE I SAID, IT'S A STUPID HOLIDAY.
ZRM ZRM ZRM ZRM
BESIDES THAT ONE GIRL IN THE GARBAGE BAG. SHE WAS GREAT.
I'M SORRY WE HAD TO LEAVE, TOMURA SHIGARAKI. THERE WERE PRO HEROES.
NOT INTO IT... SO TERRIBLE.
SKCH SKCH
PARDON MY CARELESS-NESS. I WILL SCOUT AHEAD NEXT TIME.
SKCH
I'M NOT TALKING ABOUT THAT.
I MEAN, YOUR COSTUME. WHAT EVEN ARE YOU? EVERYONE ELSE HAD A COHESIVE THEME, AT LEAST.
IS THAT A SMOCK? LIKE FOR HOUSE-WIVES? REALLY?
I APOLOGIZE. IT WAS ALL I HAD.
WHAT-EVER.
LISTEN. NOW THAT WE GET HOW THIS DUMB HALLOWEEN THING WORKS, WE'RE GOING ALL OUT NEXT YEAR.
SKCH
SKCH
OH.
KUROGIRI WAS RELIEVED TO LEARN THAT TOMURA SHIGARAKI MAY HAVE ENJOYED HIMSELF.

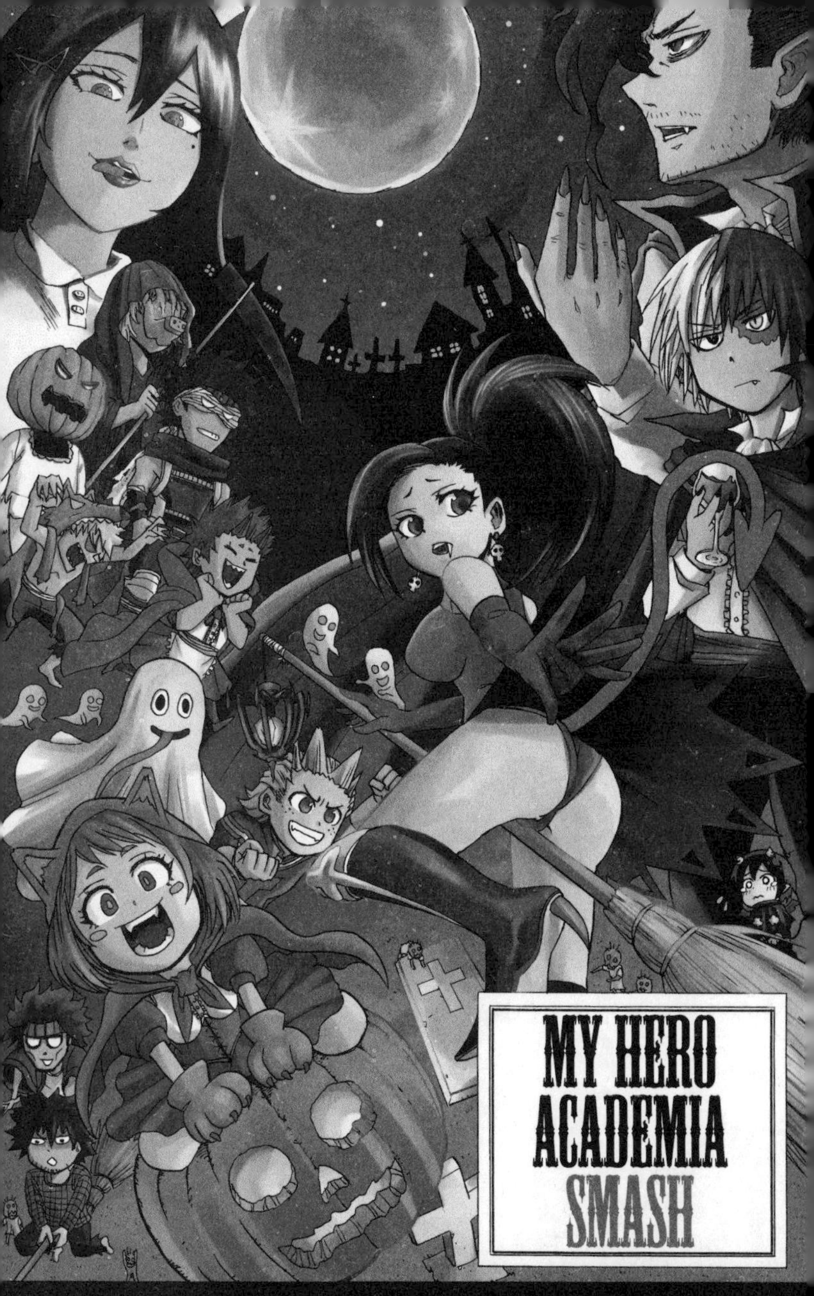
MY HERO
ACADEMIA
SMASH

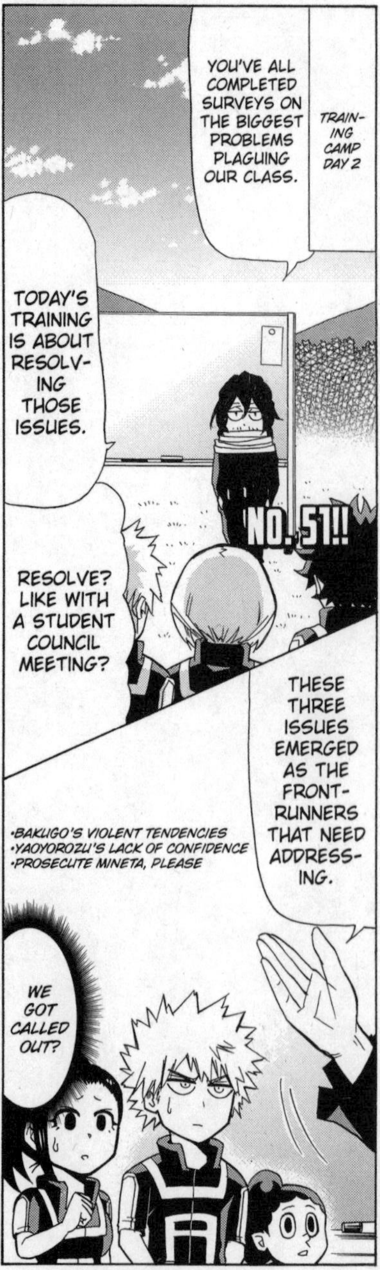
TRAINING CAMP DAY 2
YOU'VE ALL COMPLETED SURVEYS ON THE BIGGEST PROBLEMS PLAGUING OUR CLASS.
TODAY'S TRAINING IS ABOUT RESOLVING THOSE ISSUES.
NO. 51!!
RESOLVE? LIKE WITH A STUDENT COUNCIL MEETING?
THESE THREE ISSUES EMERGED AS THE FRONT-RUNNERS THAT NEED ADDRESSING.
·BAKUGO'S VIOLENT TENDENCIES
·YAOYOROZU'S LACK OF CONFIDENCE
·PROSECUTE MINETA, PLEASE
WE GOT CALLED OUT?

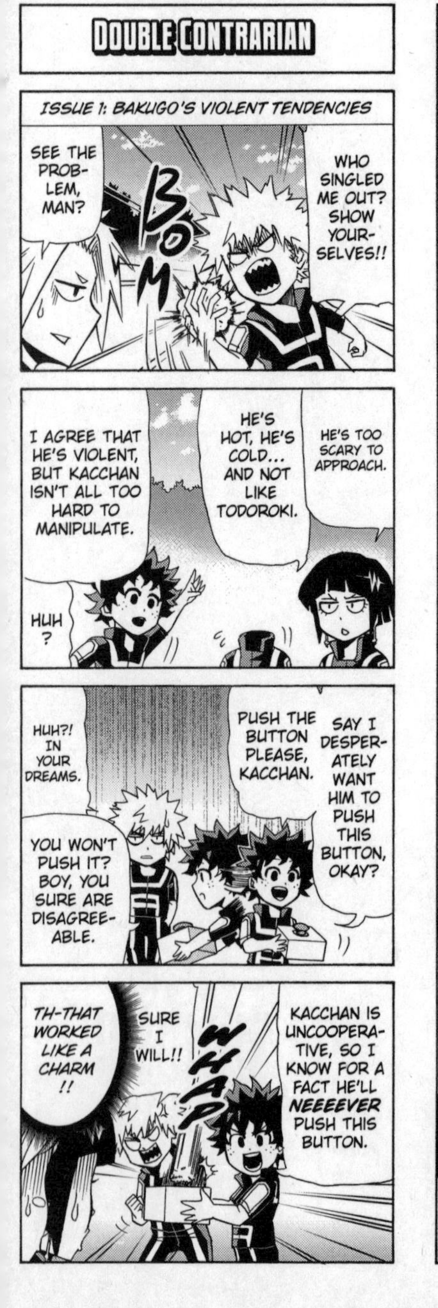
DOUBLE CONTRARIAN
ISSUE 1: BAKUGO'S VIOLENT TENDENCIES
WHO SINGLED ME OUT? SHOW YOURSELVES!!
BOOM
SEE THE PROBLEM, MAN?
HE'S TOO SCARY TO APPROACH.
HE'S HOT, HE'S COLD... AND NOT LIKE TODOROKI.
I AGREE THAT HE'S VIOLENT, BUT KACCHAN ISN'T ALL TOO HARD TO MANIPULATE.
HUH?
SAY I DESPERATELY WANT HIM TO PUSH THIS BUTTON, OKAY?
PUSH THE BUTTON PLEASE, KACCHAN.
HUH?! IN YOUR DREAMS.
YOU WON'T PUSH IT? BOY, YOU SURE ARE DISAGREEABLE.
KACCHAN IS UNCOOPERATIVE, SO I KNOW FOR A FACT HE'LL NEEEEEVER PUSH THIS BUTTON.
WHAP
SURE I WILL!!
TH-THAT WORKED LIKE A CHARM!!

KACCHAN: EXPOSED

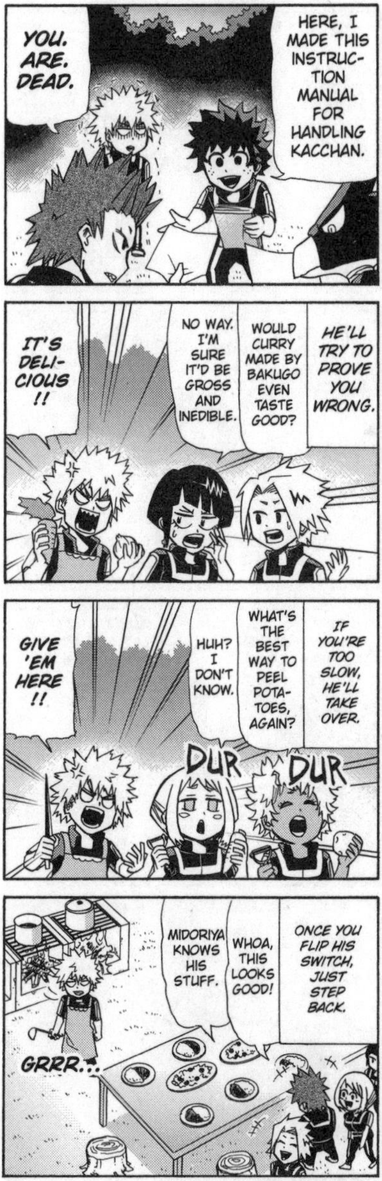
HERE, I MADE THIS INSTRUCTION MANUAL FOR HANDLING KACCHAN.
YOU. ARE. DEAD.
HE'LL TRY TO PROVE YOU WRONG.
WOULD CURRY MADE BY BAKUGO EVEN TASTE GOOD?
NO WAY. I'M SURE IT'D BE GROSS AND INEDIBLE.
IT'S DELICIOUS!!
IF YOU'RE TOO SLOW, HE'LL TAKE OVER.
WHAT'S THE BEST WAY TO PEEL POTATOES, AGAIN?
HUH? I DON'T KNOW.
DUR
DUR
GIVE 'EM HERE!!
ONCE YOU FLIP HIS SWITCH, JUST STEP BACK.
WHOA, THIS LOOKS GOOD!
MIDORIYA KNOWS HIS STUFF.
GRRR...

DE-MOTIVATIONAL

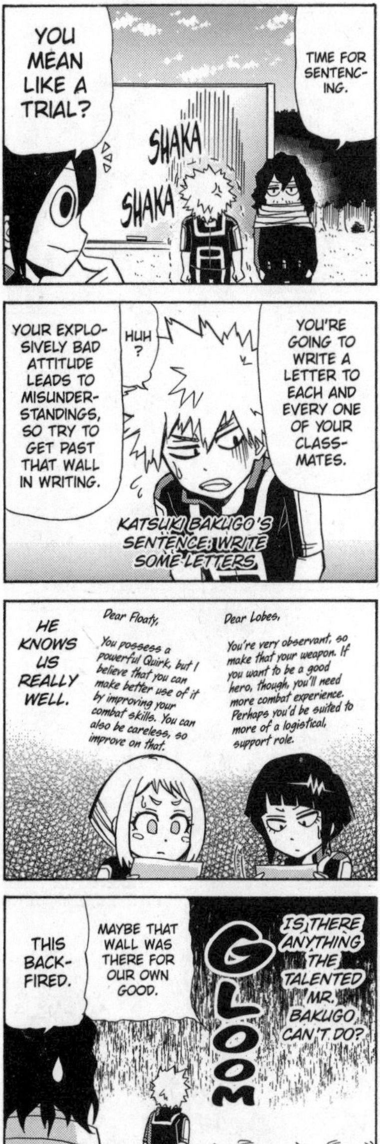
TIME FOR SENTENCING.
SHAKA
SHAKA
YOU MEAN LIKE A TRIAL?
YOU'RE GOING TO WRITE A LETTER TO EACH AND EVERY ONE OF YOUR CLASSMATES.
HUH?
YOUR EXPLOSIVELY BAD ATTITUDE LEADS TO MISUNDERSTANDINGS, SO TRY TO GET PAST THAT WALL IN WRITING.
KATSUKI BAKUGO'S SENTENCE: WRITE SOME LETTERS
Dear Lobes,
You're very observant, so make that your weapon. If you want to be a good hero, though, you'll need more combat experience. Perhaps you'd be suited to more of a logistical, support role.
Dear Floaty,
You possess a powerful Quirk, but I believe that you can make better use of it by improving your combat skills. You can also be careless, so improve on that.
HE KNOWS US REALLY WELL.
IS THERE ANYTHING THE TALENTED MR. BAKUGO CAN'T DO?
GLOOM
MAYBE THAT WALL WAS THERE FOR OUR OWN GOOD.
THIS BACKFIRED.

Full Circle

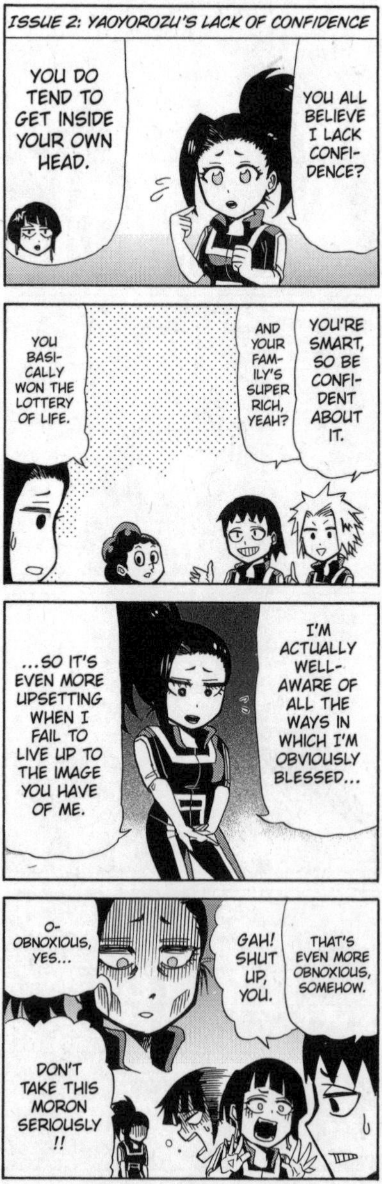
ISSUE 2: YAOYOROZU'S LACK OF CONFIDENCE
YOU ALL BELIEVE I LACK CONFIDENCE?
YOU DO TEND TO GET INSIDE YOUR OWN HEAD.
YOU'RE SMART, SO BE CONFIDENT ABOUT IT.
AND YOUR FAMILY'S SUPER RICH, YEAH?
YOU BASICALLY WON THE LOTTERY OF LIFE.
I'M ACTUALLY WELL-AWARE OF ALL THE WAYS IN WHICH I'M OBVIOUSLY BLESSED...
...SO IT'S EVEN MORE UPSETTING WHEN I FAIL TO LIVE UP TO THE IMAGE YOU HAVE OF ME.
THAT'S EVEN MORE OBNOXIOUS, SOMEHOW.
GAH! SHUT UP, YOU.
O-OBNOXIOUS, YES...
DON'T TAKE THIS MORON SERIOUSLY!!

Maslow's Hierarchy

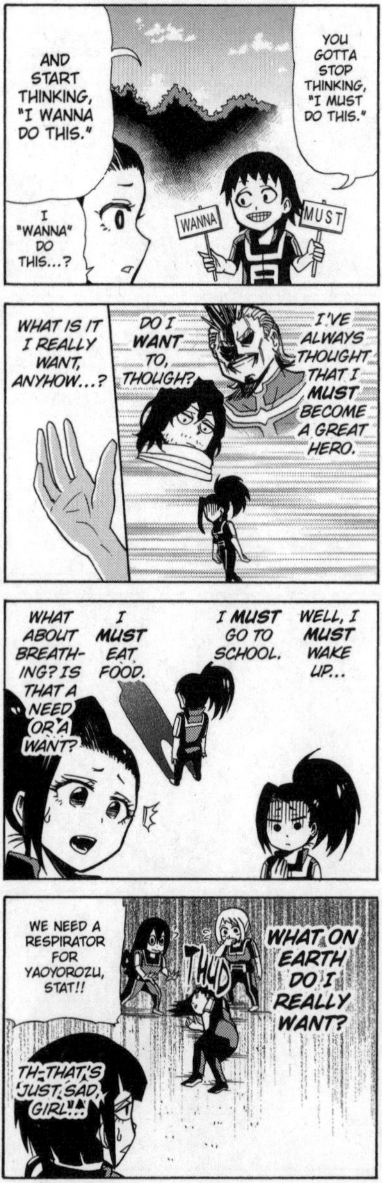
YOU GOTTA STOP THINKING, "I MUST DO THIS."
AND START THINKING, "I WANNA DO THIS."
MUST
WANNA
I "WANNA" DO THIS...?
I'VE ALWAYS THOUGHT THAT I MUST BECOME A GREAT HERO.
DO I WANT TO, THOUGH?
WHAT IS IT I REALLY WANT, ANYHOW...?
WELL, I MUST WAKE UP...
I MUST GO TO SCHOOL.
I MUST EAT FOOD.
WHAT ABOUT BREATHING? IS THAT A NEED OR A WANT?
WHAT ON EARTH DO I REALLY WANT?
THUD
WE NEED A RESPIRATOR FOR YAOYOROZU, STAT!!
TH-THAT'S JUST SAD, GIRL...

THE SIMPLE LIFE

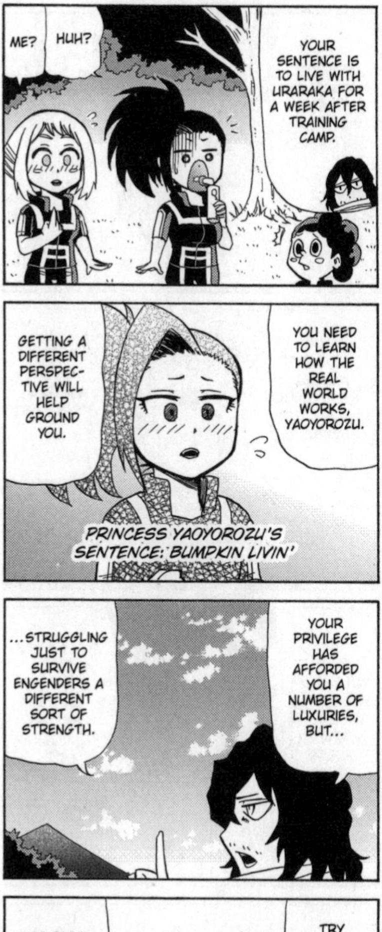
YOUR SENTENCE IS TO LIVE WITH URARAKA FOR A WEEK AFTER TRAINING CAMP.
HUH?
ME?
YOU NEED TO LEARN HOW THE REAL WORLD WORKS, YAOYOROZU.
GETTING A DIFFERENT PERSPEC-TIVE WILL HELP GROUND YOU.
PRINCESS YAOYOROZU'S SENTENCE: BUMPKIN LIVIN'
YOUR PRIVILEGE HAS AFFORDED YOU A NUMBER OF LUXURIES, BUT...
...STRUGGLING JUST TO SURVIVE ENGENDERS A DIFFERENT SORT OF STRENGTH.
TRY LEARNING THAT LESSON.
I'm ready to learn.
NOD
SO GLAD MY POVERTY WILL BE OF SERVICE. YEP. THAT'S NOT OFFENSIVE AT ALL...
SEE NO. 54!!

MALE VIEWERS AGE 8 TO 16

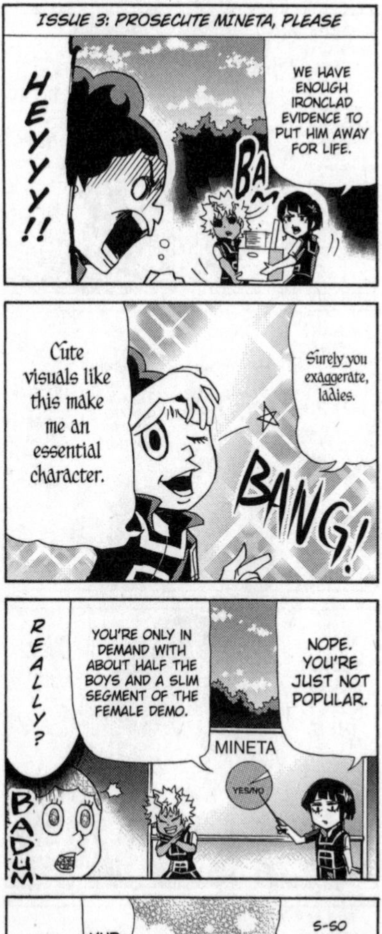
ISSUE 3: PROSECUTE MINETA, PLEASE
WE HAVE ENOUGH IRONCLAD EVIDENCE TO PUT HIM AWAY FOR LIFE.
BAM
HEYYY!!
Surely you exaggerate, ladies.
BANG!
Cute visuals like this make me an essential character.
NOPE. YOU'RE JUST NOT POPULAR.
MINETA
YES/NO
YOU'RE ONLY IN DEMAND WITH ABOUT HALF THE BOYS AND A SLIM SEGMENT OF THE FEMALE DEMO.
REALLY?
BADUM
S-SO THE MEN RESPECT ME AS THEIR MOUTH-PIECE?
YUP.
CHEER UP. I LIKE YOU PLENTY.
NOT NEARLY ALL OF THEM, THOUGH!!

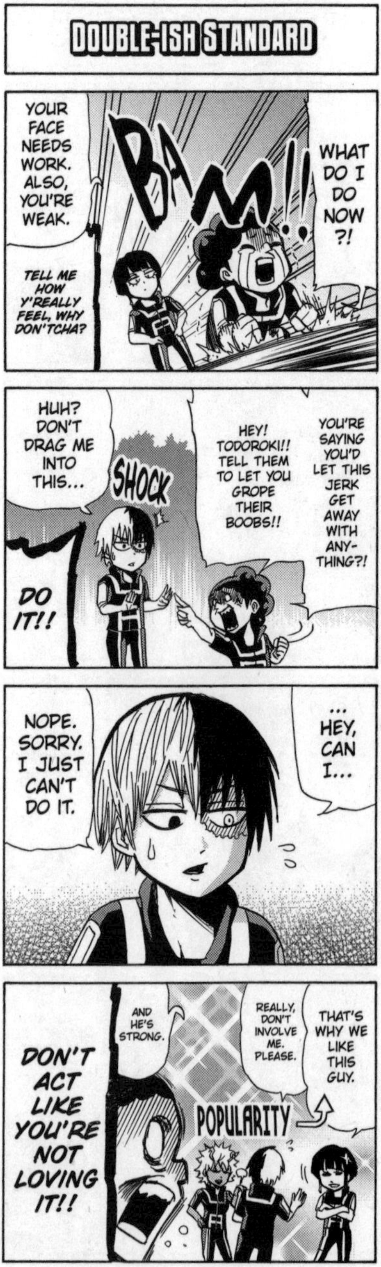
DOUBLE-ISH STANDARD
WHAT DO I DO NOW?!
BAM!!
YOUR FACE NEEDS WORK. ALSO, YOU'RE WEAK.
TELL ME HOW Y'REALLY FEEL, WHY DON'TCHA?
YOU'RE SAYING YOU'D LET THIS JERK GET AWAY WITH ANY-THING?!
HEY! TODOROKI!! TELL THEM TO LET YOU GROPE THEIR BOOBS!!
SHOCK
HUH? DON'T DRAG ME INTO THIS...
DO IT!!
... HEY, CAN I...
NOPE. SORRY. I JUST CAN'T DO IT.
THAT'S WHY WE LIKE THIS GUY.
REALLY, DON'T INVOLVE ME. PLEASE.
AND HE'S STRONG.
POPULARITY
DON'T ACT LIKE YOU'RE NOT LOVING IT!!

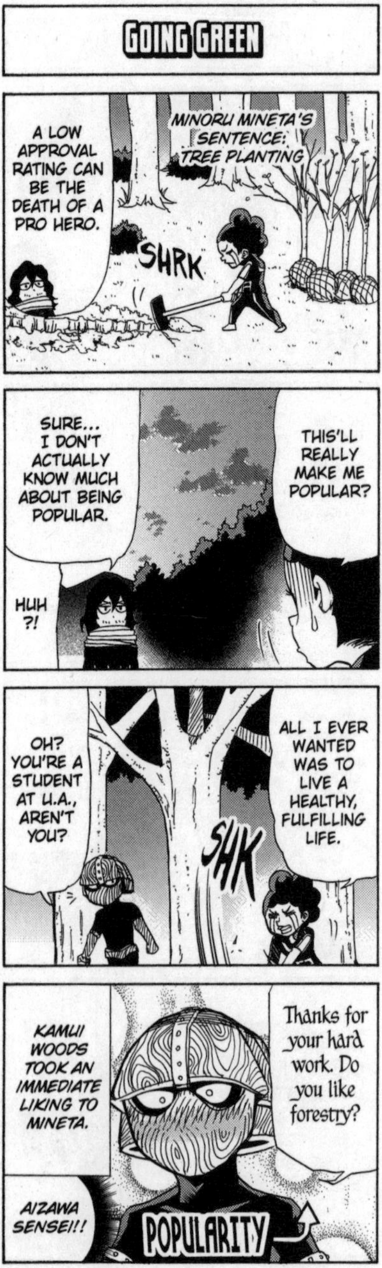
GOING GREEN
MINORU MINETA'S SENTENCE: TREE PLANTING
A LOW APPROVAL RATING CAN BE THE DEATH OF A PRO HERO.
SHRK
THIS'LL REALLY MAKE ME POPULAR?
SURE... I DON'T ACTUALLY KNOW MUCH ABOUT BEING POPULAR.
HUH?!
ALL I EVER WANTED WAS TO LIVE A HEALTHY, FULFILLING LIFE.
SHK
OH? YOU'RE A STUDENT AT U.A., AREN'T YOU?
Thanks for your hard work. Do you like forestry?
KAMUI WOODS TOOK AN IMMEDIATE LIKING TO MINETA.
POPULARITY
AIZAWA SENSEI!!

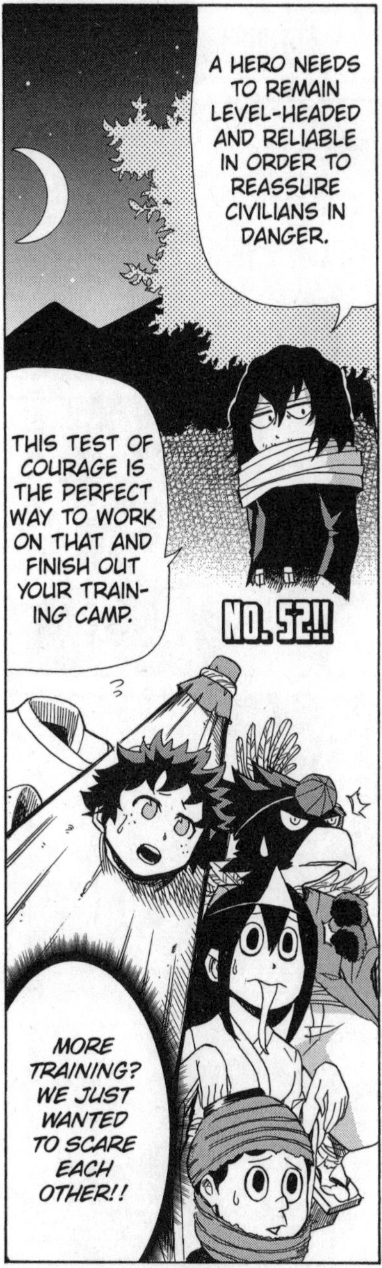
A HERO NEEDS TO REMAIN LEVEL-HEADED AND RELIABLE IN ORDER TO REASSURE CIVILIANS IN DANGER.
THIS TEST OF COURAGE IS THE PERFECT WAY TO WORK ON THAT AND FINISH OUT YOUR TRAIN-ING CAMP.
NO. 52!!
MORE TRAINING? WE JUST WANTED TO SCARE EACH OTHER!!

ONCE MORE, WITH FEELING

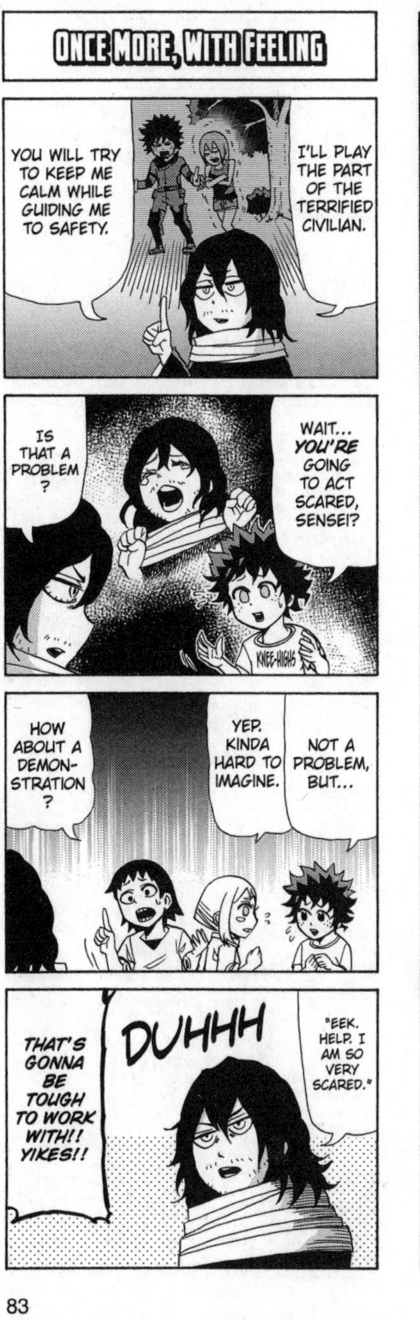
I'LL PLAY THE PART OF THE TERRIFIED CIVILIAN.
YOU WILL TRY TO KEEP ME CALM WHILE GUIDING ME TO SAFETY.
WAIT... *YOU'RE* GOING TO ACT SCARED, SENSEI?
IS THAT A PROBLEM?
KNEE-HIGHS
NOT A PROBLEM, BUT...
YEP. KINDA HARD TO IMAGINE.
HOW ABOUT A DEMONSTRATION?
"EEK. HELP. I AM SO VERY SCARED."
DUHHH
THAT'S GONNA BE TOUGH TO WORK WITH!! YIKES!!

Lesson Plan

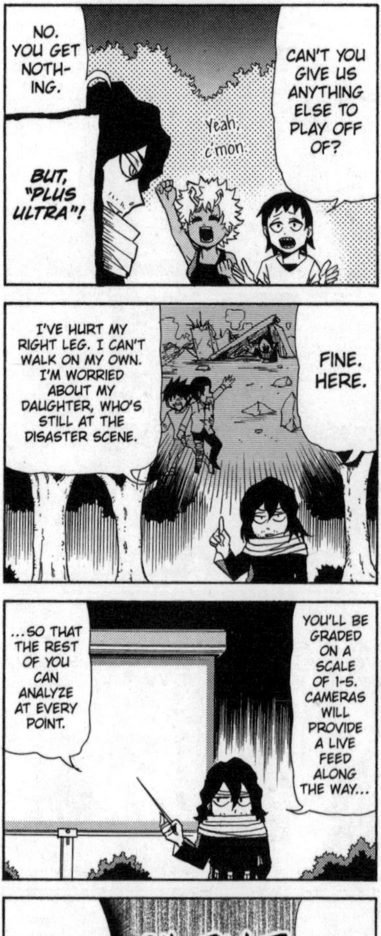
CAN'T YOU GIVE US ANYTHING ELSE TO PLAY OFF OF?
Yeah, c'mon.
NO. YOU GET NOTHING.
BUT, "PLUS ULTRA"!
FINE. HERE.
I'VE HURT MY RIGHT LEG. I CAN'T WALK ON MY OWN. I'M WORRIED ABOUT MY DAUGHTER, WHO'S STILL AT THE DISASTER SCENE.
YOU'LL BE GRADED ON A SCALE OF 1-5. CAMERAS WILL PROVIDE A LIVE FEED ALONG THE WAY...
...SO THAT THE REST OF YOU CAN ANALYZE AT EVERY POINT.
OKAY? BEGIN!!
SILENT
THIS IS JUST LIKE A NORMAL DAY OF SCHOOL!!
KNEE-HIGHS

Nothing to Work With

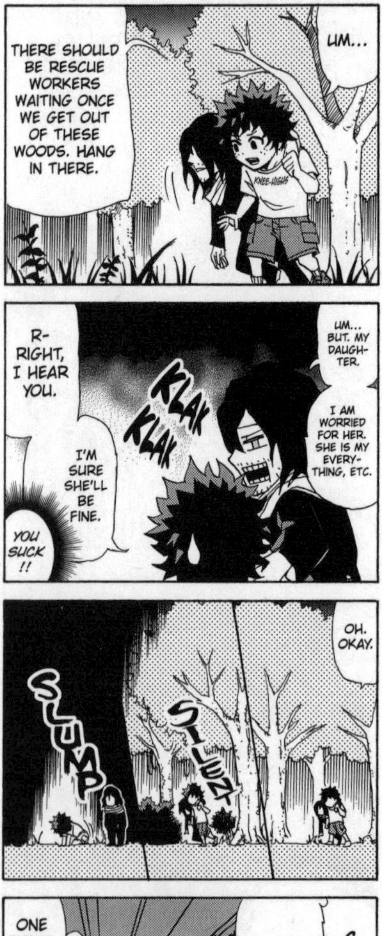
UM...
THERE SHOULD BE RESCUE WORKERS WAITING ONCE WE GET OUT OF THESE WOODS. HANG IN THERE.
KNEE-HIGHS
UM... BUT. MY DAUGHTER.
I AM WORRIED FOR HER. SHE IS MY EVERYTHING, ETC.
KLAK KLAK
R-RIGHT, I HEAR YOU.
I'M SURE SHE'LL BE FINE.
YOU SUCK!!
OH. OKAY.
SILENT
SLUMP
GAHHH!!
KEEP IT TOGETHER, MIDORIYA!!
ONE POINT.
BACK AT YOU, SENSEI!!
KNEE-HIGHS

'TIS BUT A FLESH WOUND

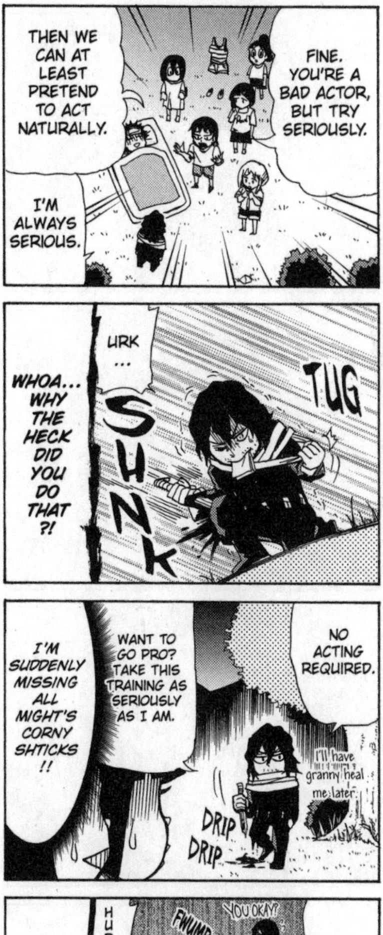
FINE. YOU'RE A BAD ACTOR, BUT TRY SERIOUSLY.
THEN WE CAN AT LEAST PRETEND TO ACT NATURALLY.
I'M ALWAYS SERIOUS.
TUG
URK...
SHUNK
WHOA... WHY THE HECK DID YOU DO THAT?!
NO ACTING REQUIRED.
I'll have granny heal me later.
WANT TO GO PRO? TAKE THIS TRAINING AS SERIOUSLY AS I AM.
DRIP DRIP
I'M SUDDENLY MISSING ALL MIGHT'S CORNY SHTICKS!!
YOU OKAY?
UGH... FEELING DIZZY.
FWUMP
WOBBLE
HURK!
ALL RIGHT, ENOUGH OF THAT!!

COLD AND WARMTH

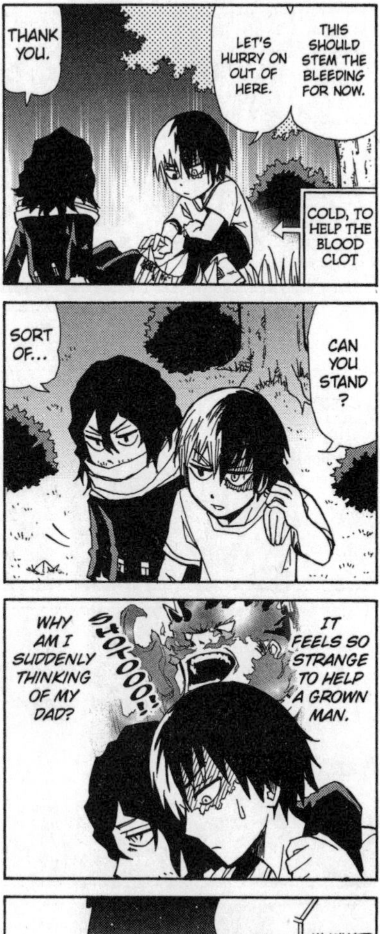
THIS SHOULD STEM THE BLEEDING FOR NOW.
LET'S HURRY ON OUT OF HERE.
THANK YOU.
COLD, TO HELP THE BLOOD CLOT
CAN YOU STAND?
SORT OF...
IT FEELS SO STRANGE TO HELP A GROWN MAN.
SHOTOOO!!
WHY AM I SUDDENLY THINKING OF MY DAD?
W-WHAT? WHY'S THIS HAPPENING?
IS TODOROKI CRYING?
SNIFFLE
KNEE-HIGHS
HE'S STARVED FOR SOME FATHERLY WARMTH!!

Kindred Spirits

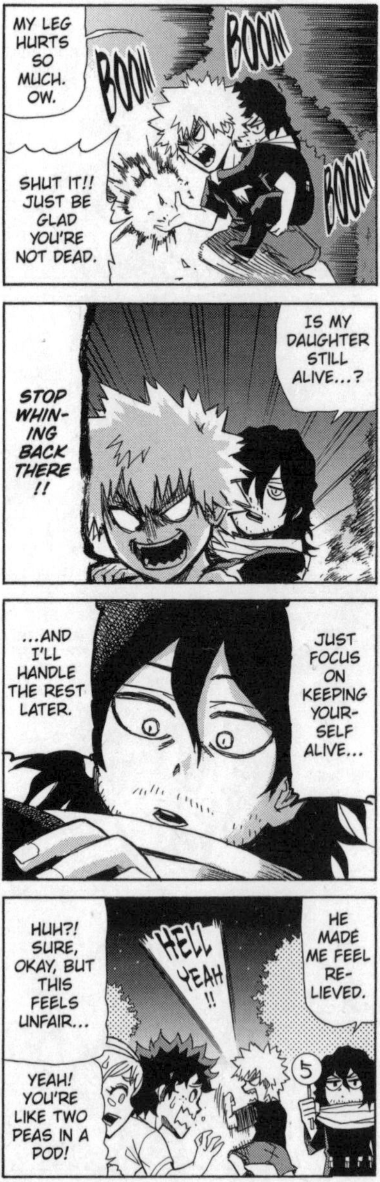
BOOM
BOOM
BOOM
MY LEG HURTS SO MUCH. OW.
SHUT IT!! JUST BE GLAD YOU'RE NOT DEAD.
IS MY DAUGHTER STILL ALIVE...?
STOP WHINING BACK THERE!!
JUST FOCUS ON KEEPING YOURSELF ALIVE...
...AND I'LL HANDLE THE REST LATER.
HE MADE ME FEEL RELIEVED.
HELL YEAH!!
HUH?! SURE, OKAY, BUT THIS FEELS UNFAIR...
5
YEAH! YOU'RE LIKE TWO PEAS IN A POD!

He's No Bakugo

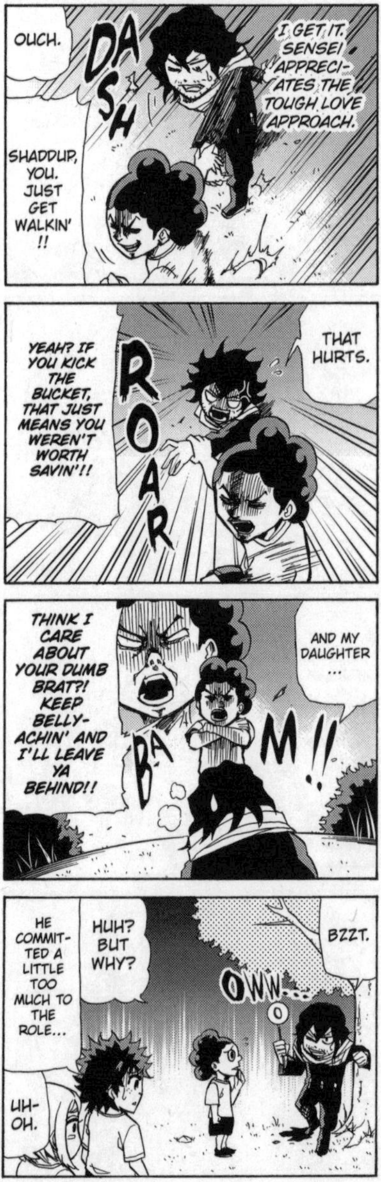
I GET IT. SENSEI APPRECIATES THE TOUGH LOVE APPROACH.
DASH
OUCH.
SHADDUP, YOU. JUST GET WALKIN'!!
THAT HURTS.
ROAR
YEAH? IF YOU KICK THE BUCKET, THAT JUST MEANS YOU WEREN'T WORTH SAVIN'!!
AND MY DAUGHTER...
BAM!!
THINK I CARE ABOUT YOUR DUMB BRAT?! KEEP BELLYACHIN' AND I'LL LEAVE YA BEHIND!!
BZZT.
OWW...
0
HUH? BUT WHY?
HE COMMITTED A LITTLE TOO MUCH TO THE ROLE...
UH-OH.

Petty Might

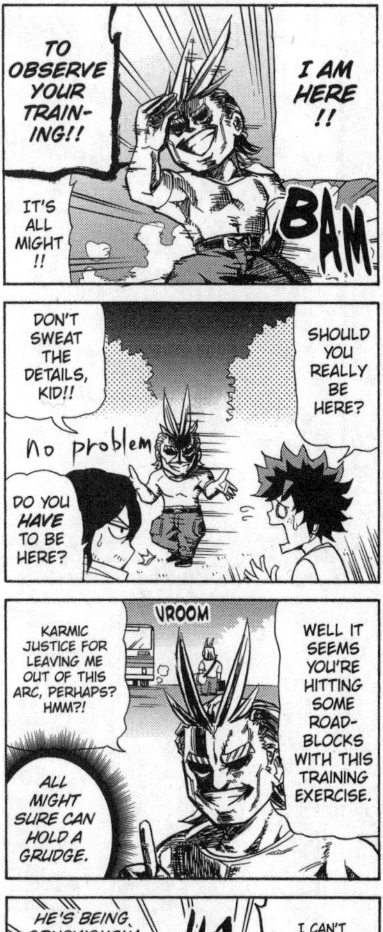
I AM HERE!!
TO OBSERVE YOUR TRAINING!!
BAM
IT'S ALL MIGHT!!
SHOULD YOU REALLY BE HERE?
DON'T SWEAT THE DETAILS, KID!!
no problem
DO YOU HAVE TO BE HERE?
VROOM
WELL IT SEEMS YOU'RE HITTING SOME ROADBLOCKS WITH THIS TRAINING EXERCISE.
KARMIC JUSTICE FOR LEAVING ME OUT OF THIS ARC, PERHAPS? HMM?!
ALL MIGHT SURE CAN HOLD A GRUDGE.
I CAN'T JUST SIT BY WITHOUT HELPING, SO ALLOW ME TO DEMONSTRATE HOW THE NUMBER ONE HERO GETS THE JOB DONE!!
HA
HE'S BEING OBNOXIOUSLY PUSHY ABOUT IT, BUT WE CAN'T WAIT TO SEE.

Appalled Might

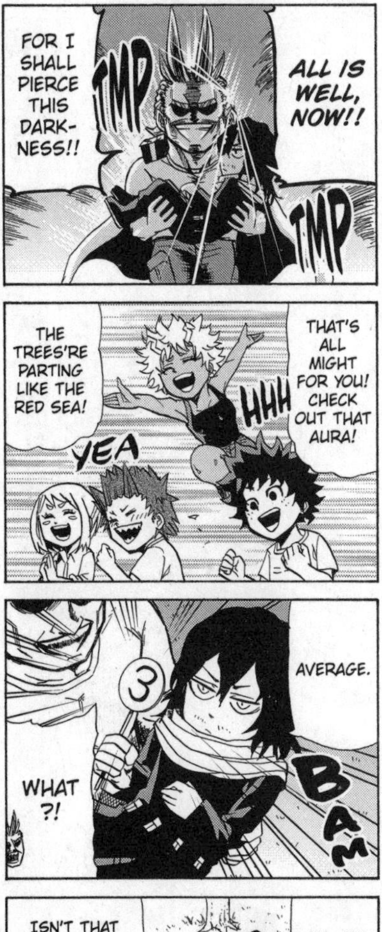
ALL IS WELL, NOW!!
TMP
FOR I SHALL PIERCE THIS DARKNESS!!
TMP
THAT'S ALL MIGHT FOR YOU! CHECK OUT THAT AURA!
HHH
THE TREES'RE PARTING LIKE THE RED SEA!
YEA
AVERAGE.
BAM
WHAT?!
ALL YOU DID WAS CARRY ME OUT OF THERE.
ISN'T THAT REASSURING ENOUGH WHEN ALL MIGHT'S THE ONE DOING THE CARRYING?
EXACTLY. NOT MUCH OF A "DEMONSTRATION" IF IT RELIES ON THE RESCUER BEING ALL MIGHT.
THAT'S... A GOOD POINT.

TOMURA SHIGARAKI

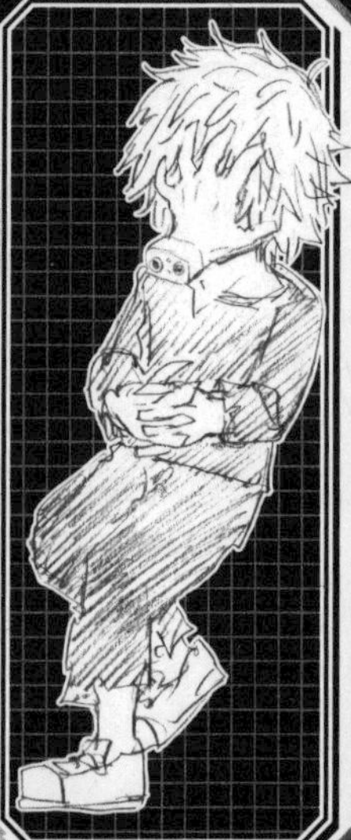

CENTRAL FIGURE IN THE LEAGUE OF VILLAINS.

THIS TROUBLEMAKER KNOWS HE'S MAIN-ANTAGONIST MATERIAL, SO HE'S ONLY WILLING TO FOLLOW HIS OWN RULES!! IN *SMASH!!*, THOUGH, HE'S REMARKABLY UNAWARE OF HOW BIZARRE HIS OWN RULES ARE!! TOMURA'S A QUICK STUDY WITH KILLER INTUITION, SO WATCH OUT, BECAUSE THIS MAN-CHILD IS GOING PLACES!!

IF HE WERE TO COMMIT EVIL ON PRINCIPLE INSTEAD OF JUST PASSION, WHO KNOWS HOW BAD THINGS MIGHT GET...

KUROGIRI

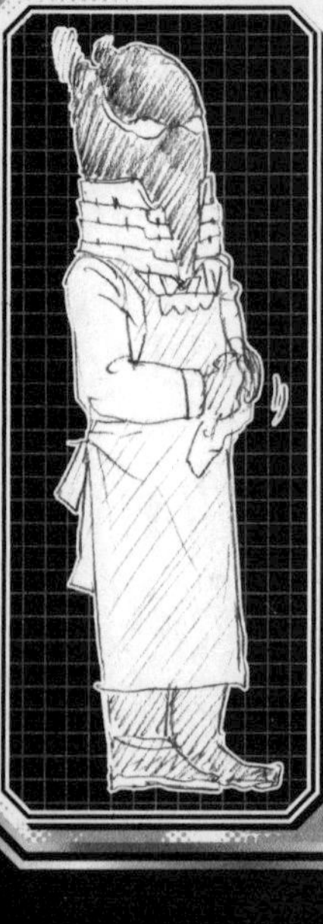

THE LEAGUE OF VILLAINS' PRIMARY ADVISER.

HE'S THERE TO SCOLD, FORGIVE, PROVIDE GUIDANCE... IN *SMASH!!*, HE'S LESS OF A STRATEGIST AND MORE OF A PARENTAL FIGURE!! KUROGIRI NEVER GETS TOO PUSHY, SO HE'S OFTEN ON THE LOSING END OF DISAGREEMENTS. DEALING WITH THE OTHER WACKY VILLAINS AND THEIR ANTICS DAY AFTER DAY MUST GIVE HIM HEARTBURN. EVEN TAKING INTO ACCOUNT THOSE ON THE HERO SIDE OF THE EQUATION, KUROGIRI IS ONE OF THE MOST HONEST, UPRIGHT CHARACTERS, DESPITE BEING A VILLAIN!!

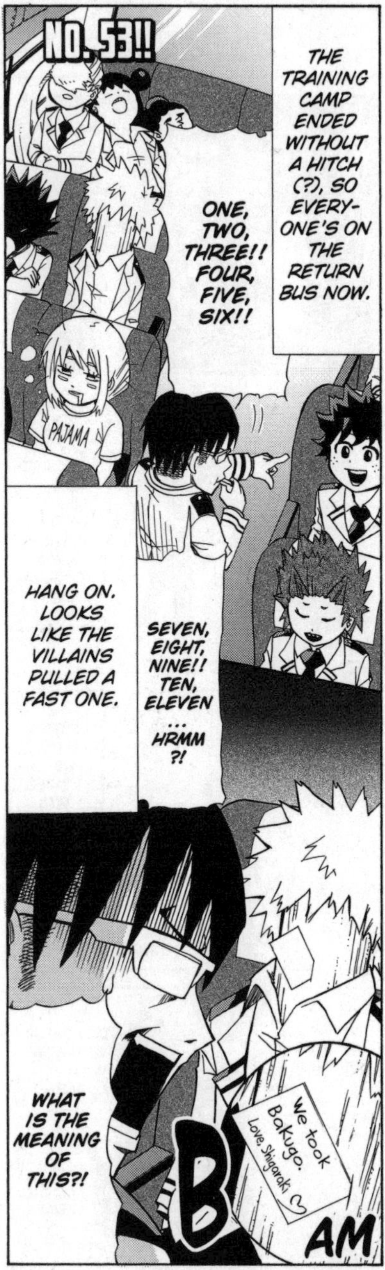
No. 53!!
THE TRAINING CAMP ENDED WITHOUT A HITCH (?), SO EVERYONE'S ON THE RETURN BUS NOW.
ONE, TWO, THREE!! FOUR, FIVE, SIX!!
PAJAMA
SEVEN, EIGHT, NINE!! TEN, ELEVEN ... HRMM ?!
HANG ON. LOOKS LIKE THE VILLAINS PULLED A FAST ONE.
We took Bakugo. Love, Shigaraki
BAM
WHAT IS THE MEANING OF THIS?!

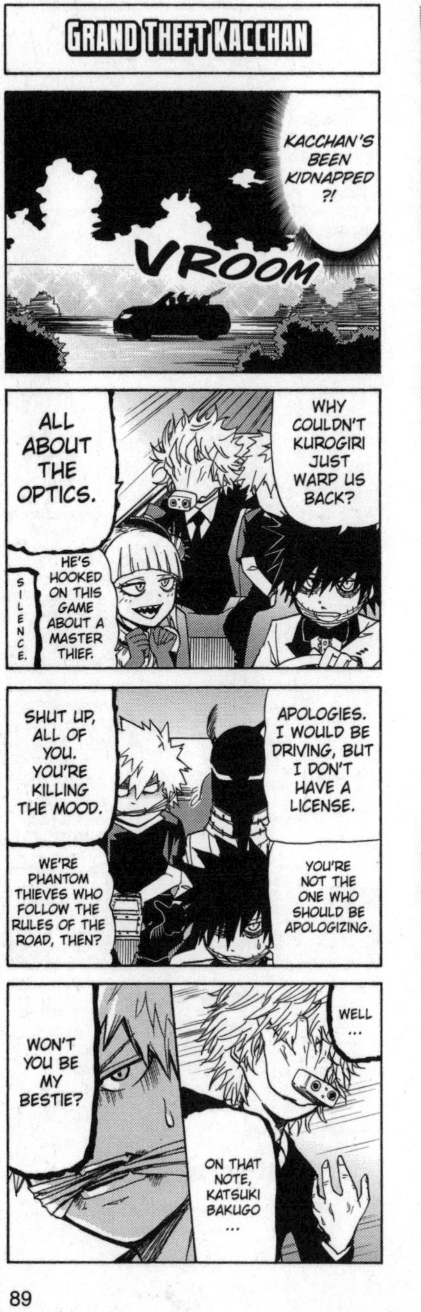
GRAND THEFT KACCHAN
KACCHAN'S BEEN KIDNAPPED ?!
VROOM
WHY COULDN'T KUROGIRI JUST WARP US BACK?
ALL ABOUT THE OPTICS.
HE'S HOOKED ON THIS GAME ABOUT A MASTER THIEF.
SILENCE.
APOLOGIES. I WOULD BE DRIVING, BUT I DON'T HAVE A LICENSE.
SHUT UP, ALL OF YOU. YOU'RE KILLING THE MOOD.
YOU'RE NOT THE ONE WHO SHOULD BE APOLOGIZING.
WE'RE PHANTOM THIEVES WHO FOLLOW THE RULES OF THE ROAD, THEN?
WELL ...
ON THAT NOTE, KATSUKI BAKUGO ...
WON'T YOU BE MY BESTIE?

SALES PITCH

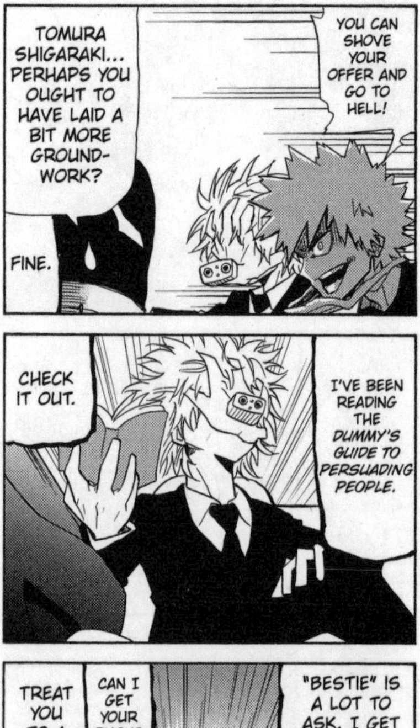
YOU CAN SHOVE YOUR OFFER AND GO TO HELL!
TOMURA SHIGARAKI... PERHAPS YOU OUGHT TO HAVE LAID A BIT MORE GROUND-WORK?
FINE.
I'VE BEEN READING THE *DUMMY'S GUIDE TO PERSUADING PEOPLE.*
CHECK IT OUT.
"BESTIE" IS A LOT TO ASK. I GET IT. HOW ABOUT WE HANG OUT, SAY, ONCE A MONTH?
NOPE.
CAN I GET YOUR PHONE NUM-BER?
NOPE.
TREAT YOU TO A MEAL?
NOPE.
B-BUT THE BOOK SAID TO ASK FOR SMALLER THINGS AFTER SOMEONE REJECTS THE BIG REQUEST.
SKCH SKCH SKCH SKCH
DABI. YOU'RE AWFULLY CHATTY FOR A GUY WHO GOT WHUPPED BY A SCHOOL-TEACHER.
WHY WOULD ANYONE WANT A MEAL WITH YOU? GROSS.
VROOOM
GO TO HELL.

GOOD COP x 4

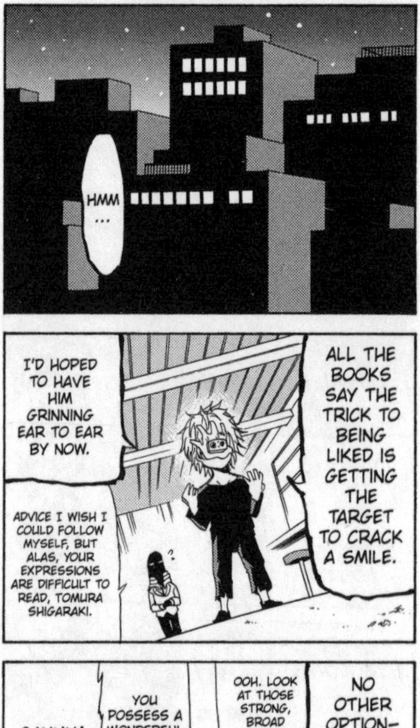
HMM ...
ALL THE BOOKS SAY THE TRICK TO BEING LIKED IS GETTING THE TARGET TO CRACK A SMILE.
I'D HOPED TO HAVE HIM GRINNING EAR TO EAR BY NOW.
ADVICE I WISH I COULD FOLLOW MYSELF, BUT ALAS, YOUR EXPRESSIONS ARE DIFFICULT TO READ, TOMURA SHIGARAKI.
NO OTHER OPTION—WE'LL PRAISE HIM.
OOH. LOOK AT THOSE STRONG, BROAD SHOULDERS.
YOU POSSESS A WONDERFUL QUIRK, I MUST SAY.
GAHHH! CUT IT OUT!!
YOU'RE HAND-SOME, BAKUGO.
NICE KICKS, KID.
FINE!! I'LL EAT A DUMB MEAL WITH YOU LOSERS!!
N-NO! I'M JUST HUNGRY!!
OH, THAT WORKED REMARK-ABLY WELL!!

ART OF THE DEAL

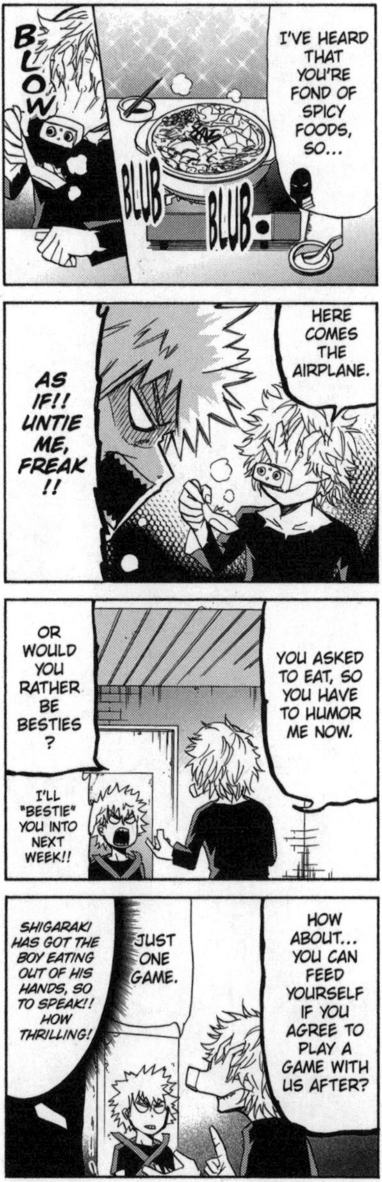
I'VE HEARD THAT YOU'RE FOND OF SPICY FOODS, SO...
BLUB
BLUB
BLOW
HERE COMES THE AIRPLANE.
AS IF!! UNTIE ME, FREAK!!
YOU ASKED TO EAT, SO YOU HAVE TO HUMOR ME NOW.
OR WOULD YOU RATHER BE BESTIES?
I'LL "BESTIE" YOU INTO NEXT WEEK!!
HOW ABOUT... YOU CAN FEED YOURSELF IF YOU AGREE TO PLAY A GAME WITH US AFTER?
JUST ONE GAME.
SHIGARAKI HAS GOT THE BOY EATING OUT OF HIS HANDS, SO TO SPEAK!! HOW THRILLING!

WHO'S THE REAL VILLAIN?

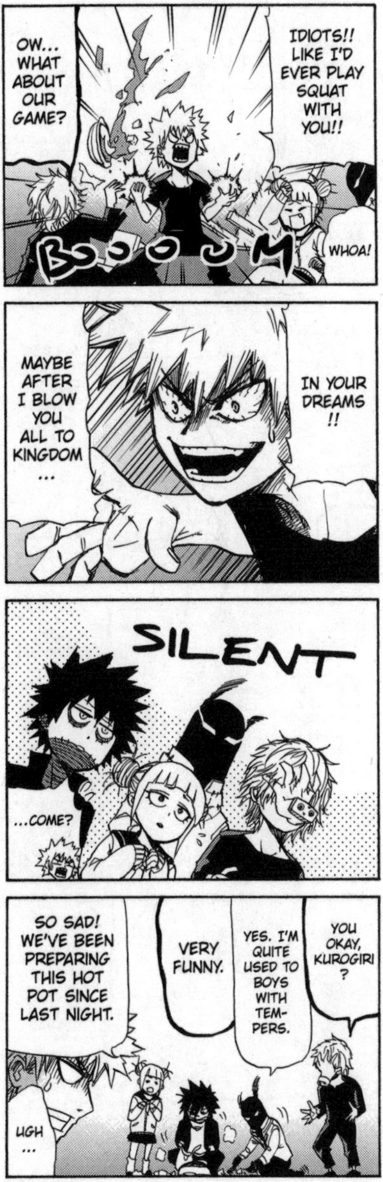
IDIOTS!! LIKE I'D EVER PLAY SQUAT WITH YOU!!
OW... WHAT ABOUT OUR GAME?
WHOA!
BOOOOM
IN YOUR DREAMS!!
MAYBE AFTER I BLOW YOU ALL TO KINGDOM...
SILENT
...COME?
YOU OKAY, KUROGIRI?
YES. I'M QUITE USED TO BOYS WITH TEMPERS.
VERY FUNNY.
SO SAD! WE'VE BEEN PREPARING THIS HOT POT SINCE LAST NIGHT.
UGH...

FIRST TIME PLAYERS

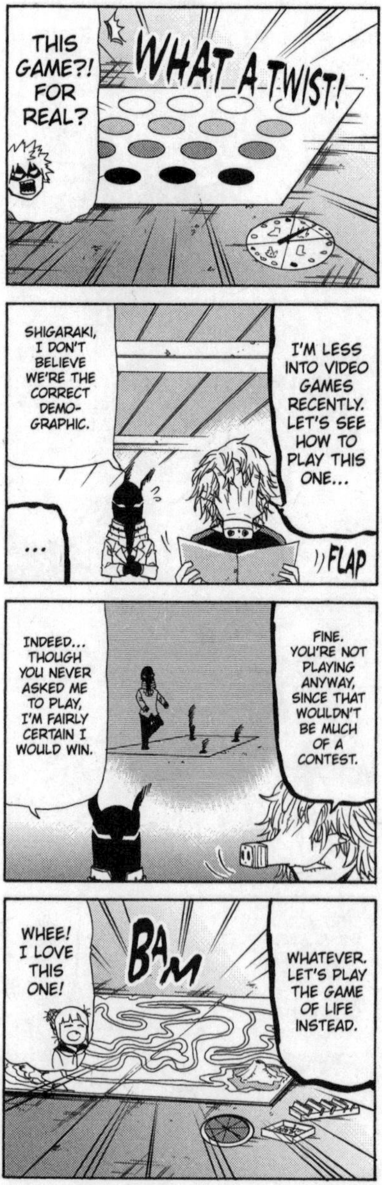
WHAT A TWIST!
THIS GAME?! FOR REAL?
I'M LESS INTO VIDEO GAMES RECENTLY. LET'S SEE HOW TO PLAY THIS ONE...
SHIGARAKI, I DON'T BELIEVE WE'RE THE CORRECT DEMOGRAPHIC.
FLAP
...
FINE. YOU'RE NOT PLAYING ANYWAY, SINCE THAT WOULDN'T BE MUCH OF A CONTEST.
INDEED... THOUGH YOU NEVER ASKED ME TO PLAY, I'M FAIRLY CERTAIN I WOULD WIN.
WHATEVER. LET'S PLAY THE GAME OF LIFE INSTEAD.
BAM
WHEE! I LOVE THIS ONE!

ART OF THE DEAL, PART 2

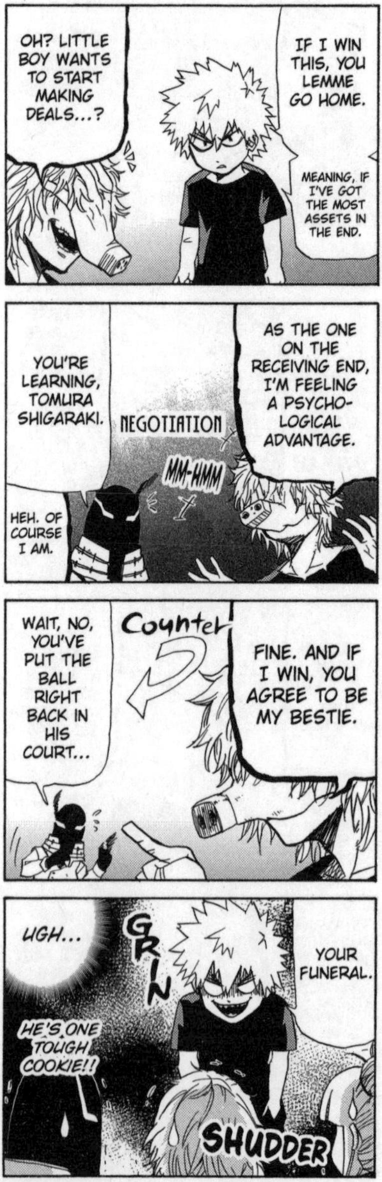
IF I WIN THIS, YOU LEMME GO HOME.
MEANING, IF I'VE GOT THE MOST ASSETS IN THE END.
OH? LITTLE BOY WANTS TO START MAKING DEALS...?
AS THE ONE ON THE RECEIVING END, I'M FEELING A PSYCHOLOGICAL ADVANTAGE.
NEGOTIATION
MM-HMM
YOU'RE LEARNING, TOMURA SHIGARAKI.
HEH. OF COURSE I AM.
FINE. AND IF I WIN, YOU AGREE TO BE MY BESTIE.
Counter
WAIT, NO, YOU'VE PUT THE BALL RIGHT BACK IN HIS COURT...
YOUR FUNERAL.
GRIN
UGH...
HE'S ONE TOUGH COOKIE!!
SHUDDER

APTITUDE

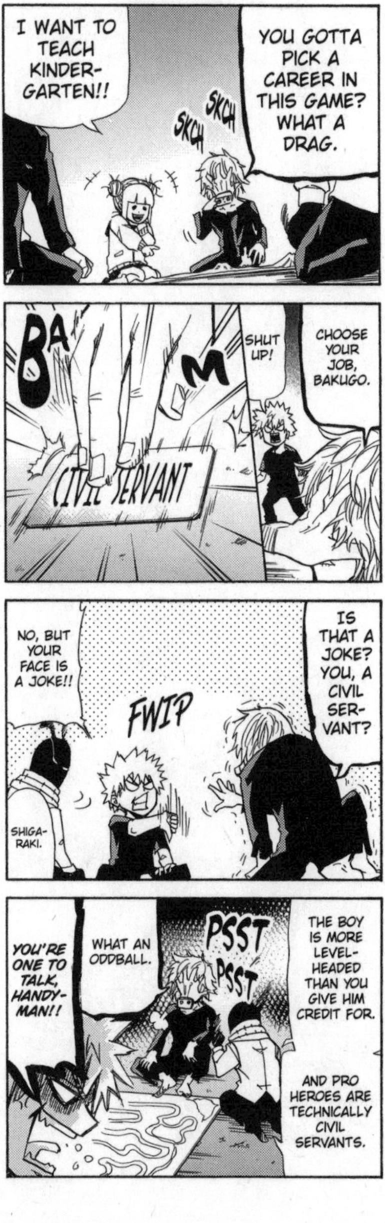
YOU GOTTA PICK A CAREER IN THIS GAME? WHAT A DRAG.
SKCH
SKCH
I WANT TO TEACH KINDERGARTEN!!
CHOOSE YOUR JOB, BAKUGO.
SHUT UP!
BAM
CIVIL SERVANT
IS THAT A JOKE? YOU, A CIVIL SERVANT?
NO, BUT YOUR FACE IS A JOKE!!
FWIP
SHIGARAKI.
THE BOY IS MORE LEVEL-HEADED THAN YOU GIVE HIM CREDIT FOR.
PSST
PSST
WHAT AN ODDBALL.
YOU'RE ONE TO TALK, HANDYMAN!!
AND PRO HEROES ARE TECHNICALLY CIVIL SERVANTS.

SECRET YUPPIE

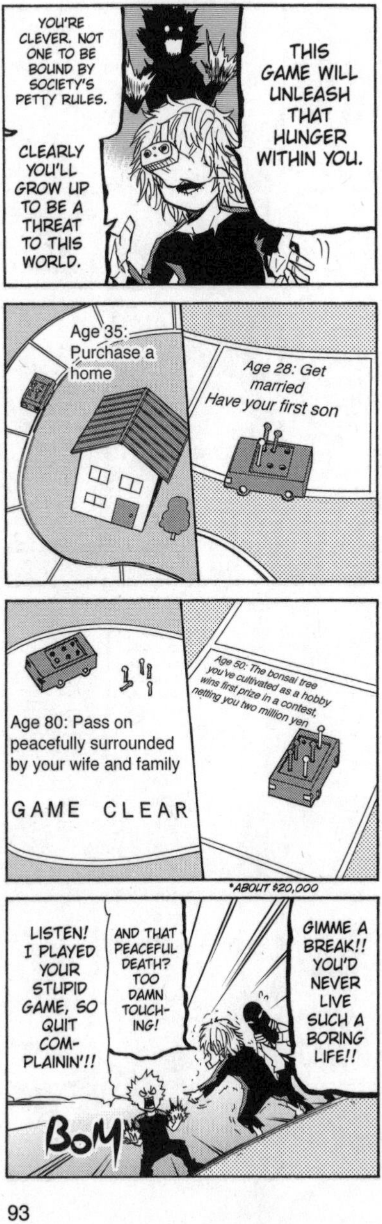
THIS GAME WILL UNLEASH THAT HUNGER WITHIN YOU.
YOU'RE CLEVER. NOT ONE TO BE BOUND BY SOCIETY'S PETTY RULES.
CLEARLY YOU'LL GROW UP TO BE A THREAT TO THIS WORLD.
Age 28: Get married
Have your first son
Age 35: Purchase a home
Age 50: The bonsai tree you've cultivated as a hobby wins first prize in a contest, netting you two million yen
Age 80: Pass on peacefully surrounded by your wife and family
GAME CLEAR
*ABOUT $20,000
GIMME A BREAK!! YOU'D NEVER LIVE SUCH A BORING LIFE!!
AND THAT PEACEFUL DEATH? TOO DAMN TOUCHING!
LISTEN! I PLAYED YOUR STUPID GAME, SO QUIT COMPLAININ'!!
BOM

PLAYDATE'S END

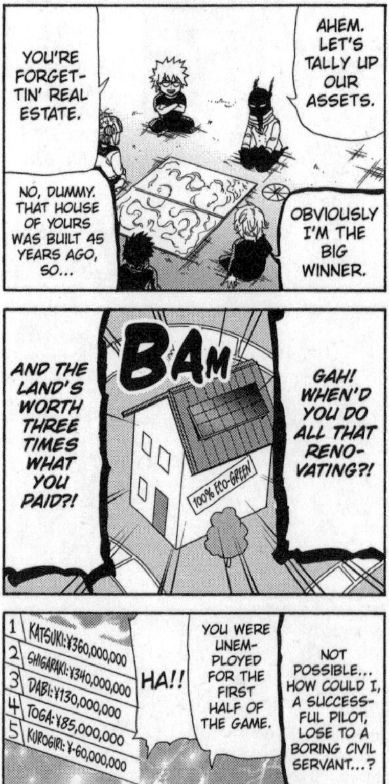
AHEM. LET'S TALLY UP OUR ASSETS.
OBVIOUSLY I'M THE BIG WINNER.
YOU'RE FORGET-TIN' REAL ESTATE.
NO, DUMMY. THAT HOUSE OF YOURS WAS BUILT 45 YEARS AGO, SO...
GAH! WHEN'D YOU DO ALL THAT RENO-VATING?!
BAM
100% ECO-GREEN
AND THE LAND'S WORTH THREE TIMES WHAT YOU PAID?!
NOT POSSIBLE... HOW COULD I, A SUCCESS-FUL PILOT, LOSE TO A BORING CIVIL SERVANT...?
YOU WERE UNEM-PLOYED FOR THE FIRST HALF OF THE GAME.
HA!!
1 KATSUKI: ¥360,000,000
2 SHIGARAKI: ¥340,000,000
3 DABI: ¥130,000,000
4 TOGA: ¥85,000,000
5 KUROGIRI: ¥-60,000,000

*IN DOLLARS, 3.6 MILLION, 3.4 MILLION, 1.3 MILLION, 850,000 AND -600,000

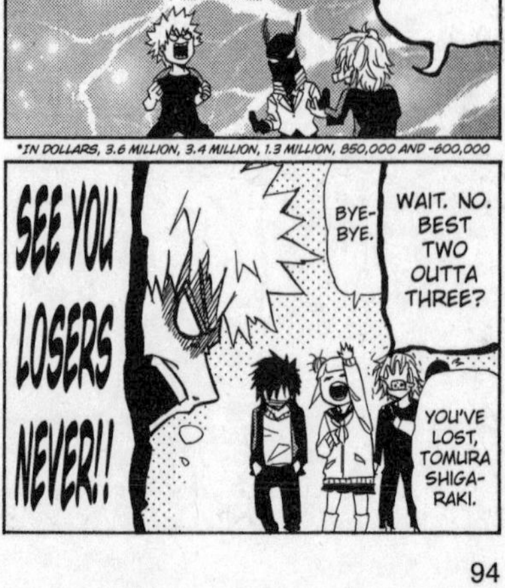
WAIT. NO. BEST TWO OUTTA THREE?
BYE-BYE.
SEE YOU LOSERS NEVER!!
YOU'VE LOST, TOMURA SHIGA-RAKI.

BRIEF DEBRIEFING

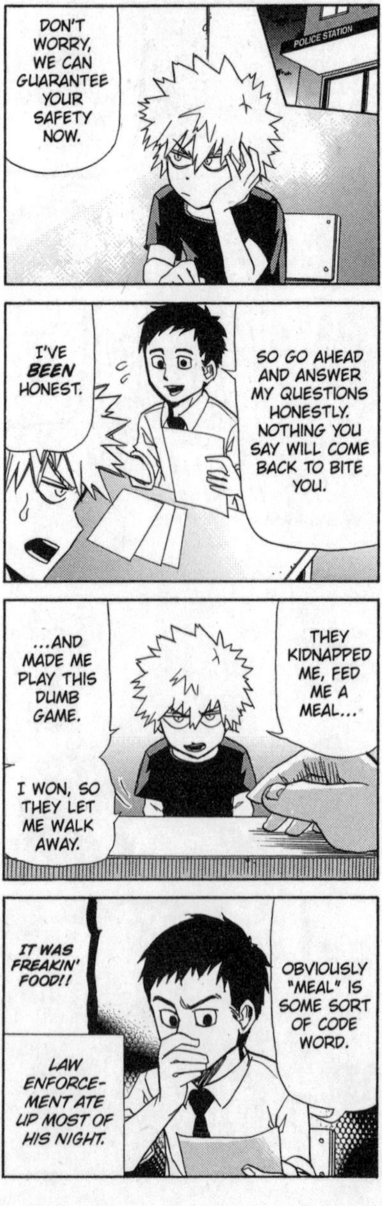
POLICE STATION
DON'T WORRY, WE CAN GUARANTEE YOUR SAFETY NOW.
SO GO AHEAD AND ANSWER MY QUESTIONS HONESTLY. NOTHING YOU SAY WILL COME BACK TO BITE YOU.
I'VE BEEN HONEST.
THEY KIDNAPPED ME, FED ME A MEAL...
...AND MADE ME PLAY THIS DUMB GAME.
I WON, SO THEY LET ME WALK AWAY.
OBVIOUSLY "MEAL" IS SOME SORT OF CODE WORD.
IT WAS FREAKIN' FOOD!!
LAW ENFORCE-MENT ATE UP MOST OF HIS NIGHT.

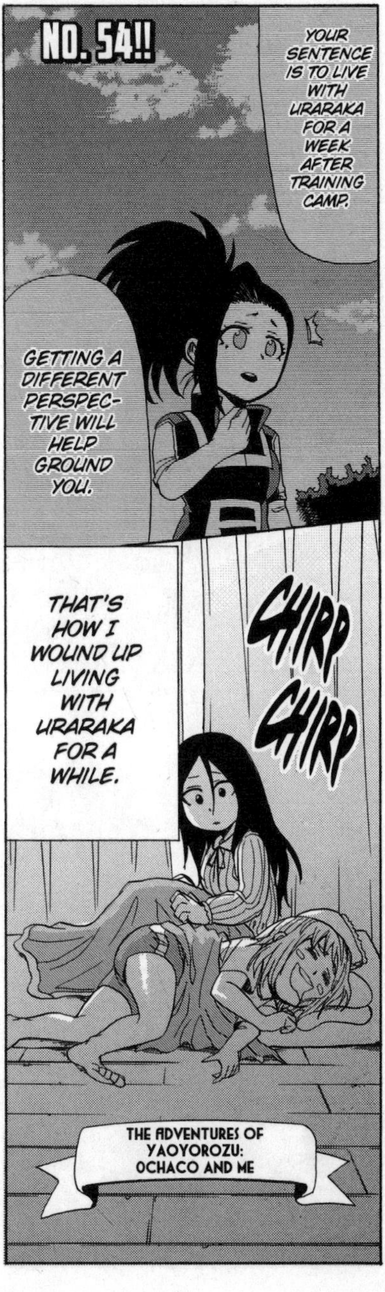
No. 54!!
YOUR SENTENCE IS TO LIVE WITH URARAKA FOR A WEEK AFTER TRAINING CAMP.
GETTING A DIFFERENT PERSPECTIVE WILL HELP GROUND YOU.
THAT'S HOW I WOUND UP LIVING WITH URARAKA FOR A WHILE.
CHIRP CHIRP
THE ADVENTURES OF YAOYOROZU: OCHACO AND ME

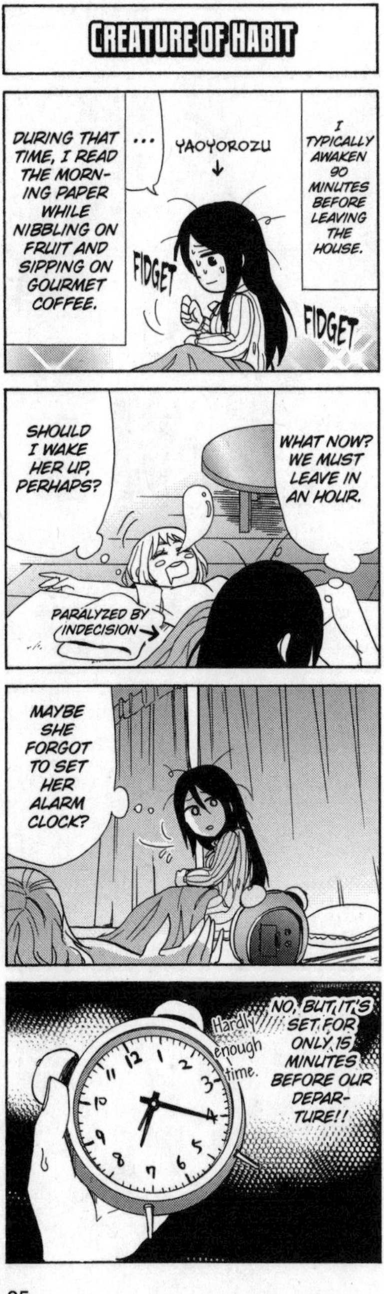
CREATURE OF HABIT
I TYPICALLY AWAKEN 90 MINUTES BEFORE LEAVING THE HOUSE.
YAOYOROZU
...
DURING THAT TIME, I READ THE MORNING PAPER WHILE NIBBLING ON FRUIT AND SIPPING ON GOURMET COFFEE.
FIDGET
FIDGET
WHAT NOW? WE MUST LEAVE IN AN HOUR.
SHOULD I WAKE HER UP, PERHAPS?
PARALYZED BY INDECISION
MAYBE SHE FORGOT TO SET HER ALARM CLOCK?
NO, BUT IT'S SET FOR ONLY 15 MINUTES BEFORE OUR DEPARTURE!!
Hardly enough time.

Culture Shock

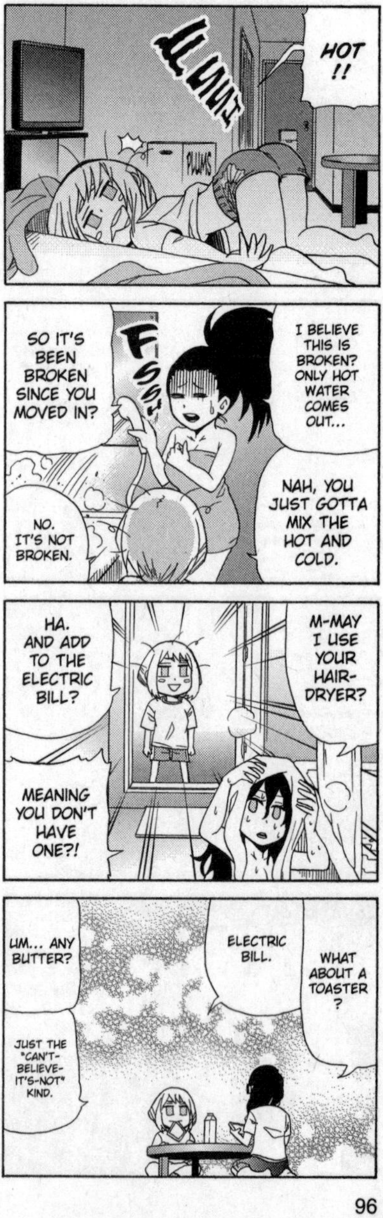
HOT!!
PLUMS
I BELIEVE THIS IS BROKEN? ONLY HOT WATER COMES OUT...
FSSH
SO IT'S BEEN BROKEN SINCE YOU MOVED IN?
NAH, YOU JUST GOTTA MIX THE HOT AND COLD.
NO. IT'S NOT BROKEN.
M-MAY I USE YOUR HAIR-DRYER?
HA. AND ADD TO THE ELECTRIC BILL?
MEANING YOU DON'T HAVE ONE?!
WHAT ABOUT A TOASTER?
ELECTRIC BILL.
UM... ANY BUTTER?
JUST THE "CAN'T-BELIEVE-IT'S-NOT" KIND.

Train-Fu Master

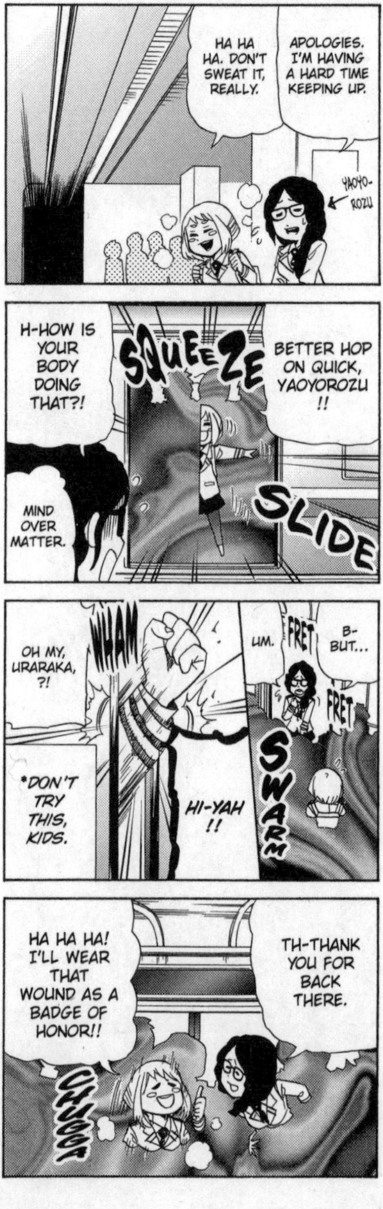
APOLOGIES. I'M HAVING A HARD TIME KEEPING UP.
HA HA HA. DON'T SWEAT IT, REALLY.
YAOYOROZU
BETTER HOP ON QUICK, YAOYOROZU!!
SQUEEZE
H-HOW IS YOUR BODY DOING THAT?!
SLIDE
MIND OVER MATTER.
B-BUT...
FRET
UM.
FRET
SWARM
WHAM
OH MY, URARAKA, ?!
HI-YAH!!
*DON'T TRY THIS, KIDS.
TH-THANK YOU FOR BACK THERE.
HA HA HA! I'LL WEAR THAT WOUND AS A BADGE OF HONOR!!
CHUGGA

LIFE HACK

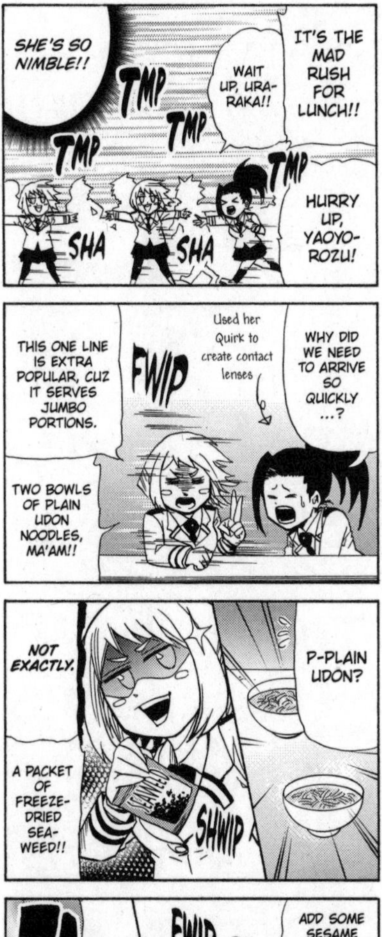
IT'S THE MAD RUSH FOR LUNCH!!
WAIT UP, URARAKA!!
TMP
SHE'S SO NIMBLE!!
TMP
TMP
TMP
HURRY UP, YAOYOROZU!
SHA
SHA
WHY DID WE NEED TO ARRIVE SO QUICKLY ...?
Used her Quirk to create contact lenses
FWIP
THIS ONE LINE IS EXTRA POPULAR, CUZ IT SERVES JUMBO PORTIONS.
TWO BOWLS OF PLAIN UDON NOODLES, MA'AM!!
P-PLAIN UDON?
NOT EXACTLY.
A PACKET OF FREEZE-DRIED SEAWEED!!
SHWIP
ADD SOME SESAME SEEDS, RED GINGER, CRUNCHY TEMPURA BITS AND...
FWIP
FWIP
BAM!
TA
DA
OCHACO'S DELUXE URARA-NOODLES!!

LIFESTYLE OF THE POOR AND FABULOUS

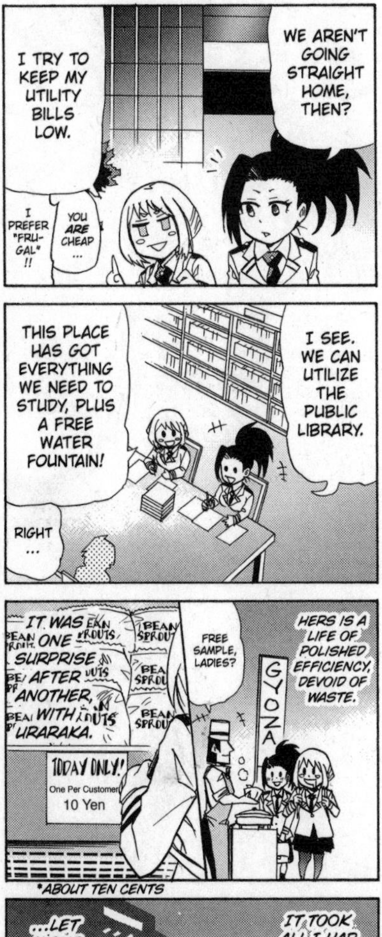
WE AREN'T GOING STRAIGHT HOME, THEN?
I TRY TO KEEP MY UTILITY BILLS LOW.
YOU ARE CHEAP...
I PREFER "FRUGAL"!!
I SEE. WE CAN UTILIZE THE PUBLIC LIBRARY.
THIS PLACE HAS GOT EVERYTHING WE NEED TO STUDY, PLUS A FREE WATER FOUNTAIN!
RIGHT...
HERS IS A LIFE OF POLISHED EFFICIENCY, DEVOID OF WASTE.
GYOZA
FREE SAMPLE, LADIES?
IT WAS ONE SURPRISE AFTER ANOTHER, WITH URARAKA.
BEAN SPROUTS
TODAY ONLY!
One Per Customer
10 Yen
IT TOOK ALL I HAD JUST TO KEEP UP...
...LET ALONE COME UP WITH ANY IDEAS OF MY OWN.

*ABOUT TEN CENTS

Camel, Meet Eye of Needle

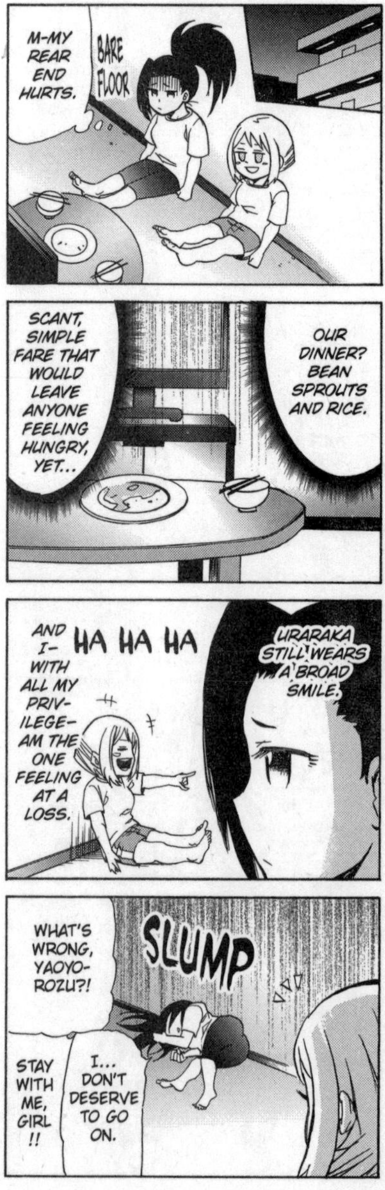
BARE FLOOR
M-MY REAR END HURTS.
OUR DINNER? BEAN SPROUTS AND RICE.
SCANT, SIMPLE FARE THAT WOULD LEAVE ANYONE FEELING HUNGRY, YET...
URARAKA STILL WEARS A BROAD SMILE.
HA HA HA
AND I— WITH ALL MY PRIVILEGE— AM THE ONE FEELING AT A LOSS.
SLUMP
WHAT'S WRONG, YAOYOROZU?!
I... DON'T DESERVE TO GO ON.
STAY WITH ME, GIRL!!

Glitch in the Momotrix

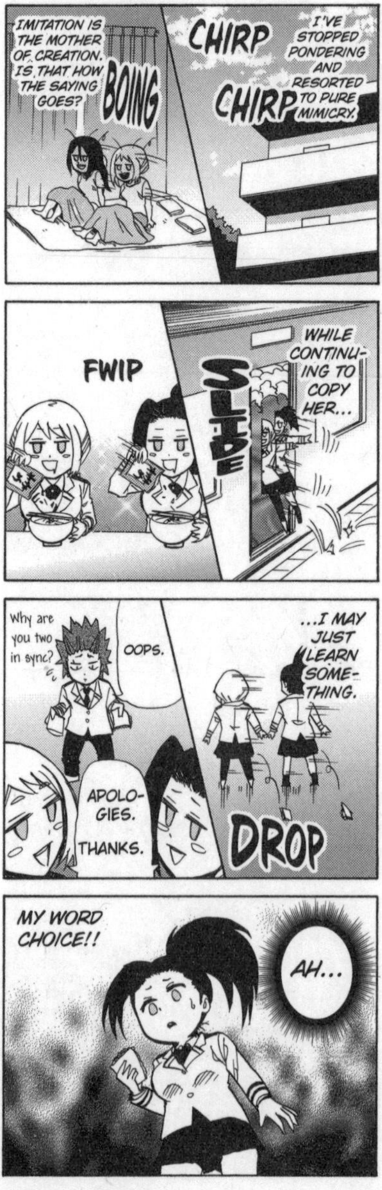
I'VE STOPPED PONDERING AND RESORTED TO PURE MIMICRY.
CHIRP
CHIRP
BOING
IMITATION IS THE MOTHER OF CREATION. IS THAT HOW THE SAYING GOES?
WHILE CONTINUING TO COPY HER...
SLIDE
FWIP
...I MAY JUST LEARN SOMETHING.
DROP
OOPS.
Why are you two in sync?
APOLOGIES.
THANKS.
AH...
MY WORD CHOICE!!

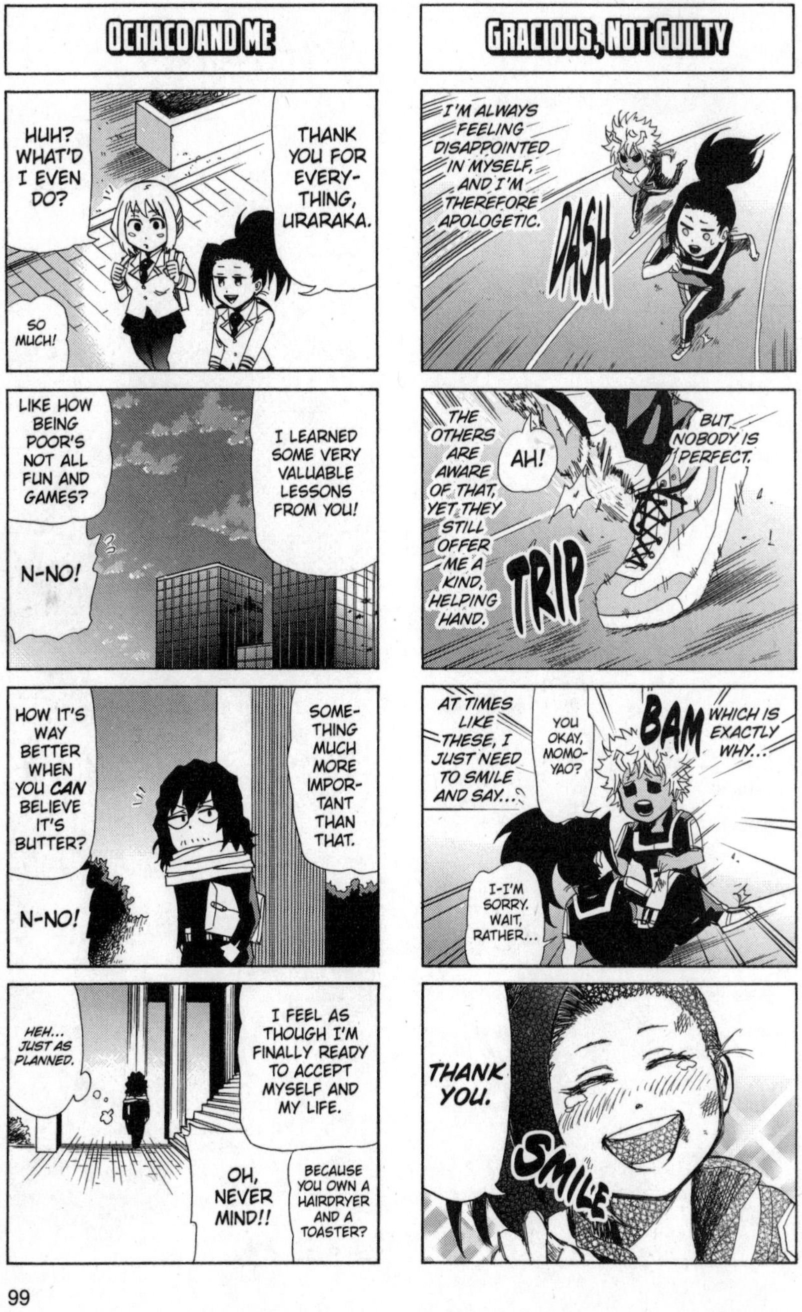
GRACIOUS, NOT GUILTY
I'M ALWAYS FEELING DISAPPOINTED IN MYSELF, AND I'M THEREFORE APOLOGETIC.
DASH
BUT NOBODY IS PERFECT.
AH!
THE OTHERS ARE AWARE OF THAT, YET THEY STILL OFFER ME A KIND, HELPING HAND.
TRIP
WHICH IS EXACTLY WHY...
BAM
YOU OKAY, MOMO-YAO?
AT TIMES LIKE THESE, I JUST NEED TO SMILE AND SAY...
I-I'M SORRY. WAIT, RATHER...
THANK YOU.
SMILE
OCHACO AND ME
THANK YOU FOR EVERYTHING, URARAKA.
HUH? WHAT'D I EVEN DO?
SO MUCH!
I LEARNED SOME VERY VALUABLE LESSONS FROM YOU!
LIKE HOW BEING POOR'S NOT ALL FUN AND GAMES?
N-NO!
SOMETHING MUCH MORE IMPORTANT THAN THAT.
HOW IT'S WAY BETTER WHEN YOU *CAN* BELIEVE IT'S BUTTER?
N-NO!
I FEEL AS THOUGH I'M FINALLY READY TO ACCEPT MYSELF AND MY LIFE.
BECAUSE YOU OWN A HAIRDRYER AND A TOASTER?
OH, NEVER MIND!!
HEH... JUST AS PLANNED.

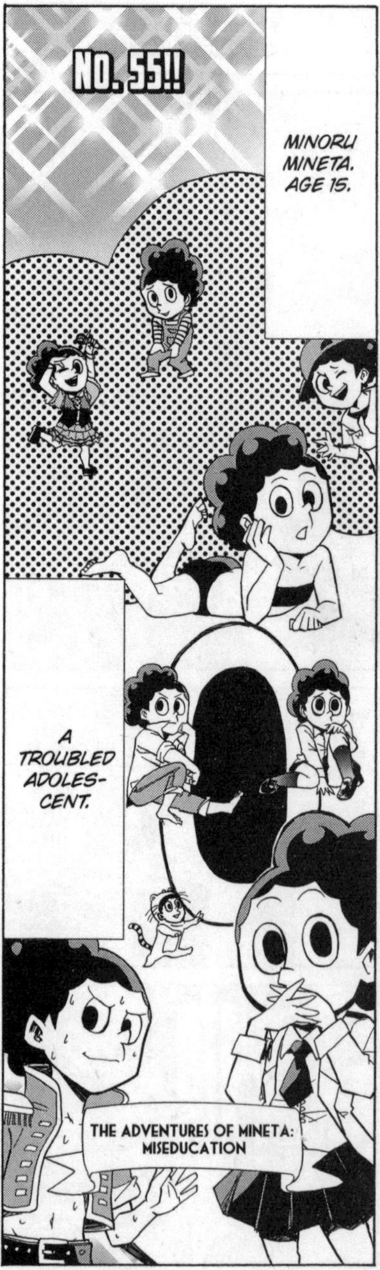
NO. 55!!
MINORU MINETA. AGE 15.
A TROUBLED ADOLES-CENT.
THE ADVENTURES OF MINETA: MISEDUCATION

FACING FACTS

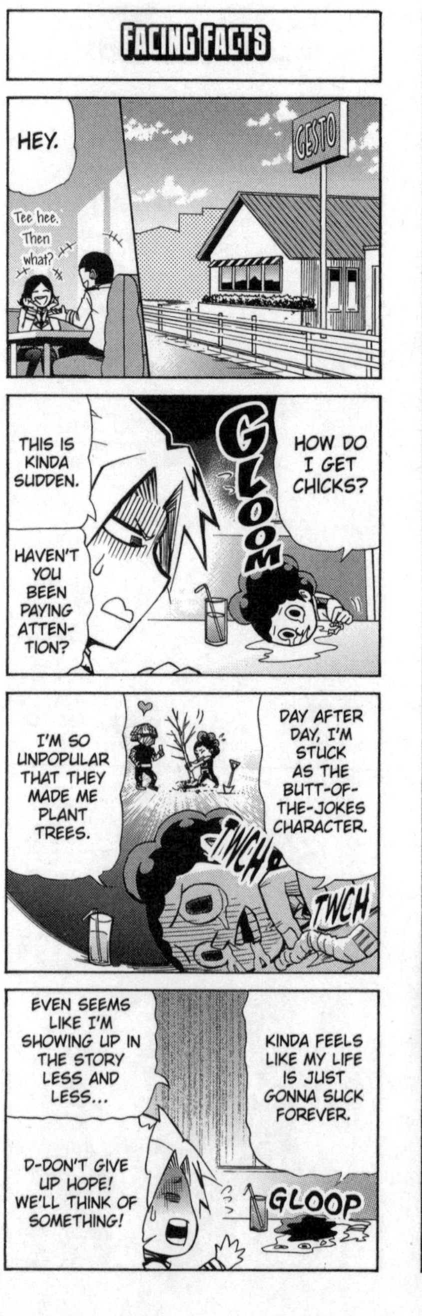
HEY.
Tee hee. Then what?
HOW DO I GET CHICKS?
GLOOM
THIS IS KINDA SUDDEN.
HAVEN'T YOU BEEN PAYING ATTEN-TION?
DAY AFTER DAY, I'M STUCK AS THE BUTT-OF-THE-JOKES CHARACTER.
I'M SO UNPOPULAR THAT THEY MADE ME PLANT TREES.
TWCH
TWCH
KINDA FEELS LIKE MY LIFE IS JUST GONNA SUCK FOREVER.
EVEN SEEMS LIKE I'M SHOWING UP IN THE STORY LESS AND LESS...
GLOOP
D-DON'T GIVE UP HOPE! WE'LL THINK OF SOMETHING!

TRAGIC

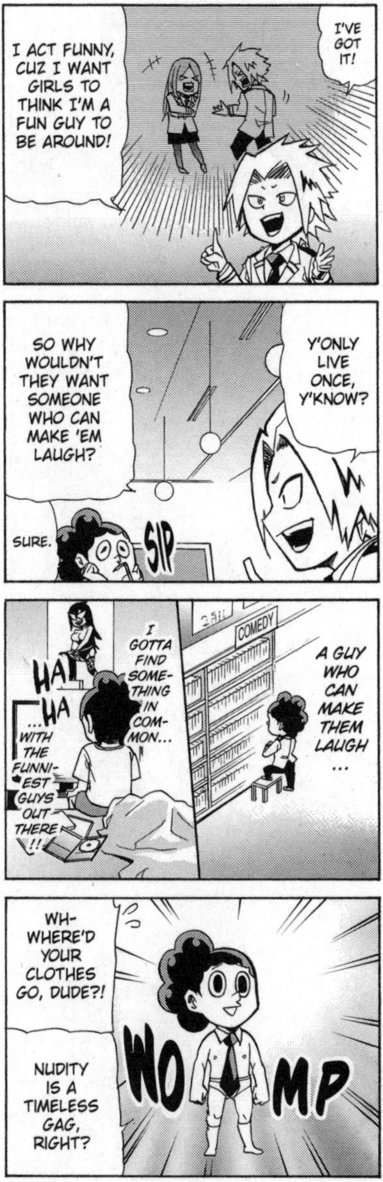
I'VE GOT IT!
I ACT FUNNY, CUZ I WANT GIRLS TO THINK I'M A FUN GUY TO BE AROUND!
Y'ONLY LIVE ONCE, Y'KNOW?
SO WHY WOULDN'T THEY WANT SOMEONE WHO CAN MAKE 'EM LAUGH?
SIP
SURE.
COMEDY
A GUY WHO CAN MAKE THEM LAUGH...
I GOTTA FIND SOMETHING IN COMMON...
HA HA
...WITH THE FUNNIEST GUYS OUT THERE!!
WH-WHERE'D YOUR CLOTHES GO, DUDE?!
WOMP
NUDITY IS A TIMELESS GAG, RIGHT?

BEFORE/AFTER

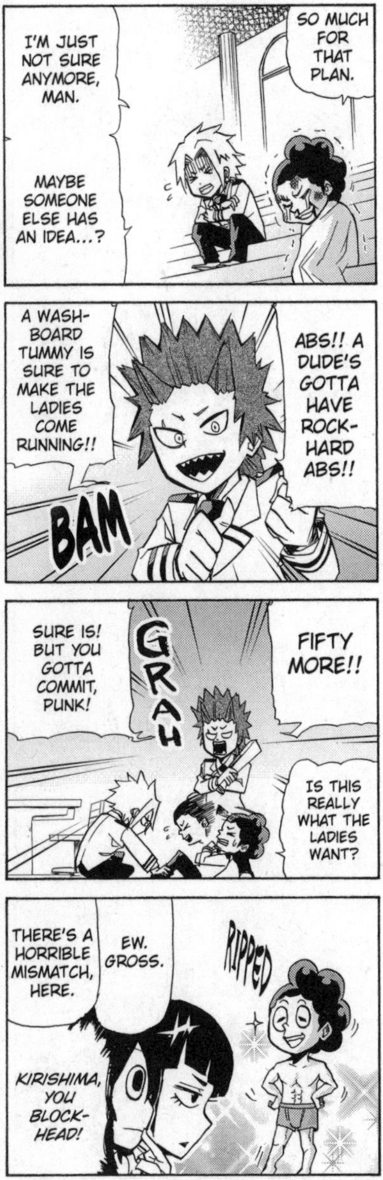
SO MUCH FOR THAT PLAN.
I'M JUST NOT SURE ANYMORE, MAN.
MAYBE SOMEONE ELSE HAS AN IDEA...?
ABS!! A DUDE'S GOTTA HAVE ROCK-HARD ABS!!
A WASHBOARD TUMMY IS SURE TO MAKE THE LADIES COME RUNNING!!
BAM
FIFTY MORE!!
GRAH
SURE IS! BUT YOU GOTTA COMMIT, PUNK!
IS THIS REALLY WHAT THE LADIES WANT?
RIPPED
EW. GROSS.
THERE'S A HORRIBLE MISMATCH, HERE.
KIRISHIMA, YOU BLOCKHEAD!

DAMNED IF YOU DON'T

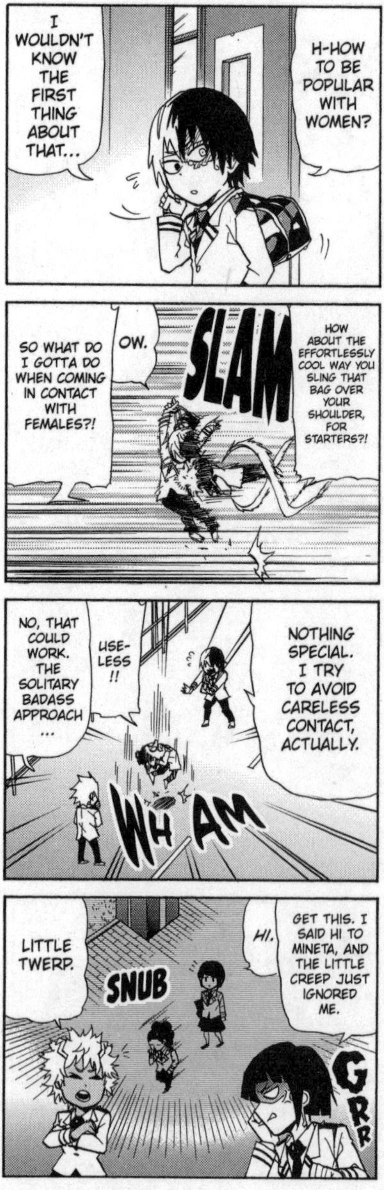
H-HOW TO BE POPULAR WITH WOMEN?
I WOULDN'T KNOW THE FIRST THING ABOUT THAT...
HOW ABOUT THE EFFORTLESSLY COOL WAY YOU SLING THAT BAG OVER YOUR SHOULDER, FOR STARTERS?!
SLAM
OW.
SO WHAT DO I GOTTA DO WHEN COMING IN CONTACT WITH FEMALES?!
NOTHING SPECIAL. I TRY TO AVOID CARELESS CONTACT, ACTUALLY.
USE-LESS!!
NO, THAT COULD WORK. THE SOLITARY BADASS APPROACH...
WHAM
GET THIS. I SAID HI TO MINETA, AND THE LITTLE CREEP JUST IGNORED ME.
HI.
GRR
SNUB
LITTLE TWERP.

ADVICE FROM BAKUGO...'S FRIEND

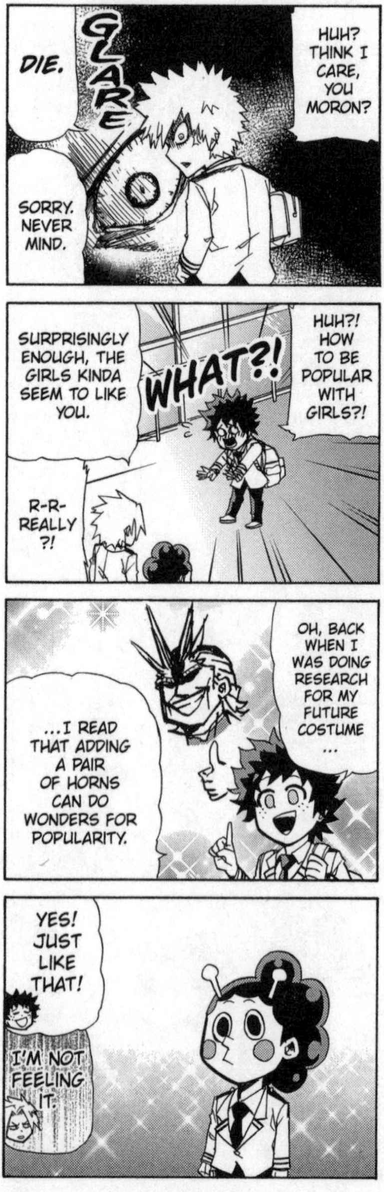
HUH? THINK I CARE, YOU MORON?
GLARE
DIE.
SORRY. NEVER MIND.
HUH?! HOW TO BE POPULAR WITH GIRLS?!
WHAT?!
SURPRISINGLY ENOUGH, THE GIRLS KINDA SEEM TO LIKE YOU.
R-R-REALLY?!
OH, BACK WHEN I WAS DOING RESEARCH FOR MY FUTURE COSTUME...
...I READ THAT ADDING A PAIR OF HORNS CAN DO WONDERS FOR POPULARITY.
YES! JUST LIKE THAT!
I'M NOT FEELING IT.

GOING VIRAL

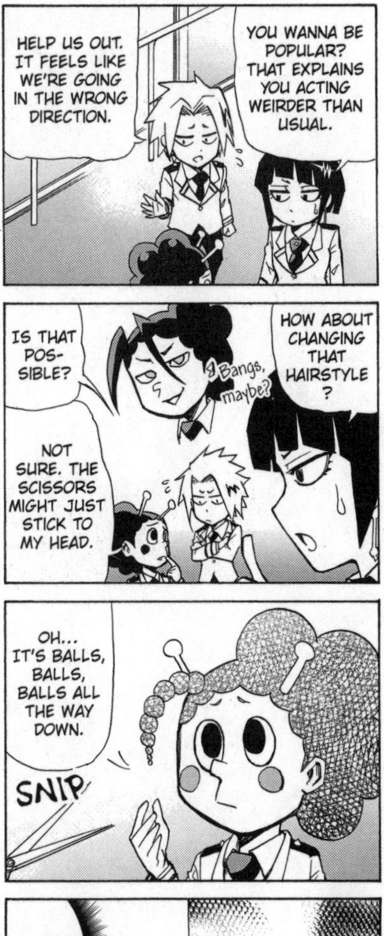

YOU WANNA BE POPULAR? THAT EXPLAINS YOU ACTING WEIRDER THAN USUAL.
HELP US OUT. IT FEELS LIKE WE'RE GOING IN THE WRONG DIRECTION.
HOW ABOUT CHANGING THAT HAIRSTYLE?
Bangs, maybe?
IS THAT POS-SIBLE?
NOT SURE. THE SCISSORS MIGHT JUST STICK TO MY HEAD.
OH... IT'S BALLS, BALLS, BALLS ALL THE WAY DOWN.
SNIP
KINDA WENT IN THE AMOEBA DIRECTION.
THAT DIDN'T WORK.

ULTIMINETA

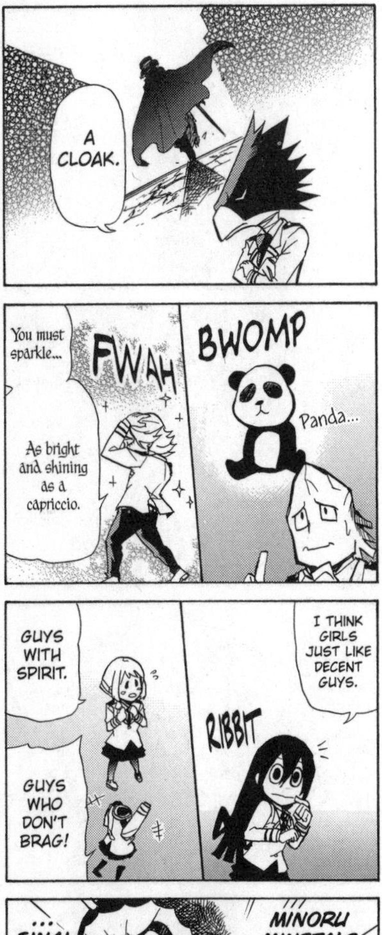

A CLOAK.
BWOMP
Panda...
You must sparkle...
FWAH
As bright and shining as a capriccio.
I THINK GIRLS JUST LIKE DECENT GUYS.
RIBBIT
GUYS WITH SPIRIT.
GUYS WHO DON'T BRAG!
MINORU MINETA'S ...
... FINAL FORM.
TA DA AAA

Letting Go

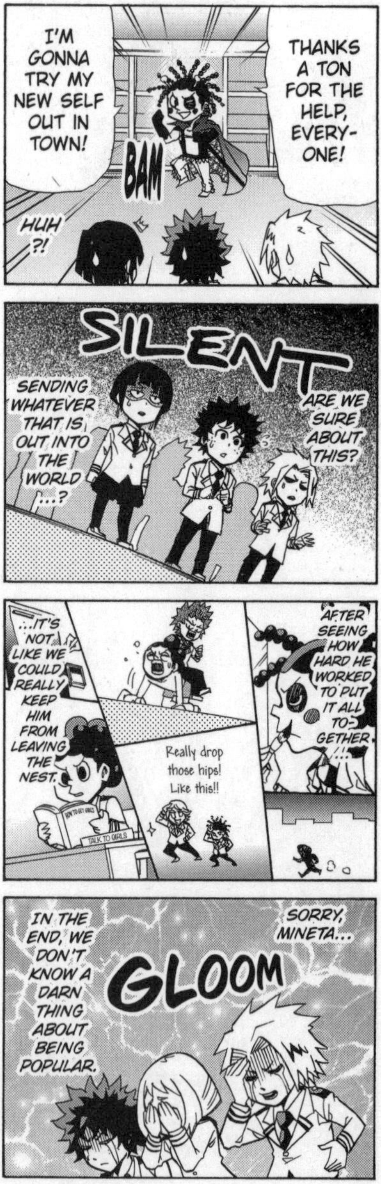

THANKS A TON FOR THE HELP, EVERYONE!
I'M GONNA TRY MY NEW SELF OUT IN TOWN!
BAM
HUH?!
SILENT
ARE WE SURE ABOUT THIS?
SENDING WHATEVER THAT IS OUT INTO THE WORLD...?
AFTER SEEING HOW HARD HE WORKED TO PUT IT ALL TOGETHER...!
Really drop those hips! Like this!!
...IT'S NOT LIKE WE COULD REALLY KEEP HIM FROM LEAVING THE NEST.
TALK TO GIRLS
SORRY, MINETA...
GLOOM
IN THE END, WE DON'T KNOW A DARN THING ABOUT BEING POPULAR.

Live to Perv Another Day

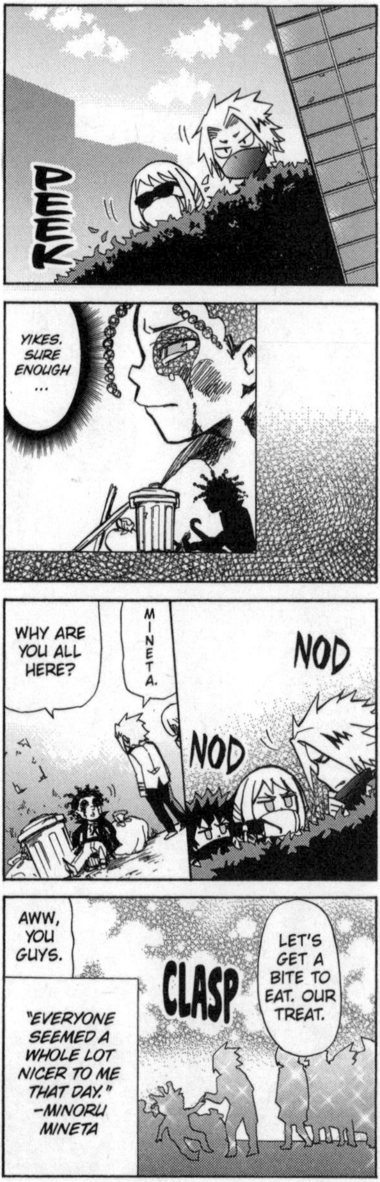

PEEK
YIKES. SURE ENOUGH...
NOD
NOD
MINETA.
WHY ARE YOU ALL HERE?
LET'S GET A BITE TO EAT. OUR TREAT.
CLASP
AWW, YOU GUYS.
"EVERYONE SEEMED A WHOLE LOT NICER TO ME THAT DAY." -MINORU MINETA

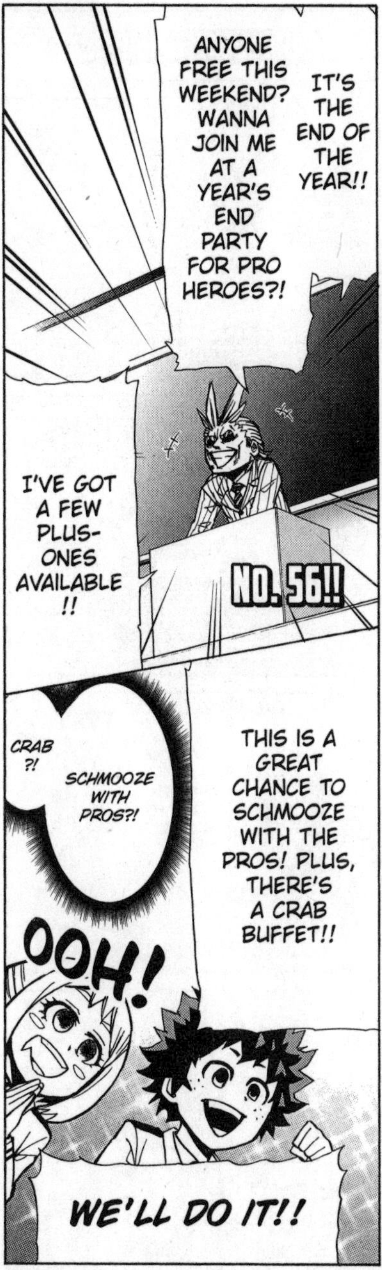
IT'S THE END OF THE YEAR!!
ANYONE FREE THIS WEEKEND? WANNA JOIN ME AT A YEAR'S END PARTY FOR PRO HEROES?!
NO. 56!!
I'VE GOT A FEW PLUS-ONES AVAILABLE!!
THIS IS A GREAT CHANCE TO SCHMOOZE WITH THE PROS! PLUS, THERE'S A CRAB BUFFET!!
SCHMOOZE WITH PROS?!
CRAB?!
OOH!
WE'LL DO IT!!

QUIRK: TUP-R-WARE

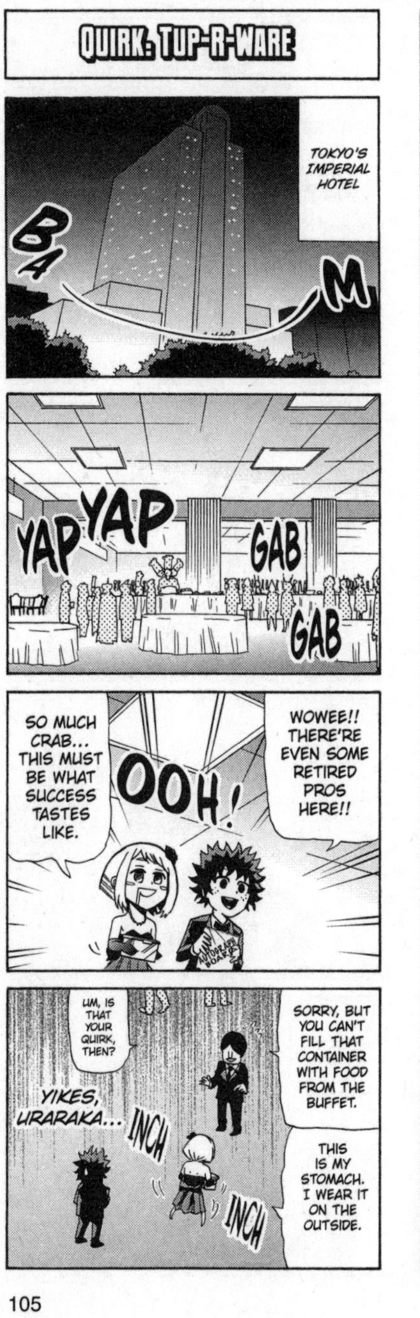
TOKYO'S IMPERIAL HOTEL
BAM
GAB
GAB
YAP YAP
WOWEE!! THERE'RE EVEN SOME RETIRED PROS HERE!!
OOH!
SO MUCH CRAB... THIS MUST BE WHAT SUCCESS TASTES LIKE.
AUTOGRAPH BOARD
SORRY, BUT YOU CAN'T FILL THAT CONTAINER WITH FOOD FROM THE BUFFET.
THIS IS MY STOMACH. I WEAR IT ON THE OUTSIDE.
UM, IS THAT YOUR QUIRK, THEN?
YIKES, URARAKA...
INCH
INCH

INFLUENCED

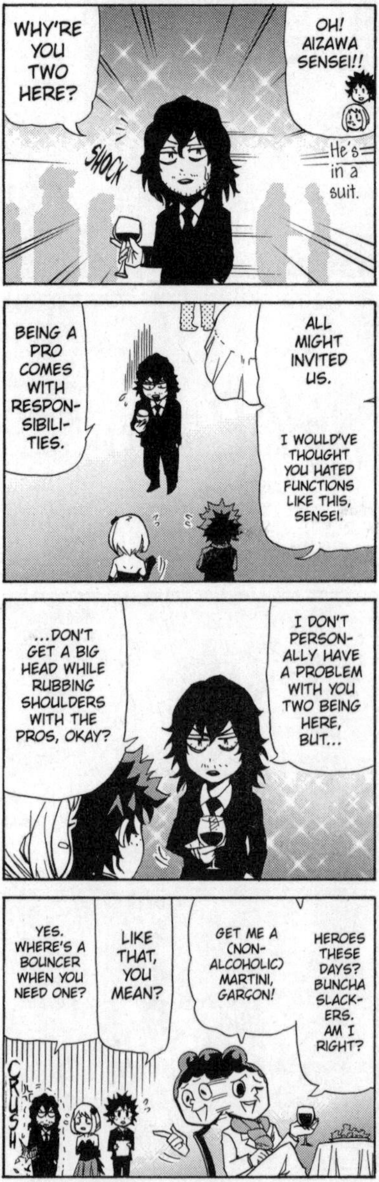
OH! AIZAWA SENSEI!!
WHY'RE YOU TWO HERE?
He's in a suit.
SHOCK
ALL MIGHT INVITED US.
I WOULD'VE THOUGHT YOU HATED FUNCTIONS LIKE THIS, SENSEI.
BEING A PRO COMES WITH RESPONSIBILITIES.
I DON'T PERSONALLY HAVE A PROBLEM WITH YOU TWO BEING HERE, BUT...
...DON'T GET A BIG HEAD WHILE RUBBING SHOULDERS WITH THE PROS, OKAY?
HEROES THESE DAYS? BUNCHA SLACKERS. AM I RIGHT?
GET ME A (NON-ALCOHOLIC) MARTINI, GARÇON!
LIKE THAT, YOU MEAN?
YES. WHERE'S A BOUNCER WHEN YOU NEED ONE?
CRUSH

INFLUENCED, PART 2

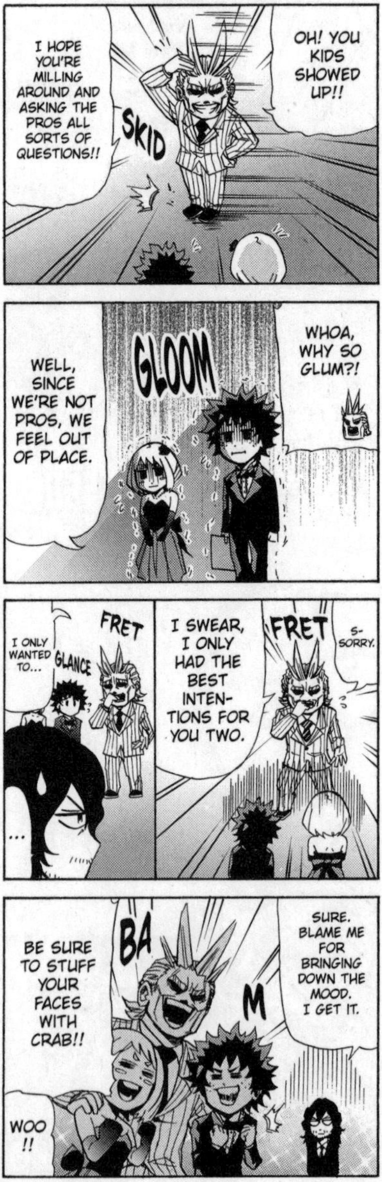
OH! YOU KIDS SHOWED UP!!
SKID
I HOPE YOU'RE MILLING AROUND AND ASKING THE PROS ALL SORTS OF QUESTIONS!!
WHOA, WHY SO GLUM?!
GLOOM
WELL, SINCE WE'RE NOT PROS, WE FEEL OUT OF PLACE.
S-SORRY.
FRET
I SWEAR, I ONLY HAD THE BEST INTENTIONS FOR YOU TWO.
FRET
GLANCE
I ONLY WANTED TO...
...
SURE. BLAME ME FOR BRINGING DOWN THE MOOD. I GET IT.
BA
M
BE SURE TO STUFF YOUR FACES WITH CRAB!!
WOO!!

WHAT A WORLD

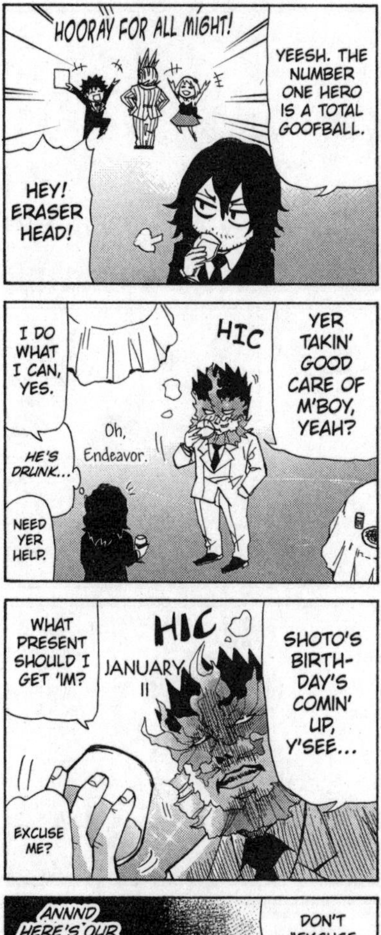
HOORAY FOR ALL MIGHT!
YEESH. THE NUMBER ONE HERO IS A TOTAL GOOFBALL.
HEY! ERASER HEAD!
YER TAKIN' GOOD CARE OF M'BOY, YEAH?
HIC
I DO WHAT I CAN, YES.
Oh, Endeavor.
HE'S DRUNK...
NEED YER HELP.
SHOTO'S BIRTH-DAY'S COMIN' UP, Y'SEE...
HIC
JANUARY 11
WHAT PRESENT SHOULD I GET 'IM?
EXCUSE ME?
DON'T "EXCUSE ME" ME. YER HIS TEACHER. Y'SHOULD KNOW!!
WHY NOT JUST ASK HIM YOURSEL-
ARE YOU THE ONE PAYING HIS TUITION? NO? DIDN'T THINK SO.
ANNND HERE'S OUR NUMBER TWO HERO... THIS COUNTRY'S DOOMED.

CLEANS UP NICE

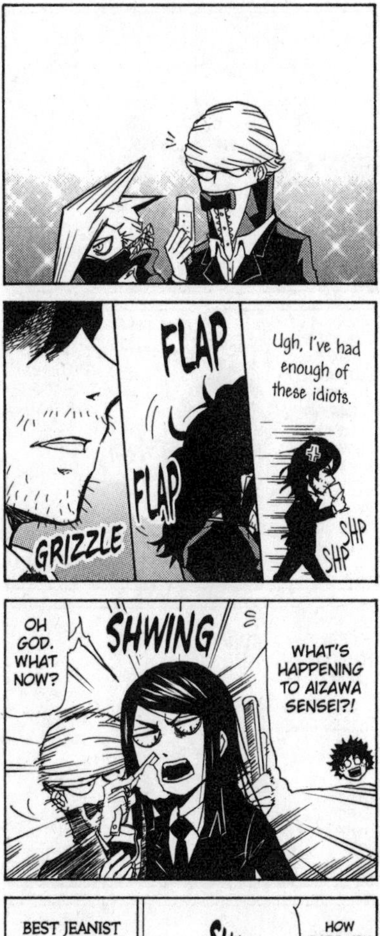
Ugh, I've had enough of these idiots.
FLAP
FLAP
SHP SHP
GRIZZLE
WHAT'S HAPPENING TO AIZAWA SENSEI?!
SHWING
OH GOD. WHAT NOW?
HOW DARE YOU MAKE ME PRESENTABLE!!
SUAVE
HMPH.
BEST JEANIST
LOVER OF THE PRIM AND THE PROPER. HE CAN'T BEAR TO IGNORE THE DISHEVELED.

LOST IN TRANSLATION

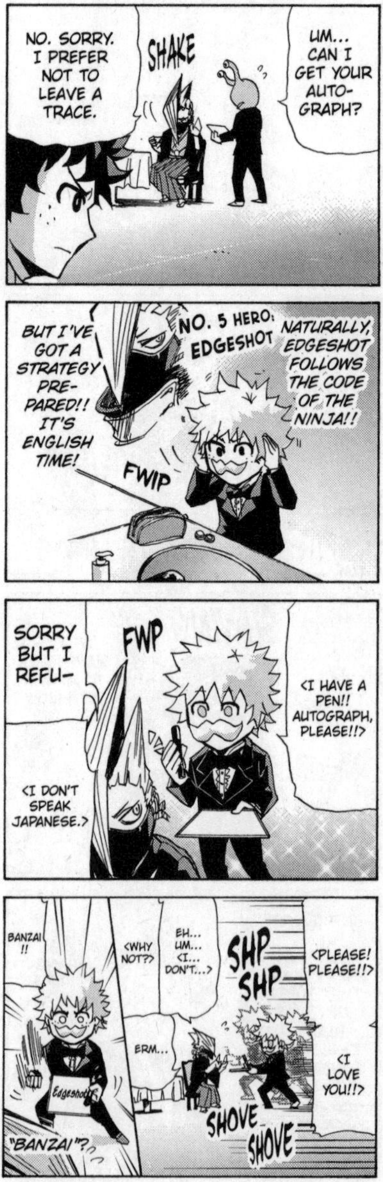
UM... CAN I GET YOUR AUTO-GRAPH?
SHAKE
NO. SORRY. I PREFER NOT TO LEAVE A TRACE.
NATURALLY, EDGESHOT FOLLOWS THE CODE OF THE NINJA!!
NO. 5 HERO: EDGESHOT
BUT I'VE GOT A STRATEGY PRE-PARED!! IT'S ENGLISH TIME!
FWIP
<I HAVE A PEN!! AUTOGRAPH, PLEASE!!>
FWP
SORRY BUT I REFU-
<I DON'T SPEAK JAPANESE.>
<PLEASE! PLEASE!!>
SHP SHP
EH... UM... <I... DON'T...>
<WHY NOT?>
BANZAI !!
<I LOVE YOU!!>
ERM...
SHOVE SHOVE
Edgeshot
"BANZAI"?

BEST FOR LAST?

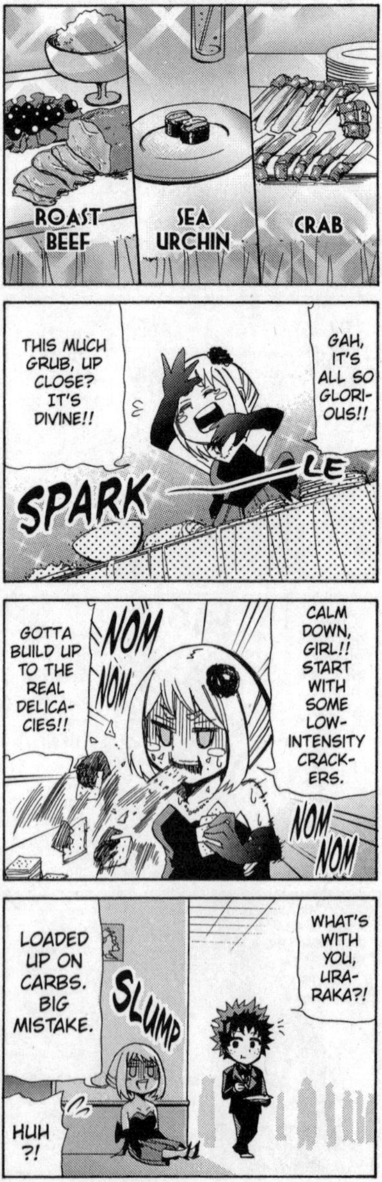
CRAB
SEA URCHIN
ROAST BEEF
GAH, IT'S ALL SO GLORI-OUS!!
THIS MUCH GRUB, UP CLOSE? IT'S DIVINE!!
SPARKLE
CALM DOWN, GIRL!! START WITH SOME LOW-INTENSITY CRACK-ERS.
NOM NOM
GOTTA BUILD UP TO THE REAL DELICA-CIES!!
NOM NOM
WHAT'S WITH YOU, URA-RAKA?!
LOADED UP ON CARBS. BIG MISTAKE.
SLUMP
HUH ?!

THE ROAD AHEAD

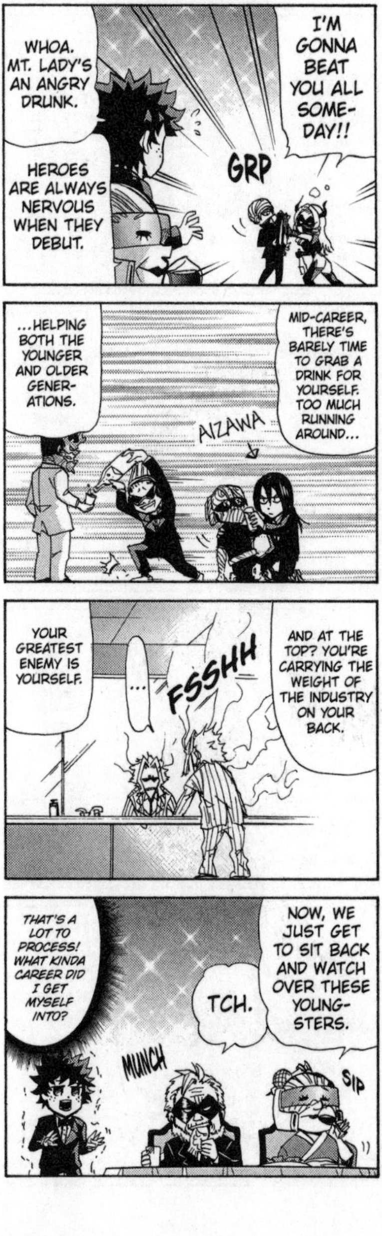
I'M GONNA BEAT YOU ALL SOME-DAY!!
WHOA. MT. LADY'S AN ANGRY DRUNK.
GRP
HEROES ARE ALWAYS NERVOUS WHEN THEY DEBUT.
MID-CAREER, THERE'S BARELY TIME TO GRAB A DRINK FOR YOURSELF. TOO MUCH RUNNING AROUND...
...HELPING BOTH THE YOUNGER AND OLDER GENER-ATIONS.
AIZAWA
AND AT THE TOP? YOU'RE CARRYING THE WEIGHT OF THE INDUSTRY ON YOUR BACK.
FSSHH
...
YOUR GREATEST ENEMY IS YOURSELF.
NOW, WE JUST GET TO SIT BACK AND WATCH OVER THESE YOUNG-STERS.
TCH.
THAT'S A LOT TO PROCESS! WHAT KINDA CAREER DID I GET MYSELF INTO?
SIP
MUNCH

LIFE'S SOLUTION: CARBS

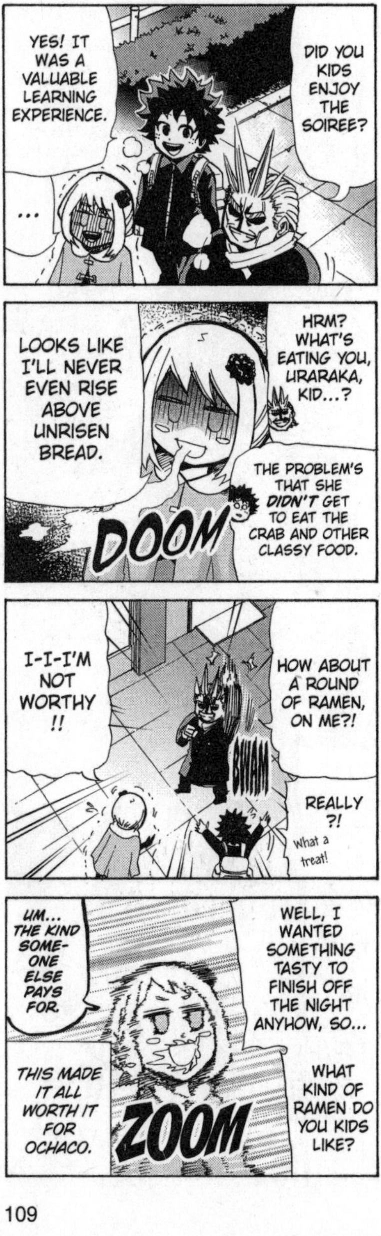
DID YOU KIDS ENJOY THE SOIREE?
YES! IT WAS A VALUABLE LEARNING EXPERIENCE.
...
HRM? WHAT'S EATING YOU, URARAKA, KID...?
LOOKS LIKE I'LL NEVER EVEN RISE ABOVE UNRISEN BREAD.
THE PROBLEM'S THAT SHE *DIDN'T* GET TO EAT THE CRAB AND OTHER CLASSY FOOD.
DOOM
HOW ABOUT A ROUND OF RAMEN, ON ME?!
I-I-I'M NOT WORTHY !!
BWAM
REALLY ?!
What a treat!
WELL, I WANTED SOMETHING TASTY TO FINISH OFF THE NIGHT ANYHOW, SO...
UM... THE KIND SOME-ONE ELSE PAYS FOR.
WHAT KIND OF RAMEN DO YOU KIDS LIKE?
ZOOM
THIS MADE IT ALL WORTH IT FOR OCHACO.

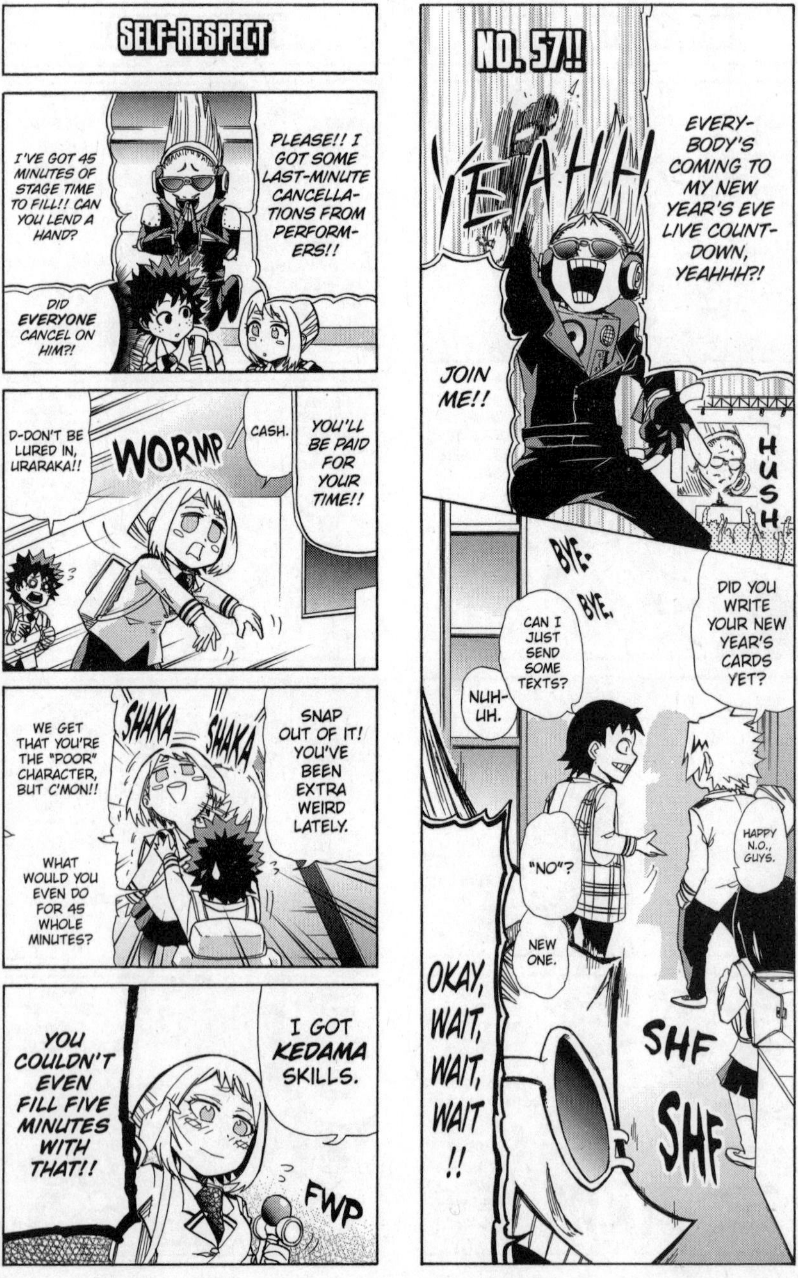
NO. 57!!
YEAHH
EVERY-BODY'S COMING TO MY NEW YEAR'S EVE LIVE COUNT-DOWN, YEAHHH?!
JOIN ME!!
HUSH
BYE.
BYE.
DID YOU WRITE YOUR NEW YEAR'S CARDS YET?
CAN I JUST SEND SOME TEXTS?
NUH-UH.
HAPPY N.O., GUYS.
"NO"?
NEW ONE.
OKAY, WAIT, WAIT, WAIT!!
SHF
SHF
SELF-RESPECT
PLEASE!! I GOT SOME LAST-MINUTE CANCELLA-TIONS FROM PERFORM-ERS!!
I'VE GOT 45 MINUTES OF STAGE TIME TO FILL!! CAN YOU LEND A HAND?
DID EVERYONE CANCEL ON HIM?!
YOU'LL BE PAID FOR YOUR TIME!!
CASH.
WORMP
D-DON'T BE LURED IN, URARAKA!!
SNAP OUT OF IT! YOU'VE BEEN EXTRA WEIRD LATELY.
SHAKA
SHAKA
WE GET THAT YOU'RE THE "POOR" CHARACTER, BUT C'MON!!
WHAT WOULD YOU EVEN DO FOR 45 WHOLE MINUTES?
I GOT KEDAMA SKILLS.
YOU COULDN'T EVEN FILL FIVE MINUTES WITH THAT!!
FWP

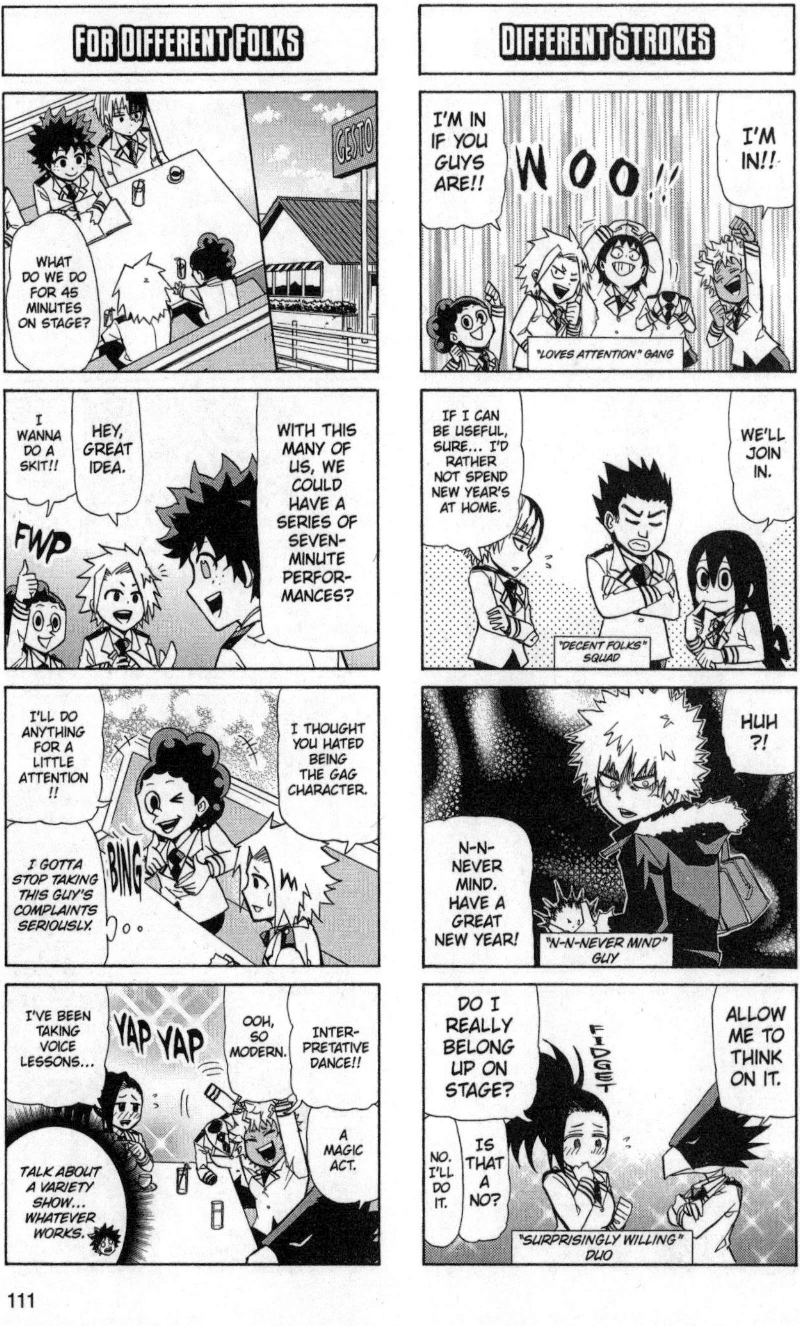
DIFFERENT STROKES
I'M IN!!
WOO!!
I'M IN IF YOU GUYS ARE!!
"LOVES ATTENTION" GANG
WE'LL JOIN IN.
IF I CAN BE USEFUL, SURE... I'D RATHER NOT SPEND NEW YEAR'S AT HOME.
"DECENT FOLKS" SQUAD
HUH?!
N-N-NEVER MIND. HAVE A GREAT NEW YEAR!
"N-N-NEVER MIND" GUY
ALLOW ME TO THINK ON IT.
FIDGET
DO I REALLY BELONG UP ON STAGE?
IS THAT A NO?
NO. I'LL DO IT.
"SURPRISINGLY WILLING" DUO
FOR DIFFERENT FOLKS
GESTO
WHAT DO WE DO FOR 45 MINUTES ON STAGE?
WITH THIS MANY OF US, WE COULD HAVE A SERIES OF SEVEN-MINUTE PERFORMANCES?
HEY, GREAT IDEA.
I WANNA DO A SKIT!!
FWP
I THOUGHT YOU HATED BEING THE GAG CHARACTER.
I'LL DO ANYTHING FOR A LITTLE ATTENTION!!
BING
I GOTTA STOP TAKING THIS GUY'S COMPLAINTS SERIOUSLY.
INTER-PRETATIVE DANCE!!
OOH, SO MODERN.
YAP YAP
I'VE BEEN TAKING VOICE LESSONS...
A MAGIC ACT.
TALK ABOUT A VARIETY SHOW... WHATEVER WORKS.

Packed House

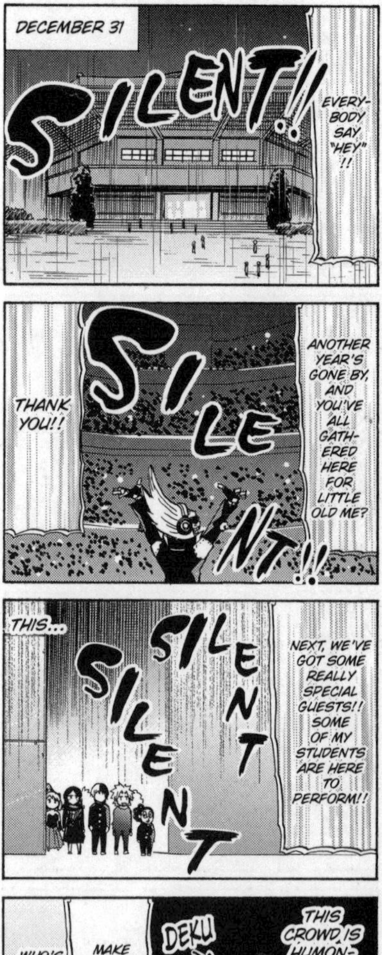
DECEMBER 31
SILENT!!
EVERY-BODY SAY "HEY"!!
ANOTHER YEAR'S GONE BY, AND YOU'VE ALL GATH-ERED HERE FOR LITTLE OLD ME?
SILENT!!
THANK YOU!!
NEXT, WE'VE GOT SOME REALLY SPECIAL GUESTS!! SOME OF MY STUDENTS ARE HERE TO PERFORM!!
SILENT
SILENT
SILENT
THIS...
THIS CROWD IS HUMON-GOUS!!
DEKU
MAKE YOUR-SELVES AT HOME, KIDS!!
WHO'S GOT AN AUDI-ENCE AT HOME, YOU CHICKEN-HEADED BOOM-BOX?!

Dragon of Desperation

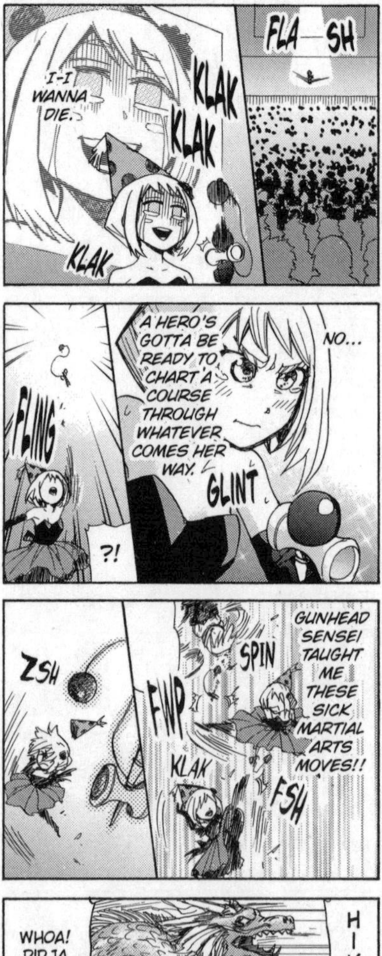
FLA SH
KLAK
KLAK
I-I WANNA DIE.
KLAK
NO...
A HERO'S GOTTA BE READY TO CHART A COURSE THROUGH WHATEVER COMES HER WAY.
GLINT
FLING
?!
GUNHEAD SENSEI TAUGHT ME THESE SICK MARTIAL ARTS MOVES!!
SPIN
FWP
FSH
KLAK
ZSH
HIYAH!
KA KLAK
WHOA! DIDJA SEE THAT DRAGON JUST NOW?!
YEAH!!

THE MAGIC FLUTE, ACT II

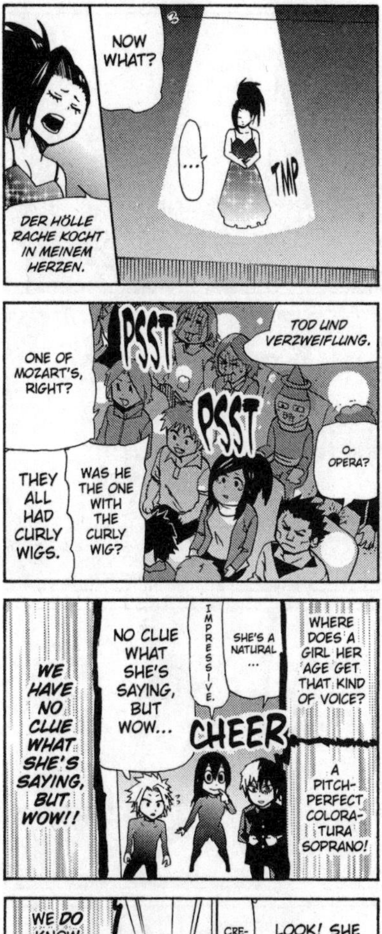
NOW WHAT?
...
TMP
DER HÖLLE RACHE KOCHT IN MEINEM HERZEN.
TOD UND VERZWEIFLUNG.
PSST
ONE OF MOZART'S, RIGHT?
O-OPERA?
PSST
WAS HE THE ONE WITH THE CURLY WIG?
THEY ALL HAD CURLY WIGS.
WHERE DOES A GIRL HER AGE GET THAT KIND OF VOICE?
SHE'S A NATURAL...
IMPRESSIVE.
NO CLUE WHAT SHE'S SAYING, BUT WOW...
CHEER
A PITCH-PERFECT COLORATURA SOPRANO!
WE HAVE NO CLUE WHAT SHE'S SAYING, BUT WOW!!
LOOK! SHE CREATED SUBTITLE CARDS! HOW CONSIDERATE!!
CRE-ATION
WE DO KNOW WHAT SHE'S SAYING NOW, AND YIKES!!
ZRM
HEAR, GODS OF REVENGE, HEAR THE MOTHER'S OATH!!
HEAR, GODS OF REVENGE, HEAR THE MOTHER'S OATH!!

ON ANOTHER LEVEL

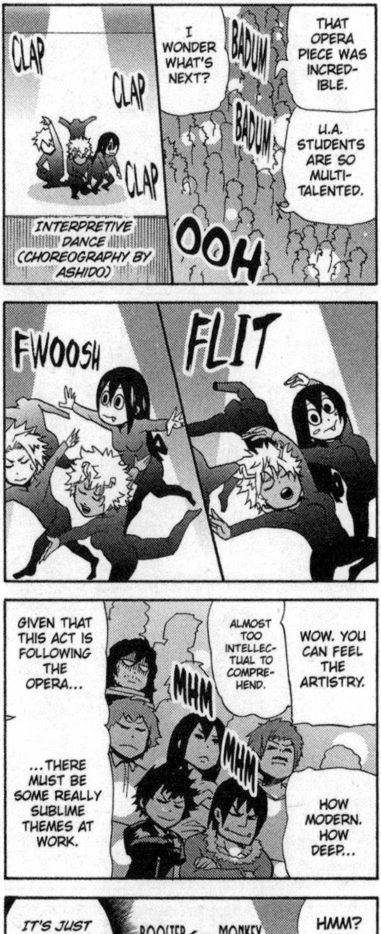
THAT OPERA PIECE WAS INCREDIBLE.
BADUM
I WONDER WHAT'S NEXT?
BADUM
U.A. STUDENTS ARE SO MULTI-TALENTED.
CLAP
CLAP
CLAP
OOH
INTERPRETIVE DANCE (CHOREOGRAPHY BY ASHIDO)
FLIT
FWOOSH
WOW. YOU CAN FEEL THE ARTISTRY.
ALMOST TOO INTELLECTUAL TO COMPREHEND.
MHM
MHM
GIVEN THAT THIS ACT IS FOLLOWING THE OPERA...
HOW MODERN. HOW DEEP...
...THERE MUST BE SOME REALLY SUBLIME THEMES AT WORK.
HMM? HANG ON, IS THAT...
ROOSTER ← MONKEY
IT'S JUST ABOUT THE LUNAR ZODIAC ANIMALS?!
FROM MONKEY TO ROOSTER?
THEME: WELCOMING THE NEW YEAR

Poof! Vanishing Confidence

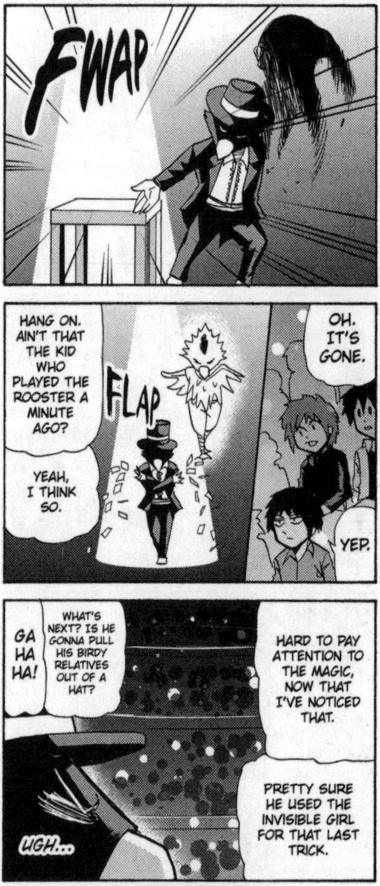

FWAP
OH. IT'S GONE.
HANG ON. AIN'T THAT THE KID WHO PLAYED THE ROOSTER A MINUTE AGO?
FLAP
YEAH, I THINK SO.
YEP.
HARD TO PAY ATTENTION TO THE MAGIC, NOW THAT I'VE NOTICED THAT.
WHAT'S NEXT? IS HE GONNA PULL HIS BIRDY RELATIVES OUT OF A HAT?
GA HA HA!
PRETTY SURE HE USED THE INVISIBLE GIRL FOR THAT LAST TRICK.
UGH...
IT'S RARE TO SEE TOKOYAMI ACTUALLY BROODING.
......
HE REALLY WAS GONNA RELEASE A FLOCK OF DOVES AT THE END.
OH.

Everyone's a Critic

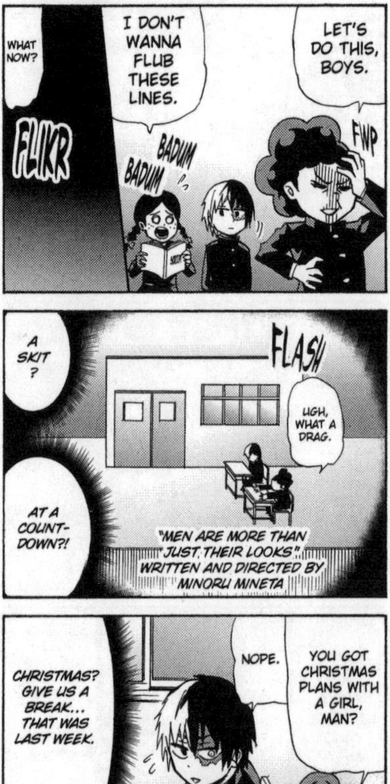

LET'S DO THIS, BOYS.
FWP
I DON'T WANNA FLUB THESE LINES.
BADUM BADUM
WHAT NOW?
FLIKR
FLASH
UGH, WHAT A DRAG.
A SKIT?
AT A COUNTDOWN?!
"MEN ARE MORE THAN JUST THEIR LOOKS" WRITTEN AND DIRECTED BY MINORU MINETA
YOU GOT CHRISTMAS PLANS WITH A GIRL, MAN?
NOPE.
CHRISTMAS? GIVE US A BREAK... THAT WAS LAST WEEK.
HOW ABOUT THAT IZUKO CHICK?
WHAT ABOUT HER?
YOU'RE GETTING WITH HER, RIGHT?
SLIDE
W-WASSUP!
ACK! IZUKO!!

LEGAL ACTION

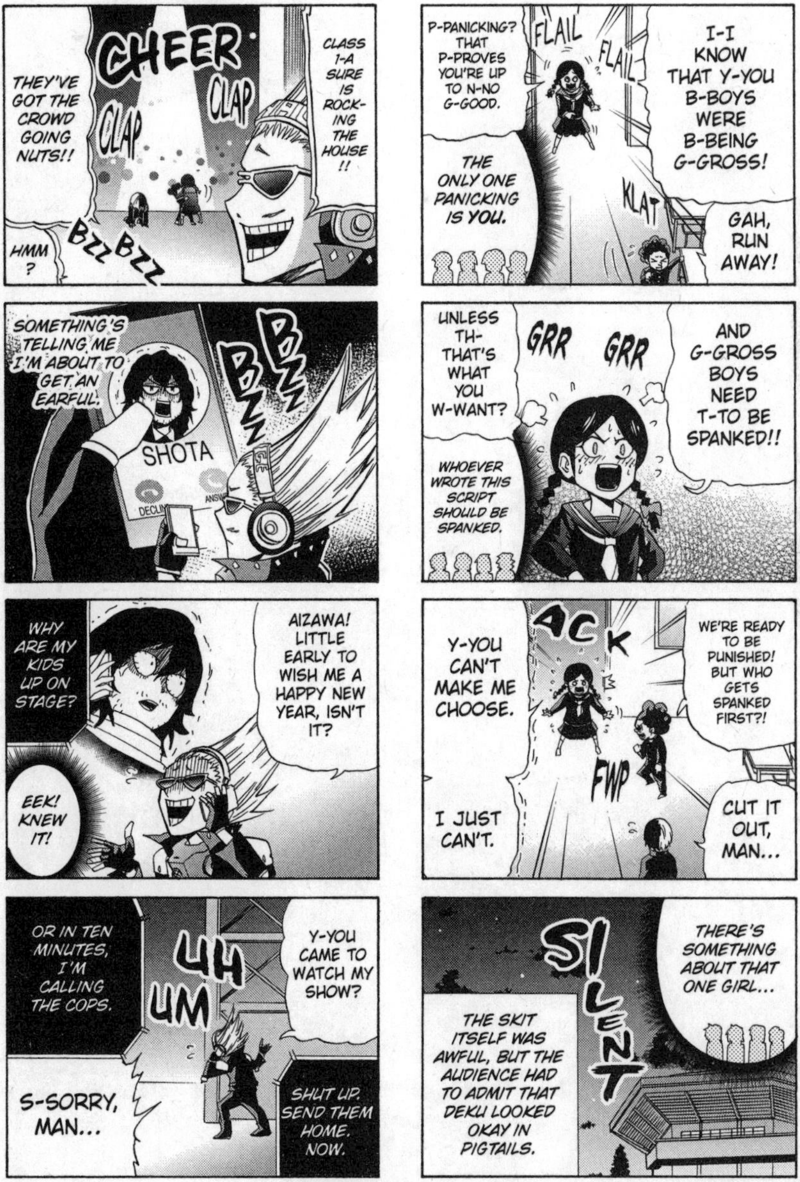
I-I KNOW THAT Y-YOU B-BOYS WERE B-BEING G-GROSS!
FLAIL
FLAIL
P-PANICKING? THAT P-PROVES YOU'RE UP TO N-NO G-GOOD.
THE ONLY ONE PANICKING IS YOU.
KLAT
GAH, RUN AWAY!
AND G-GROSS BOYS NEED T-TO BE SPANKED!!
GRR
GRR
UNLESS TH- THAT'S WHAT YOU W-WANT?
WHOEVER WROTE THIS SCRIPT SHOULD BE SPANKED.
WE'RE READY TO BE PUNISHED! BUT WHO GETS SPANKED FIRST?!
ACK
Y-YOU CAN'T MAKE ME CHOOSE.
FWP
CUT IT OUT, MAN...
I JUST CAN'T.
THERE'S SOMETHING ABOUT THAT ONE GIRL...
SILENT
THE SKIT ITSELF WAS AWFUL, BUT THE AUDIENCE HAD TO ADMIT THAT DEKU LOOKED OKAY IN PIGTAILS.
CLASS 1-A SURE IS ROCKING THE HOUSE!!
CHEER
CLAP
CLAP
THEY'VE GOT THE CROWD GOING NUTS!!
BZZ BZZ
HMM?
BZZ
BZZ
SOMETHING'S TELLING ME I'M ABOUT TO GET AN EARFUL.
SHOTA
AIZAWA! LITTLE EARLY TO WISH ME A HAPPY NEW YEAR, ISN'T IT?
WHY ARE MY KIDS UP ON STAGE?
EEK! KNEW IT!
Y-YOU CAME TO WATCH MY SHOW?
UH
UM
OR IN TEN MINUTES, I'M CALLING THE COPS.
SHUT UP. SEND THEM HOME. NOW.
S-SORRY, MAN...

VOLUME 3 - END

THE BONUS CONTENT STARTS HERE!!

THANKS IN ADVANCE IF YOU CHOOSE TO KEEP READING!!

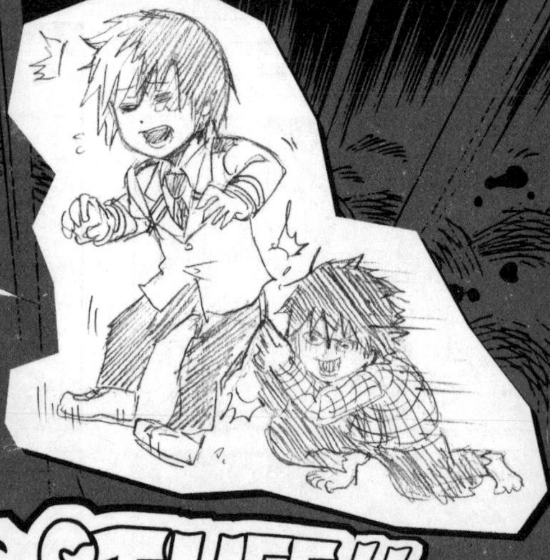

BONUS STUFF!!

MY HERO ACADEMIA SMASH

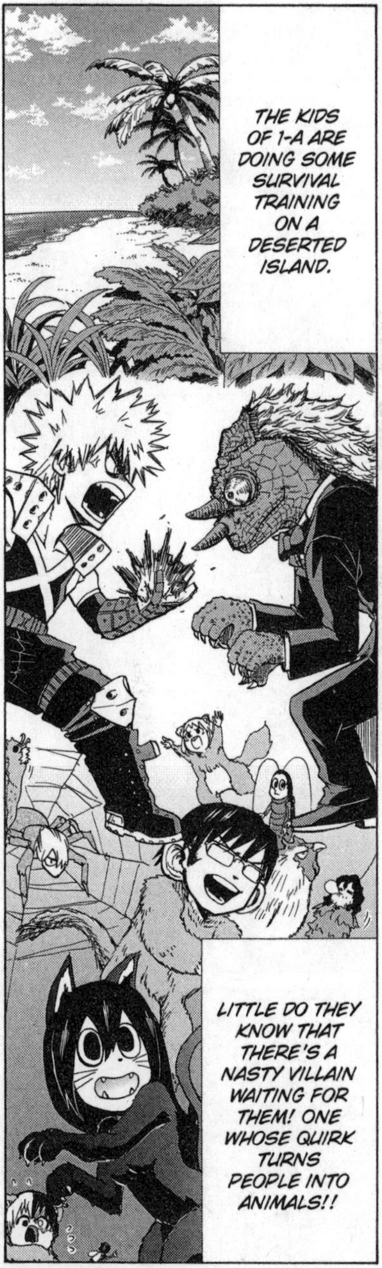
THE KIDS OF 1-A ARE DOING SOME SURVIVAL TRAINING ON A DESERTED ISLAND.
LITTLE DO THEY KNOW THAT THERE'S A NASTY VILLAIN WAITING FOR THEM! ONE WHOSE QUIRK TURNS PEOPLE INTO ANIMALS!!

PUPJIRO KIRIDOGGO

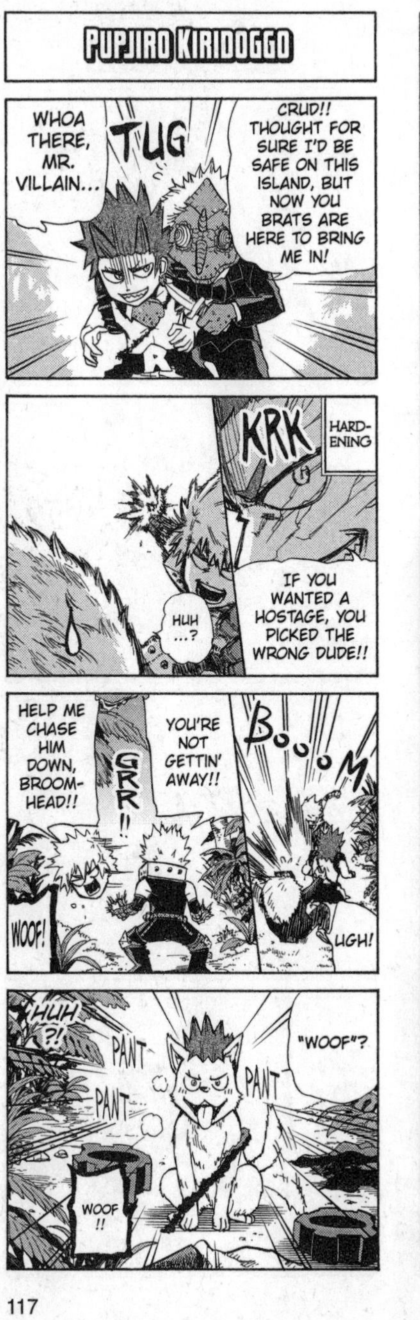
CRUD!! THOUGHT FOR SURE I'D BE SAFE ON THIS ISLAND, BUT NOW YOU BRATS ARE HERE TO BRING ME IN!
TUG
WHOA THERE, MR. VILLAIN...
HARD-ENING
KRK
IF YOU WANTED A HOSTAGE, YOU PICKED THE WRONG DUDE!!
HUH ...?
BOOOM
UGH!
YOU'RE NOT GETTIN' AWAY!!
GRR!!
HELP ME CHASE HIM DOWN, BROOM-HEAD!!
WOOF!
"WOOF"?
PANT
PANT
PANT
HUH ?!
WOOF !!

COUNTERINTUITIVE

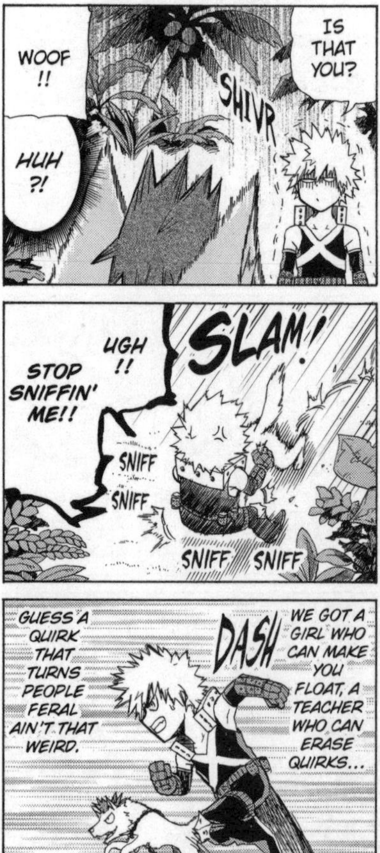
IS THAT YOU?
WOOF !!
SHIVR
HUH ?!
SLAM!
UGH !!
STOP SNIFFIN' ME!!
SNIFF
SNIFF
SNIFF SNIFF
WE GOT A GIRL WHO CAN MAKE YOU FLOAT, A TEACHER WHO CAN ERASE QUIRKS...
DASH
GUESS A QUIRK THAT TURNS PEOPLE FERAL AIN'T THAT WEIRD.
W-WHY AREN'T YOU A FROG ?!
MRROW

KOALITY TRANSFORMATION

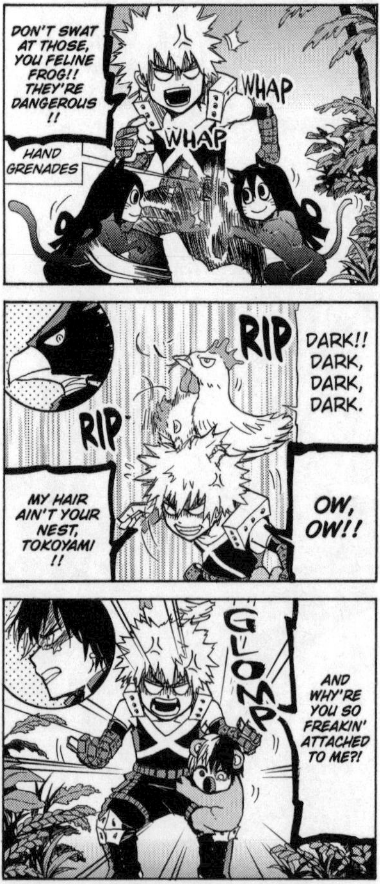
WHAP
DON'T SWAT AT THOSE, YOU FELINE FROG!! THEY'RE DANGEROUS !!
WHAP
HAND GRENADES
DARK!! DARK, DARK, DARK.
RIP
RIP
OW, OW!!
MY HAIR AIN'T YOUR NEST, TOKOYAMI !!
AND WHY'RE YOU SO FREAKIN' ATTACHED TO ME?!
GLOMP
TCH...
THIS INSANE GRIP!!
HNNGH

BAD DOG

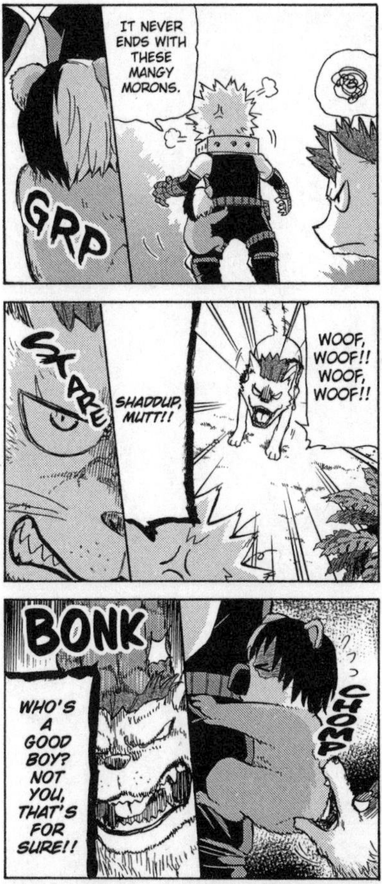
IT NEVER ENDS WITH THESE MANGY MORONS.
GRP
WOOF, WOOF!! WOOF, WOOF!!
SHADDUP, MUTT!!
STARE
CHOMP
WHO'S A GOOD BOY? NOT YOU, THAT'S FOR SURE!!
BONK
HMPH.
YEAH, WELL, PLAY DEAD FOR ALL I CARE!!

FLOORED

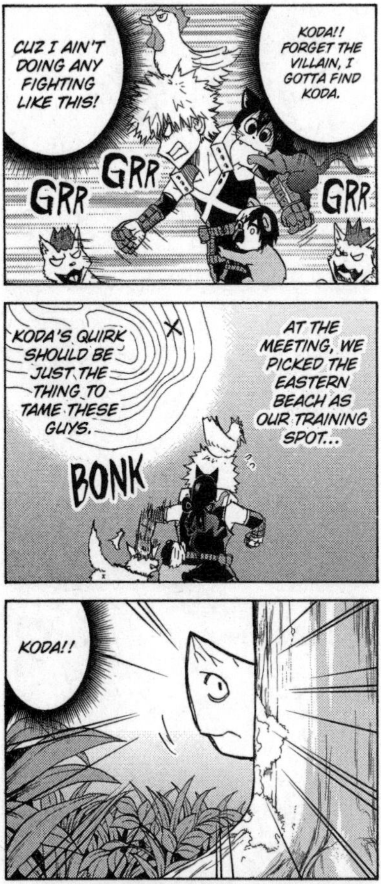
KODA!! FORGET THE VILLAIN, I GOTTA FIND KODA.
CUZ I AIN'T DOING ANY FIGHTING LIKE THIS!
GRR
GRR
GRR
AT THE MEETING, WE PICKED THE EASTERN BEACH AS OUR TRAINING SPOT...
KODA'S QUIRK SHOULD BE JUST THE THING TO TAME THESE GUYS.
BONK
KODA!!
THANK GOD-
BONK
FOR THE FIRST TIME IN KACCHAN'S LIFE, A GAG MADE HIM DO THE THING IN MANGA WHERE THE PERSON FALLS OVER BACKWARDS IN SHOCK.

BEYOND THE RAGE...

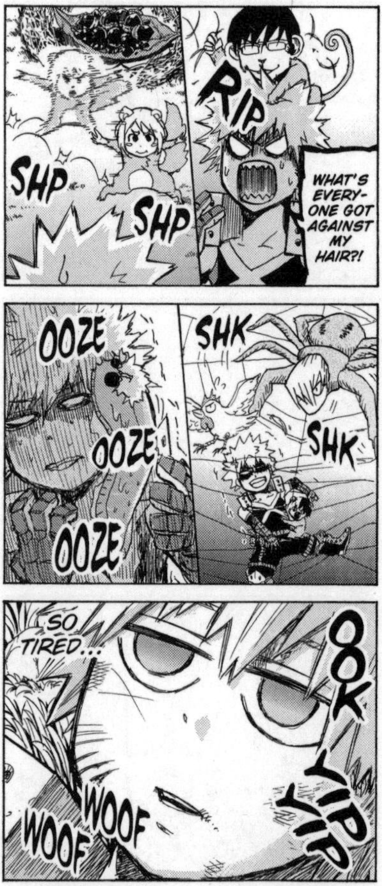
RIP
WHAT'S EVERYONE GOT AGAINST MY HAIR?!
SHP
SHP
SHK
SHK
OOZE
OOZE
OOZE
OOK
YIP
YIP
SO TIRED...
WOOF
WOOF
MY WHOLE LIFE, I'VE EXPLODED AT THINGS THAT PISS ME OFF...
BUT Y'KNOW WHAT? JUST DON'T CARE ANYMORE.
BZZZ
BNN
BZZ
BZZ

...LIES APATHY

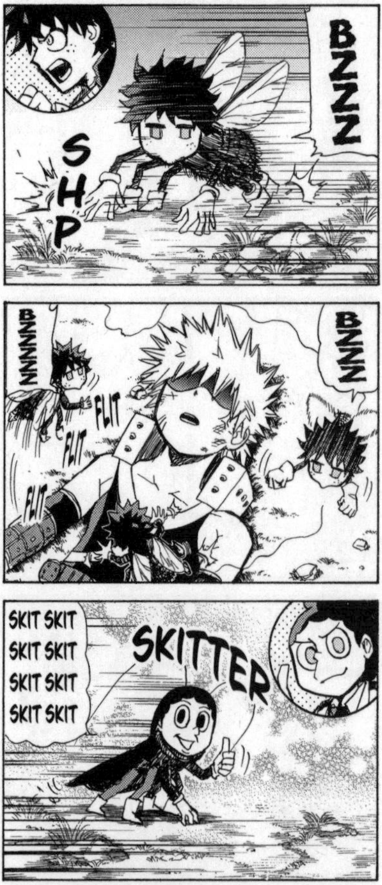
BZZZ
SHP
BZZZ
FLIT
FLIT
FLIT
BZZZZZ
SKITTER
SKIT SKIT
SKIT SKIT
SKIT SKIT
SKIT SKIT
RUB
RUB
RUB
TWITCH
DOOM
SKIT
SKIT
SKIT

REAWAKENED

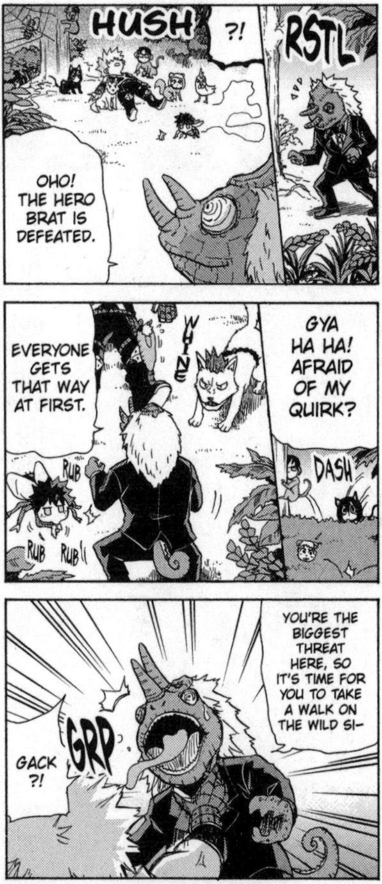
RSTL
?!
HUSH
OHO! THE HERO BRAT IS DEFEATED.
GYA HA HA! AFRAID OF MY QUIRK?
DASH
WHINE
EVERYONE GETS THAT WAY AT FIRST.
RUB
RUB RUB
YOU'RE THE BIGGEST THREAT HERE, SO IT'S TIME FOR YOU TO TAKE A WALK ON THE WILD SI-
GRP
GACK ?!
IT'S TAKING ALL I'VE GOT NOT TO BLOW YOUR HEAD CLEAN OFF.
TWITCH
GET IT?
AGH! W-WHAT'S WITH THIS KID?!
TWITCH

SAVAGED

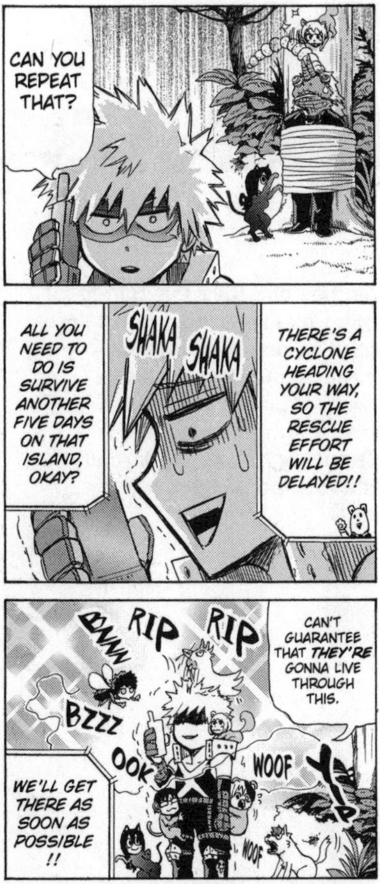
CAN YOU REPEAT THAT?
THERE'S A CYCLONE HEADING YOUR WAY, SO THE RESCUE EFFORT WILL BE DELAYED!!
SHAKA SHAKA
ALL YOU NEED TO DO IS SURVIVE ANOTHER FIVE DAYS ON THAT ISLAND, OKAY?
CAN'T GUARANTEE THAT THEY'RE GONNA LIVE THROUGH THIS.
RIP RIP
YIP
WOOF
BZZZ
OOK
WOOF
WE'LL GET THERE AS SOON AS POSSIBLE !!
AIZAWA SHOWED UP WITH THE RESCUE TEAM AND USED HIS QUIRK TO TURN EVERYONE BACK TO NORMAL.
THANKS...
RMBL
THE CLASS WAS IN GOOD SHAPE THANKS TO KATSUKI'S CAREGIVING, BUT KATSUKI HIMSELF WAS ADMITTED TO THE HOSPITAL FOR THREE WHOLE DAYS.

CONGRATS ON VOLUME 3!

Three volumes already? I've barely got anything to say at this point!! I'm just grateful to keep getting these hilarious four-panel comics week after week!! I expect nothing less from Neda!! To give you a feel for how high-quality Neda's work really is, here's a four-panel from me, Horikoshi!!

Threena Ashido
for volume 3

WOW. THAT'S A REACH.

LAUGH-A-ROKI
I don't think I've ever seen Todoroki bust out laughing.
Let's do it.
I bet he'll make an ugly face!
Todoroki!! Check it!!
Mineta: Ultimate Form.
Oh, good thinking. It's important to protect one's face.
Maybe fewer balls to improve your peripheral vision.
Laugh, dammit!!

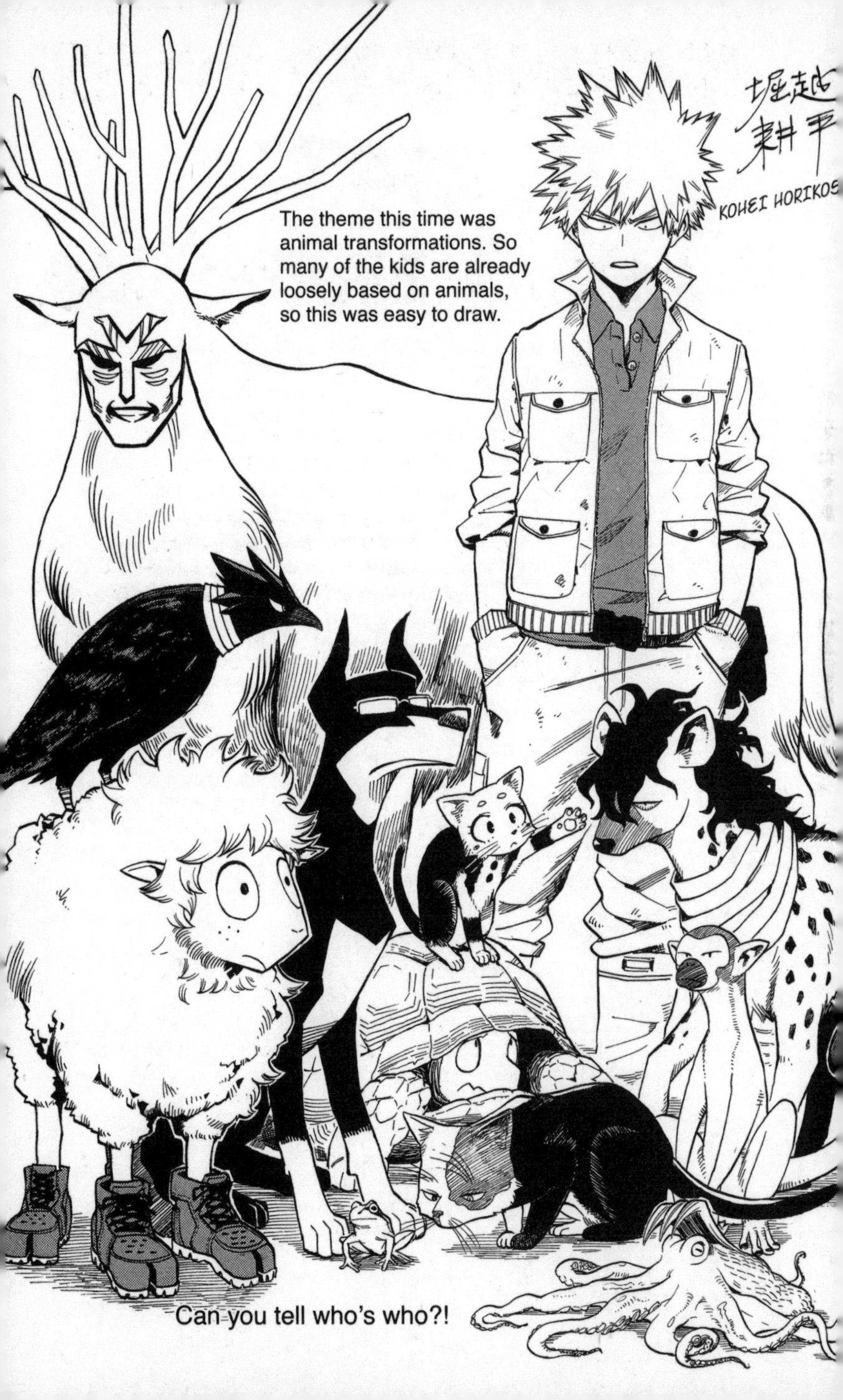
堀越耕平
KOHEI HORIKOSHI
The theme this time was animal transformations. So many of the kids are already loosely based on animals, so this was easy to draw.
Can you tell who's who?!

AFTERWORD

I KNOW THERE'S NO SUCH THING AS INFINITE BOOKSHELVES, SO I APPRECIATE YOU BUYING THREE WHOLE VOLUMES OF THIS SPIN-OFF!!

WHAT CAN I SAY AT THIS POINT, BESIDES THANK YOU!!
THANK YOU!!
THANK YOU!!
THANK YOU!!
THANK YOU!!

THE ORIGINAL PLAN WAS TO DO ONLY TWO BOOKS OF THIS, BUT IT'S THANKS TO ALL YOU READERS THAT I'VE HAD TO KEEP PRODUCING MORE.

I ACTUALLY DO THINK I'M IMPROVING LITTLE BY LITTLE, SO KEEP HOLDING ME TO THAT, PLEASE.

ALSO—AND I SAY THIS EVERY TIME—THANK YOU TO MY EDITOR KOIKE, TO HORIKOSHI AND TO EVERYONE ELSE INVOLVED WITH THE SERIES (BOW).

SEE YOU AGAIN IN VOLUME 4!!

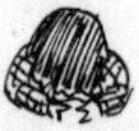

根田啓史
HIROFUMI NEDA

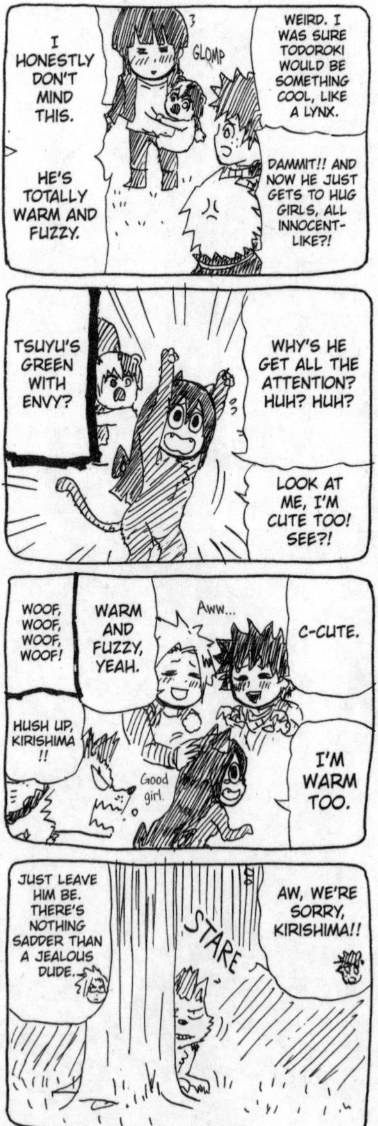
WEIRD. I WAS SURE TODOROKI WOULD BE SOMETHING COOL, LIKE A LYNX.
GLOMP
I HONESTLY DON'T MIND THIS.
DAMMIT!! AND NOW HE JUST GETS TO HUG GIRLS, ALL INNOCENT-LIKE?!
HE'S TOTALLY WARM AND FUZZY.
WHY'S HE GET ALL THE ATTENTION? HUH? HUH?
TSUYU'S GREEN WITH ENVY?
LOOK AT ME, I'M CUTE TOO! SEE?!
C-CUTE.
Aww...
WARM AND FUZZY, YEAH.
WOOF, WOOF, WOOF, WOOF!
I'M WARM TOO.
Good girl.
HUSH UP, KIRISHIMA!!
AW, WE'RE SORRY, KIRISHIMA!!
STARE
JUST LEAVE HIM BE. THERE'S NOTHING SADDER THAN A JEALOUS DUDE.

This was part of the animal-ification chapter, but it got scrapped cuz I ran out of pages.

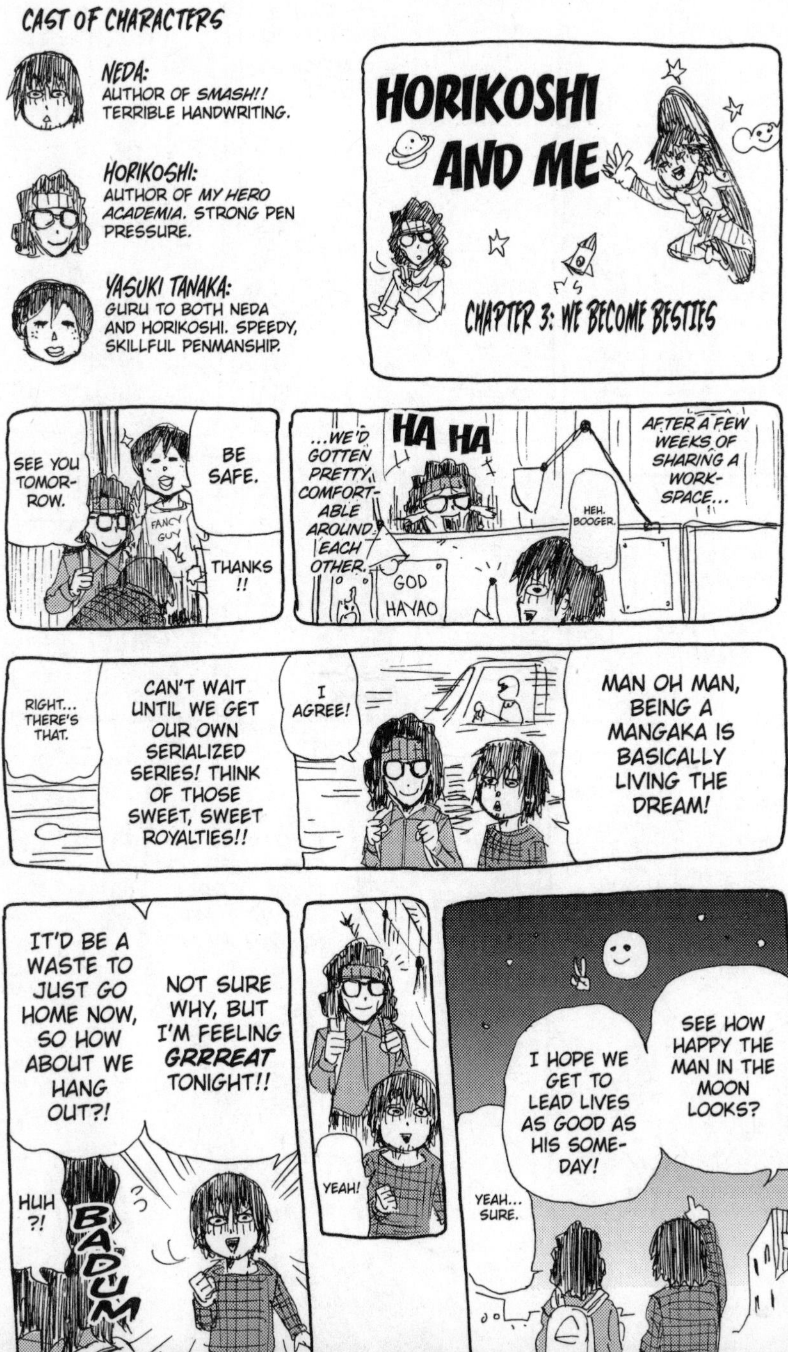
HORIKOSHI AND ME
CHAPTER 3: WE BECOME BESTIES
CAST OF CHARACTERS
NEDA:
AUTHOR OF SMASH!! TERRIBLE HANDWRITING.
HORIKOSHI:
AUTHOR OF MY HERO ACADEMIA. STRONG PEN PRESSURE.
YASUKI TANAKA:
GURU TO BOTH NEDA AND HORIKOSHI. SPEEDY, SKILLFUL PENMANSHIP.
AFTER A FEW WEEKS OF SHARING A WORKSPACE...
...WE'D GOTTEN PRETTY COMFORTABLE AROUND EACH OTHER.
HA HA
HEH. BOOGER.
GOD HAYAO
BE SAFE.
SEE YOU TOMORROW.
FANCY GUY
THANKS!!
MAN OH MAN, BEING A MANGAKA IS BASICALLY LIVING THE DREAM!
I AGREE!
CAN'T WAIT UNTIL WE GET OUR OWN SERIALIZED SERIES! THINK OF THOSE SWEET, SWEET ROYALTIES!!
RIGHT... THERE'S THAT.
SEE HOW HAPPY THE MAN IN THE MOON LOOKS?
I HOPE WE GET TO LEAD LIVES AS GOOD AS HIS SOMEDAY!
YEAH... SURE.
YEAH!
NOT SURE WHY, BUT I'M FEELING GRRREAT TONIGHT!!
IT'D BE A WASTE TO JUST GO HOME NOW, SO HOW ABOUT WE HANG OUT?!
HUH?!
BADUM

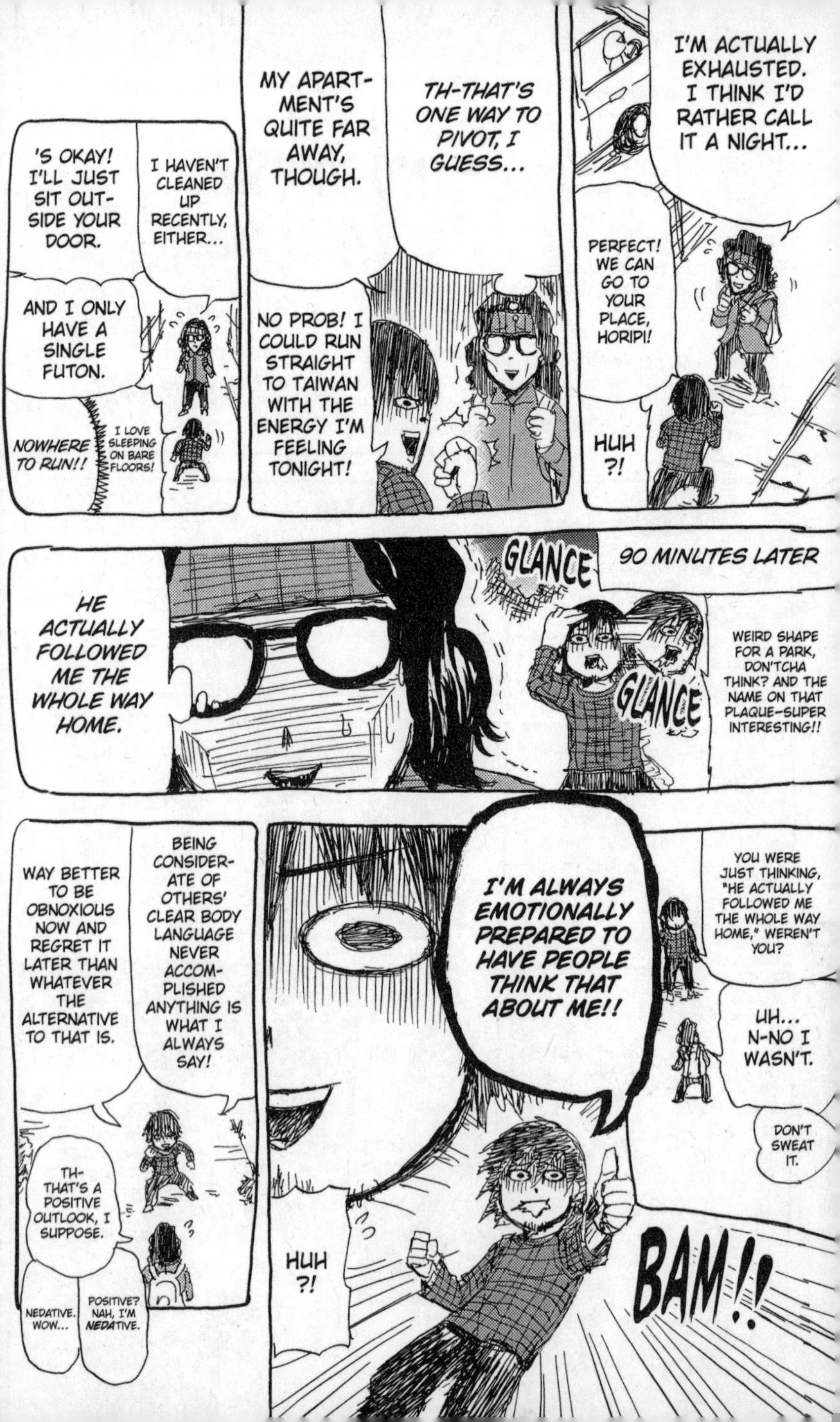
I'M ACTUALLY EXHAUSTED. I THINK I'D RATHER CALL IT A NIGHT...
PERFECT! WE CAN GO TO YOUR PLACE, HORIPI!
HUH ?!
TH-THAT'S ONE WAY TO PIVOT, I GUESS...
MY APARTMENT'S QUITE FAR AWAY, THOUGH.
NO PROB! I COULD RUN STRAIGHT TO TAIWAN WITH THE ENERGY I'M FEELING TONIGHT!
I HAVEN'T CLEANED UP RECENTLY, EITHER...
'S OKAY! I'LL JUST SIT OUTSIDE YOUR DOOR.
AND I ONLY HAVE A SINGLE FUTON.
I LOVE SLEEPING ON BARE FLOORS!
NOWHERE TO RUN!!
90 MINUTES LATER
GLANCE
WEIRD SHAPE FOR A PARK, DON'TCHA THINK? AND THE NAME ON THAT PLAQUE—SUPER INTERESTING!!
GLANCE
HE ACTUALLY FOLLOWED ME THE WHOLE WAY HOME.
YOU WERE JUST THINKING, "HE ACTUALLY FOLLOWED ME THE WHOLE WAY HOME," WEREN'T YOU?
UH... N-NO I WASN'T.
DON'T SWEAT IT.
I'M ALWAYS EMOTIONALLY PREPARED TO HAVE PEOPLE THINK THAT ABOUT ME!!
BAM!!
HUH ?!
BEING CONSIDERATE OF OTHERS' CLEAR BODY LANGUAGE NEVER ACCOMPLISHED ANYTHING IS WHAT I ALWAYS SAY!
WAY BETTER TO BE OBNOXIOUS NOW AND REGRET IT LATER THAN WHATEVER THE ALTERNATIVE TO THAT IS.
TH-THAT'S A POSITIVE OUTLOOK, I SUPPOSE.
POSITIVE? NAH, I'M NEDATIVE.
NEDATIVE. WOW...

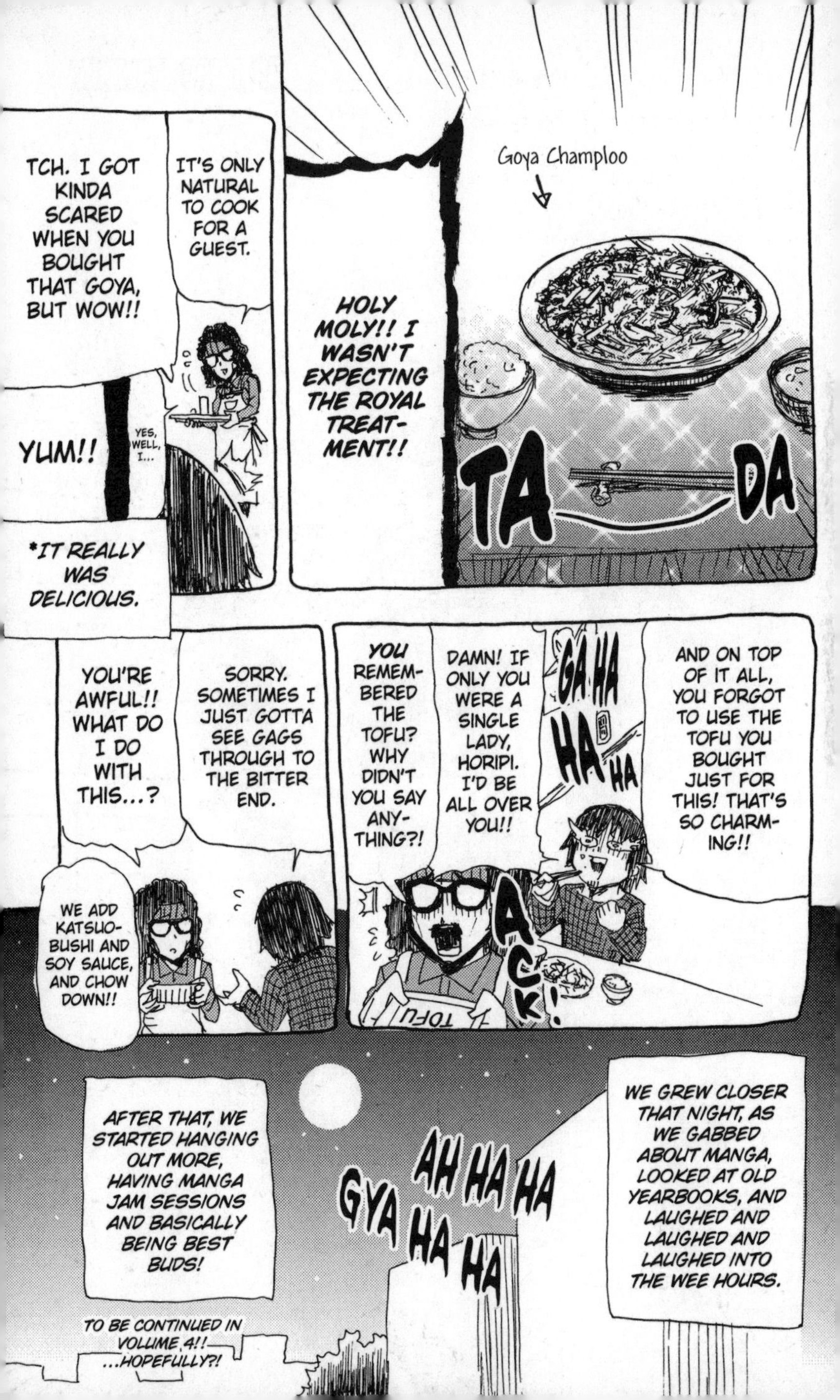
Goya Champloo
TA—DA
HOLY MOLY!! I WASN'T EXPECTING THE ROYAL TREATMENT!!
IT'S ONLY NATURAL TO COOK FOR A GUEST.
TCH. I GOT KINDA SCARED WHEN YOU BOUGHT THAT GOYA, BUT WOW!!
YES, WELL, I...
YUM!!
*IT REALLY WAS DELICIOUS.
AND ON TOP OF IT ALL, YOU FORGOT TO USE THE TOFU YOU BOUGHT JUST FOR THIS! THAT'S SO CHARMING!!
GA HA HA HA HA
DAMN! IF ONLY YOU WERE A SINGLE LADY, HORIPI. I'D BE ALL OVER YOU!!
YOU REMEMBERED THE TOFU? WHY DIDN'T YOU SAY ANYTHING?!
TACK!
TOFU
SORRY. SOMETIMES I JUST GOTTA SEE GAGS THROUGH TO THE BITTER END.
YOU'RE AWFUL!! WHAT DO I DO WITH THIS...?
WE ADD KATSUOBUSHI AND SOY SAUCE, AND CHOW DOWN!!
WE GREW CLOSER THAT NIGHT, AS WE GABBED ABOUT MANGA, LOOKED AT OLD YEARBOOKS, AND LAUGHED AND LAUGHED AND LAUGHED INTO THE WEE HOURS.
AH HA HA HA
GYA HA HA HA
AFTER THAT, WE STARTED HANGING OUT MORE, HAVING MANGA JAM SESSIONS AND BASICALLY BEING BEST BUDS!
TO BE CONTINUED IN VOLUME 4!! ...HOPEFULLY?!

ANTIHERO ACADEMIA

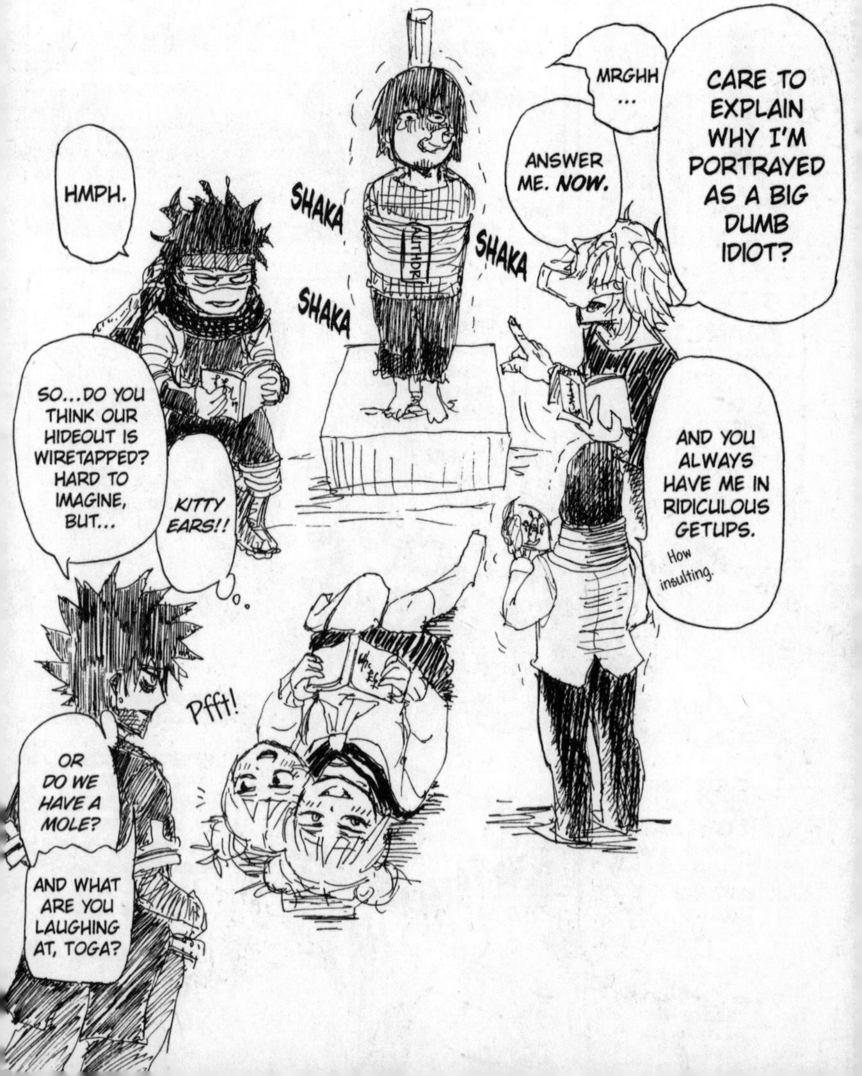

CARE TO EXPLAIN WHY I'M PORTRAYED AS A BIG DUMB IDIOT?
MRGHH ...
ANSWER ME. ***NOW.***
SHAKA
SHAKA
SHAKA
AUTHOR
HMPH.
AND YOU ALWAYS HAVE ME IN RIDICULOUS GETUPS.
How insulting.
SO...DO YOU THINK OUR HIDEOUT IS WIRETAPPED? HARD TO IMAGINE, BUT...
KITTY EARS!!
Pfft!
OR DO WE HAVE A MOLE?
AND WHAT ARE YOU LAUGHING AT, TOGA?

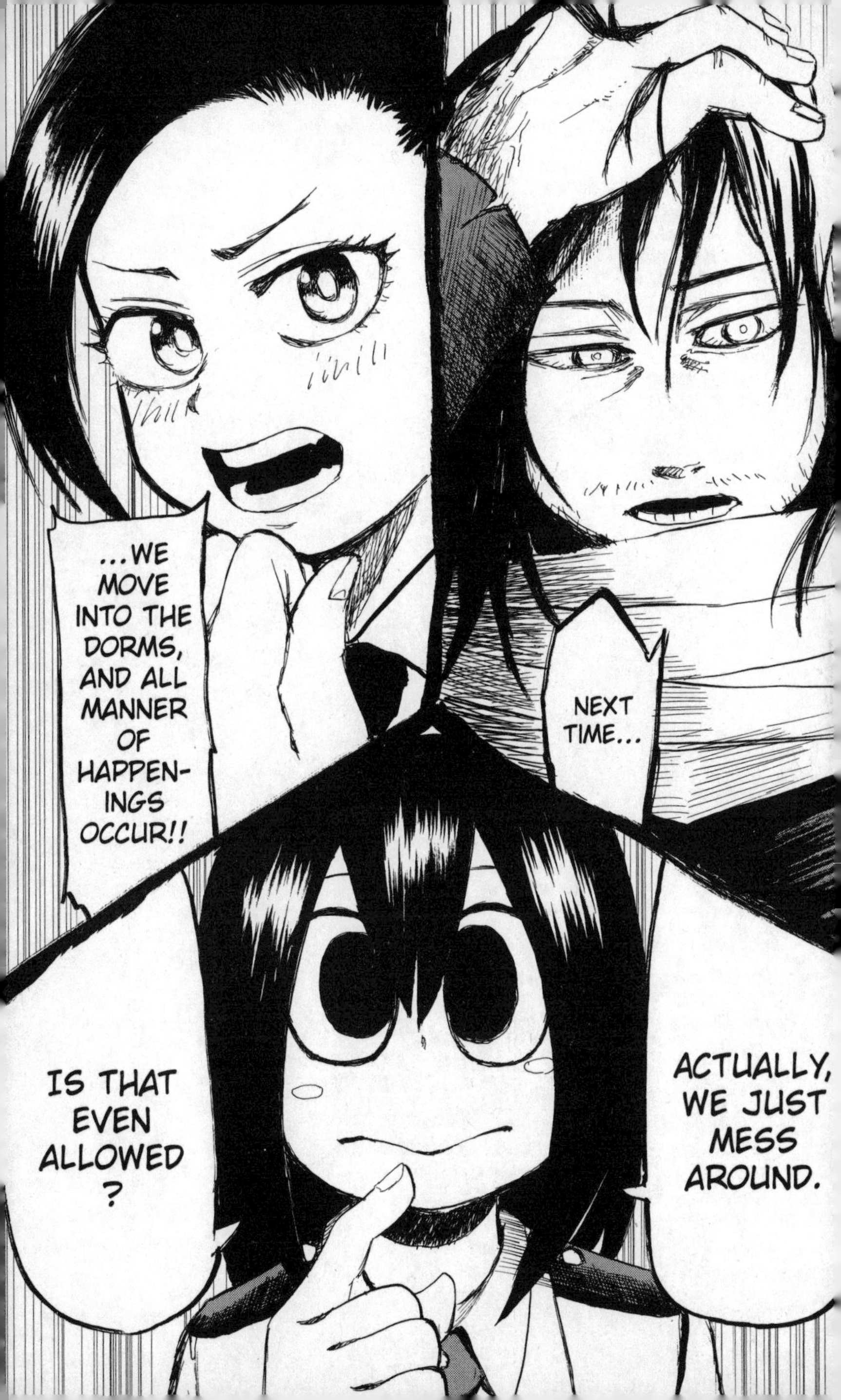
NEXT TIME...
...WE MOVE INTO THE DORMS, AND ALL MANNER OF HAPPENINGS OCCUR!!
ACTUALLY, WE JUST MESS AROUND.
IS THAT EVEN ALLOWED?

SOMETIMES THOSE WITHOUT A LEGAL WAY TO APPLY THEIR QUIRKS...

...FIND A WAY AROUND THE RULES.

MY HERO ACADEMIA
VIGILANTES

In a superpowered society, there is nothing ordinary about evil anymore. Heroes, trained and licensed to protect and defend the public against supervillains, stand above all the rest. Not everyone can be a hero, however, and there are those who would use their powers to serve the people without legal sanction. But do they fight for justice in the shadows, or for reasons known only to themselves? Whatever they fight for, they are called... Vigilantes.

MY HERO ACADEMIA
SCHOOL BRIEFS

ORIGINAL STORY BY
KOHEI HORIKOSHI

WRITTEN BY
ANRI YOSHI

Prose short stories featuring the everyday school lives of My Hero Academia's fan-favorite characters!

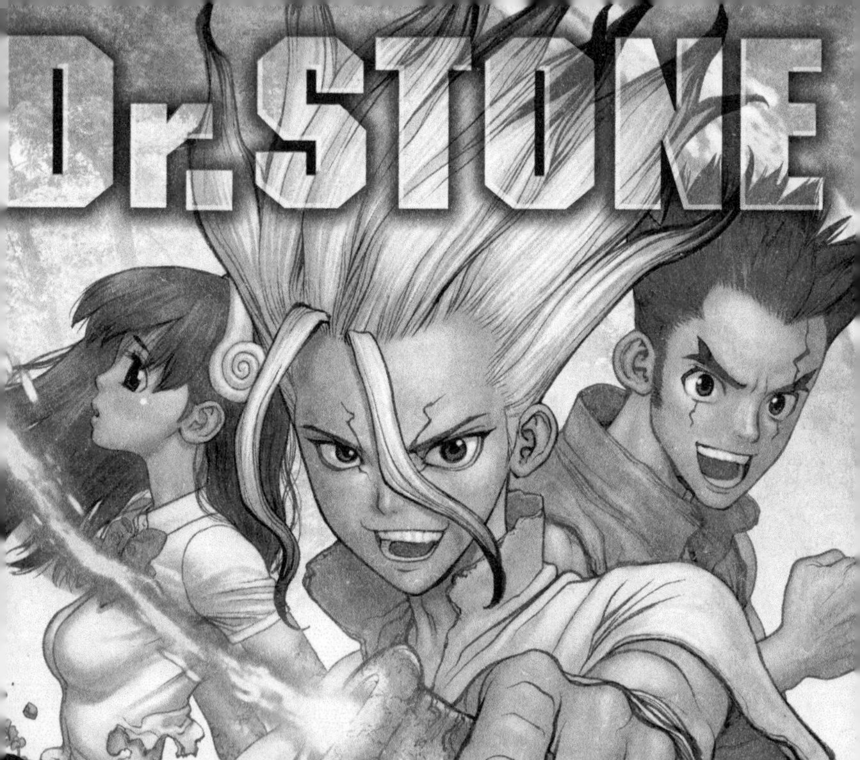

Dr. STONE

STORY BY
RIICHIRO INAGAKI

ART BY
BOICHI

ne fateful day, all of humanity turned to stone. Many millennia
ater, Taiju frees himself from petrification and finds himself
urrounded by statues. The situation looks grim—until he runs
nto his science-loving friend Senku! Together they plan to restart
ivilization with the power of science!

DEMON SLAYER
KIMETSU NO YAIBA

Story and Art by
KOYOHARU GOTOUGE

In Taisho-era Japan, kindhearted Tanjiro Kamado makes a living selling charcoal. But his peaceful life is shattered when a demon slaughters his entire family. His little sister Nezuko is the only survivor, but she has been transformed into a demon herself! Tanjiro sets out on a dangerous journey to find a way to return his sister to normal and destroy the demon who ruined his life.

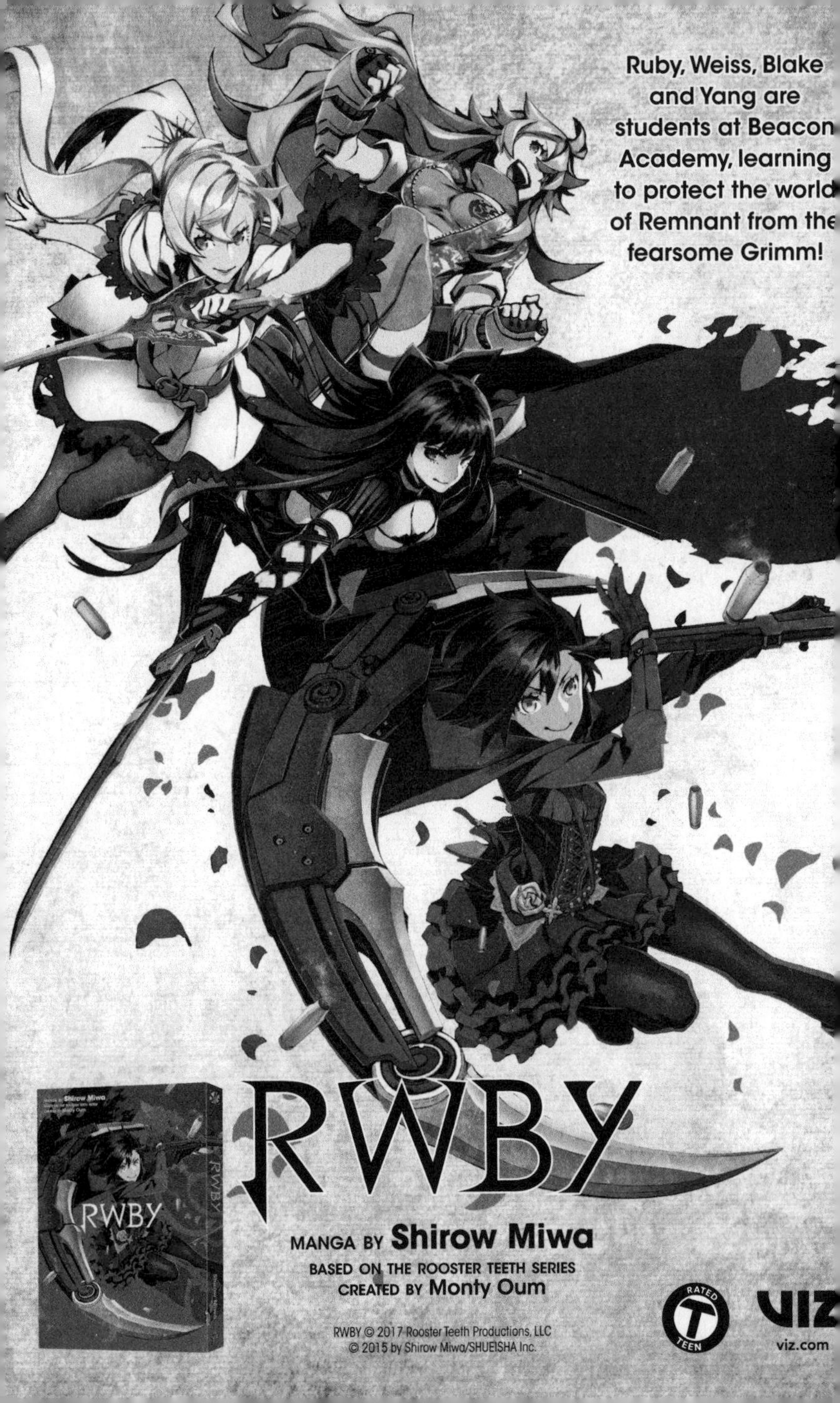
Ruby, Weiss, Blake and Yang are students at Beacon Academy, learning to protect the world of Remnant from the fearsome Grimm!
RWBY
RWBY
MANGA BY Shirow Miwa
BASED ON THE ROOSTER TEETH SERIES
CREATED BY Monty Oum
RATED T TEEN
VIZ
viz.com
RWBY © 2017 Rooster Teeth Productions, LLC
© 2015 by Shirow Miwa/SHUEISHA Inc.

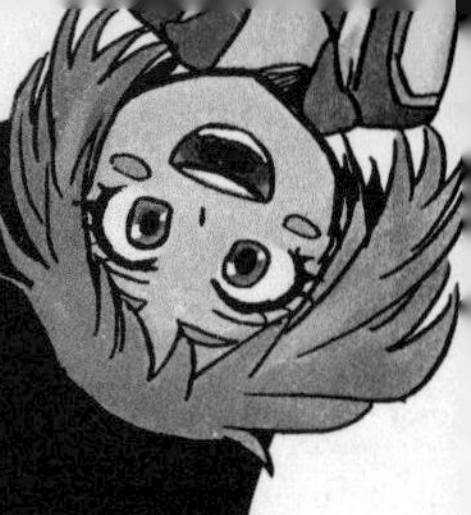

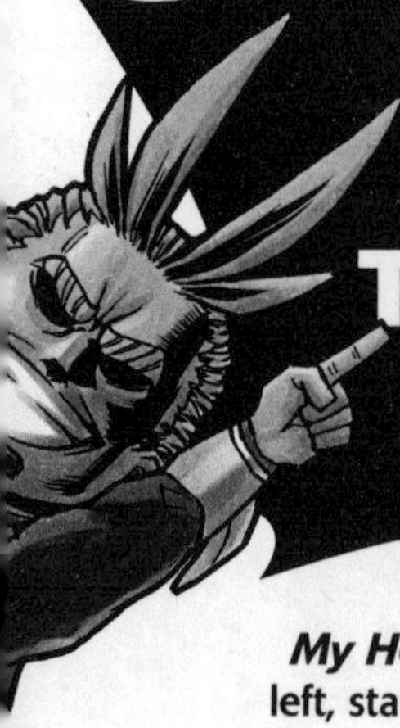

YOU'RE READING THE WRONG WAY!!

My Hero Academia: Smash!! **reads right to left, starting in the upper-right corner. Japanese is read right to left, meaning that action, sound effects and word balloon order are completely reversed from English order.**

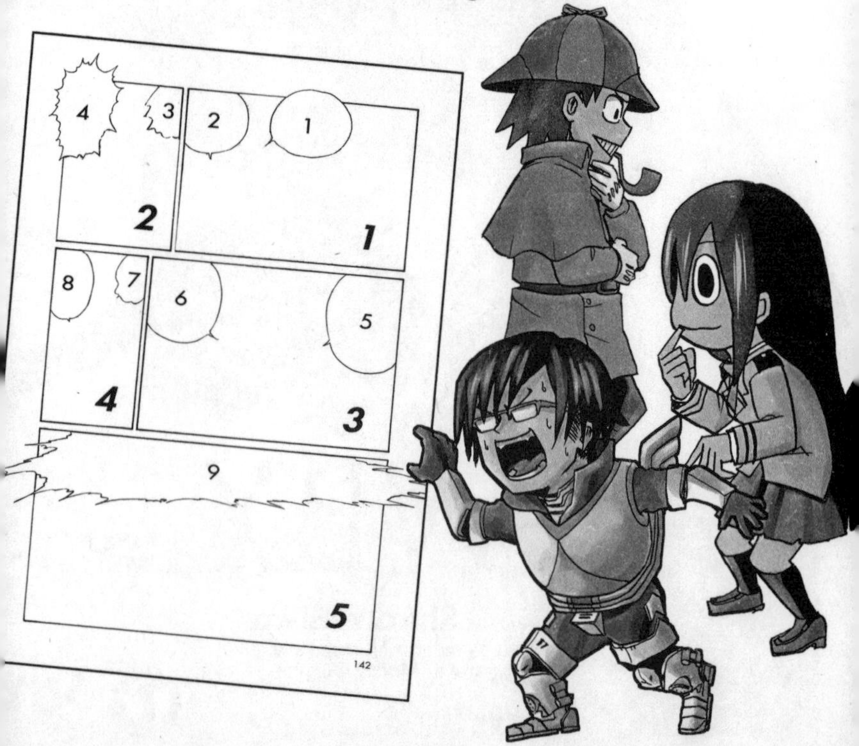
1
2
3
4
1
2
5
6
7
8
3
4
9
5
142